RosettaStone®
Language Learning   Success

Curriculum Text

Mandarin Chinese | Level 1

TRS-CHI1-4.0

ISBN 1-883972-41-8

Fairfield Language Technologies
135 West Market Street
Harrisonburg, Virginia 22801 USA

Telephone: 540-432-6166 or 800-788-0822 in U.S. and Canada
Fax: 540-432-0953
E-mail: info@RosettaStone.com
Web site: www.RosettaStone.com

目录

第三部分

第四部分

第六部分

第八部分

課文

介绍名词和介词

01　一个女孩儿
　　一个男孩儿
　　一只狗
　　一只猫

02　一个男人
　　一个女人
　　一辆汽车
　　一架飞机

03　一个球
　　一匹马
　　一架飞机
　　一头象

04　一只猫和一辆汽车
　　一个女孩儿和一个女人
　　一个男人和一个女人
　　一个男人和一个男孩儿

05　一个男孩儿和一只狗
　　一个男孩儿和一架飞机
　　一个女孩儿和一匹马
　　一个女孩儿和一只狗

06　一个骑在马上的女孩儿
　　一个骑在马上的男人
　　男孩儿身上的一个球
　　一个骑在马上的男孩儿

07　在飞机下面的一个男孩儿
　　在球下面的一个男孩儿
　　在桌子下面的一个男孩儿
　　一个男孩儿和一只狗

08　在飞机上面的一个男孩儿
　　在飞机下面的一个男孩儿
　　在桌子上面的一个男孩儿
　　在桌子下面的一个男孩儿

09　在汽车里的一个女孩儿
　　在汽车里的一个女人
　　在汽车里的一个男孩儿
　　在船上的一个男孩儿和一个女孩儿

10　一个男孩儿和一只狗
　　在飞机上面的一个男孩儿
　　在飞机下面的一个男孩儿
　　在飞机里的一个男孩儿

1-01

介紹名詞和介詞

01　一個女孩兒
　　一個男孩兒
　　一隻狗
　　一隻貓

02　一個男人
　　一個女人
　　一輛汽車
　　一架飛機

03　一個球
　　一匹馬
　　一架飛機
　　一頭象

04　一隻貓和一輛汽車
　　一個女孩兒和一個女人
　　一個男人和一個女人
　　一個男人和一個男孩兒

05　一個男孩兒和一隻狗
　　一個男孩兒和一架飛機
　　一個女孩兒和一匹馬
　　一個女孩兒和一隻狗

06　一個騎在馬上的女孩兒
　　一個騎在馬上的男人
　　男孩兒身上的一個球
　　一個騎在馬上的男孩兒

07　在飛机下面的一個男孩兒
　　在球下面的一個男孩兒
　　在桌子下面的一個男孩兒
　　一個男孩兒和一隻狗

08　在飛機上面的一個男孩兒
　　在飛機下面的一個男孩兒
　　在桌子上面的一個男孩兒
　　在桌子下面的一個男孩兒

09　在汽車裡的一個女孩兒
　　在汽車裡的一個女人
　　在汽車裡的一個男孩兒
　　在船上的一個男孩兒和一個女孩兒

10　一個男孩兒和一隻狗
　　在飛機上面的一個男孩兒
　　在飛機下面的一個男孩兒
　　在飛機裡的一個男孩兒

1-01

jiè shào míng cí hé jiè cí

01 yī gè nǚ háir
    yī gè nán háir
    yī zhī gǒu
    yī zhī māo

02 yī gè nán rén
    yī gè nǚ rén
    yī liàng qì chē
    yī jià fēi jī

03 yī gè qiú
    yī pǐ mǎ
    yī jià fēi jī
    yī tóu xiàng

04 yī zhī māo hé yī liàng qì chē
    yī gè nǚ háir hé yī gè nǚ rén
    yī gè nán rén hé yī gè nǚ rén
    yī gè nán rén hé yī gè nán háir

05 yī gè nán háir hé yī zhī gǒu
    yī gè nán háir hé yī jià fēi jī
    yī gè nǚ háir hé yī pǐ mǎ
    yī gè nǚ háir hé yī zhī gǒu

06 yī gè qí zài mǎ shàng de nǚ háir
    yī gè qí zài mǎ shàng de nán rén
    nán háir shēn shàng de yī ge qiú
    yī gè qí zài mǎ shàng de nán háir

07 zài fēi jī xià miàn de yī gè nán háir
    zài qiú xià miàn de yī gè nán háir
    zài zhuō zi xià miàn de yī gè nán háir
    yī gè nán háir hé yī zhī gǒu

08 zài fēi jī shàng miàn de yī gè nán háir
    zài fēi jī xià miàn de yī gè nán háir
    zài zhuō zi shàng miàn de yī gè nán háir
    zài zhuō zi xià miàn de yī gè nán háir

09 zài qì chē lǐ de yī gè nǚ háir
    zài qì chē lǐ de yī gè nǚ rén
    zài qì chē lǐ de yī gè nán háir
    zài chuán shàng de yī gè nán háir hé yī gè nǚ háir

10 yī gè nán háir hé yī zhī gǒu
    zài fēi jī shàng miàn de yī gè nán háir
    zài fēi jī xià miàn de yī gè nán háir
    zài fēi jī lǐ de yī gè nán háir

动词：走、跳舞、游泳、摔倒等；现在进行时

01　那个男孩儿在跳。
　　那匹马在跳。
　　那个女孩儿在跳。
　　那只狗在跳。

02　那个男孩儿在跑。
　　那个女人在跑。
　　那个女孩儿在跑。
　　那匹马在跑。

03　那个女人在跑。
　　那个女人在跳。
　　那两个女孩儿在跑。
　　那两个女孩儿在跳。

04　那两个女孩儿在走。
　　那两个女孩儿在跑。
　　那个男孩儿在跳。
　　那个男孩儿在走。

05　那个男人和那个女人在走。
　　那个男人和那个女人在跳舞。
　　那个女人在走。
　　那个女人在跳舞。

06　那个男人在看书。
　　那个女人在看书。
　　那个男人在跳舞。
　　那个女人在跳。

07　那个男人在追那个男孩儿。
　　那个男人正摔下来。
　　那个男孩儿正摔下来。
　　那两个女孩儿在追那个男孩儿。

08　那架飞机在飞。
　　那个男人在跑。
　　那个男人在跳。
　　那个男人正摔下来。

09　那个女人在游泳。
　　那个男人正摔下来。
　　那个男孩儿正摔下来。
　　那个男孩儿在游泳。

10　那条鱼在游。
　　那只鸟在飞。
　　那头牛在跑。
　　那只鹅在游。

動詞：走、跳舞、游泳、摔倒等；現在進行時

01　那個男孩兒在跳。
　　那匹馬在跳。
　　那個女孩兒在跳。
　　那隻狗在跳。

02　那個男孩兒在跑。
　　那個女人在跑。
　　那個女孩兒在跑。
　　那匹馬在跑。

03　那個女人在跑。
　　那個女人在跳。
　　那兩個女孩兒在跑。
　　那兩個女孩兒在跳。

04　那兩個女孩兒在走。
　　那兩個女孩兒在跑。
　　那個男孩兒在跳。
　　那個男孩兒在走。

05　那個男人和那個女人在走。
　　那個男人和那個女人在跳舞。
　　那個女人在走。
　　那個女人在跳舞。

06　那個男人在看書。
　　那個女人在看書。
　　那個男人在跳舞。
　　那個女人在跳。

07　那個男人在追那個男孩兒。
　　那個男人正摔下來。
　　那個男孩兒正摔下來。
　　那兩個女孩兒在追那個男孩兒。

08　那架飛機在飛。
　　那個男人在跑。
　　那個男人在跳。
　　那個男人正摔下來。

09　那個女人在游泳。
　　那個男人正摔下來。
　　那個男孩兒正摔下來。
　　那個男孩兒在游泳。

10　那條魚在游。
　　那隻鳥在飛。
　　那頭牛在跑。
　　那隻鵝在游。

1-02

dòng cí: zǒu, tiào wǔ, yóu yǒng, shuāi dǎo děng; xiàn zài jìn xíng shí

01 nà gè nán háir zài tiào.
    nà pǐ mǎ zài tiào.
    nà gè nǚ háir zài tiào.
    nà zhī gǒu zài tiào.

02 nà gè nán háir zài pǎo.
    nà gè nǚ rén zài pǎo.
    nà gè nǚ háir zài pǎo.
    nà pǐ mǎ zài pǎo.

03 nà gè nǚ rén zài pǎo.
    nà gè nǚ rén zài tiào.
    nà liǎng gè nǚ háir zài pǎo.
    nà liǎng gè nǚ háir zài tiào.

04 nà liǎng gè nǚ háir zài zǒu.
    nà liǎng gè nǚ háir zài pǎo.
    nà gè nán háir zài tiào.
    nà gè nán háir zài zǒu.

05 nà gè nán rén hé nà gè nǚ rén zài zǒu.
    nà gè nán rén hé nà gè nǚ rén zài tiào wǔ.
    nà gè nǚ rén zài zǒu.
    nà gè nǚ rén zài tiào wǔ.

06 nà gè nán rén zài kàn shū.
    nà gè nǚ rén zài kàn shū.
    nà gè nán rén zài tiào wǔ.
    nà gè nǚ rén zài tiào.

07 nà gè nán rén zài zhuī nà gè nán háir.
    nà gè nán rén zhèng shuāi xià lái.
    nà gè nán háir zhèng shuāi xià lái.
    nà liǎng gè nǚ háir zài zhuī nà gè nán háir.

08 nà jià fēi jī zài fēi.
    nà gè nán rén zài pǎo.
    nà gè nán rén zài tiào.
    nà gè nán rén zhèng shuāi xià lái.

09 nà gè nǚ rén zài yóu yǒng.
    nà gè nán rén zhèng shuāi xià lái.
    nà gè nán háir zhèng shuāi xià lái.
    nà gè nán háir zài yóu yǒng.

10 nà tiáo yú zài yóu.
    nà zhī niǎo zài fēi.
    nà tóu niú zài pǎo.
    nà zhī é zài yóu.

描述性形容词：新、旧、老等

01 那条鱼是白色的。
那辆汽车是白色的。
那辆汽车是红色的。
那只鸟是红色的。

02 那架飞机是白色的。
那架飞机是黄色的。
那辆汽车是白色的。
那辆汽车是黄色的。

03 那辆汽车是红色的。
那辆汽车是黄色的。
那辆汽车是白色的。
那辆汽车是蓝色的。

04 那辆汽车是蓝色的。
那辆汽车是黄色的。
那只猫是黑色的。
那辆汽车是黑色的。

05 那辆黄色的汽车是旧的。
那辆粉红色的汽车是旧的。
那辆蓝色的汽车是新的。
那辆红色的汽车是新的。

06 一辆旧车
一辆新车
一座老房子
一座新房子

07 一位老太太
一个年轻女人
一座老房子
一座新房子

08 一位老太太
一个年轻女人
一位老人
一个小伙子

09 那位老太太的头发是白色的。
那个女孩儿的头发是黑色的。
那个男人的头发是蓝色的。
那个男人的头发是红色的。

10 那个女人留着长发。
那个男人留着长发。
那个女人留着短发。
那个男人留着短发。

1-03

描述性形容詞：新、舊、老等

01 那條魚是白色的。
那輛汽車是白色的。
那輛汽車是紅色的。
那隻鳥是紅色的。

02 那架飛機是白色的。
那架飛機是黃色的。
那輛汽車是白色的。
那輛汽車是黃色的。

03 那輛汽車是紅色的。
那輛汽車是黃色的。
那輛汽車是白色的。
那輛汽車是藍色的。

04 那輛汽車是藍色的。
那輛汽車是黃色的。
那隻貓是黑色的。
那輛汽車是黑色的。

05 那輛黃色的汽車是舊的。
那輛粉紅色的汽車是舊的。
那輛藍色的汽車是新的。
那輛紅色的汽車是新的。

06 一輛舊車
一輛新車
一座老房子
一座新房子

07 一位老太太
一個年輕女人
一座老房子
一座新房子

08 一位老太太
一個年輕女人
一位老人
一個小夥子

09 那位老太太的頭髮是白色的。
那個女孩兒的頭髮是黑色的。
那個男人的頭髮是藍色的。
那個男人的頭髮是紅色的。

10 那個女人留著長髮。
那個男人留著長髮。
那個女人留著短髮。
那個男人留著短髮。

1-03

miáo shù xìng xíng róng cí: xīn, jiù, lǎo děng

01 nà tiáo yú shì bái sè de.
   nà liàng qì chē shì bái sè de.
   nà liàng qì chē shì hóng sè de.
   nà zhī niǎo shì hóng sè de.

02 nà jià fēi jī shì bái sè de.
   nà jià fēi jī shì huáng sè de.
   nà liàng qì chē shì bái sè de.
   nà liàng qì chē shì huáng sè de.

03 nà liàng qì chē shì hóng sè de.
   nà liàng qì chē shì huáng sè de.
   nà liàng qì chē shì bái sè de.
   nà liàng qì chē shì lán sè de.

04 nà liàng qì chē shì lán sè de.
   nà liàng qì chē shì huáng sè de.
   nà zhī māo shì hēi sè de.
   nà liàng qì chē shì hēi sè de.

05 nà liàng huáng sè de qì chē shì jiù de.
   nà liàng fěn hóng sè de qì chē shì jiù de.
   nà liàng lán sè de qì chē shì xīn de.
   nà liàng hóng sè de qì chē shì xīn de.

06 yī liàng jiù chē
   yī liàng xīn chē
   yī zuò lǎo fáng zi
   yī zuò xīn fáng zi

07 yī wèi lǎo tài tài
   yī gè nián qīng nǚ rén
   yī zuò lǎo fáng zi
   yī zuò xīn fáng zi

08 yī wèi lǎo tài tài
   yī gè nián qīng nǚ rén
   yī wèi lǎo rén
   yī gè xiǎo huǒ zi

09 nà wèi lǎo tài tài de tóu fà shì bái sè de.
   nà gè nǚ háir de tóu fà shì hēi sè de.
   nà gè nán rén de tóu fà shì lán sè de.
   nà gè nán rén de tóu fà shì hóng sè de.

10 nà gè nǚ rén liú zhe cháng fà.
   nà gè nán rén liú zhe cháng fà.
   nà gè nǚ rén liú zhe duǎn fà.
   nà gè nán rén liú zhe duǎn fà.

数字一到十

01
三
二
六
五

02
四
五和六
三
二

03
五和六
三和四
四和五
五和五

04
四和四
三、三、三
五和五
四、五、六

05
四、五、六
五、六、七
六、七、八
一、二、三

06
一、二、三
一、二、三、四
一、二、三、四、五
一、二、三、四、五、六

07
一、二、三
一、二、三、四、五
一、二、三、四、五、六、七
一、二、三、四、五、六、七、八

08
二
一、二、三、四、五、六、七、八、九、零
三
五

09
九
五
十
三

10
十
六
七
一

數字一到十

01
三
二
六
五

02
四
五和六
三
二

03
五和六
三和四
四和五
五和五

04
四和四
三、三、三
五和五
四、五、六

05
四、五、六
五、六、七
六、七、八
一、二、三

06
一、二、三
一、二、三、四
一、二、三、四、五
一、二、三、四、五、六

07
一、二、三
一、二、三、四、五
一、二、三、四、五、六、七
一、二、三、四、五、六、七、八

08
二
一、二、三、四、五、六、七、八、九、零
三
五

09
九
五
十
三

10
十
六
七
一

1-04

shù zì yī dào shí

01 sān
    èr
    liù
    wǔ

02 sì
    wǔ hé liù
    sān
    èr

03 wǔ hé liù
    sān hé sì
    sì hé wǔ
    wǔ hé wǔ

04 sì hé sì
    sān, sān, sān
    wǔ hé wǔ
    sì, wǔ, liù

05 sì, wǔ, liù
    wǔ, liù, qī
    liù, qī, bā
    yī, èr, sān

06 yī, èr, sān
    yī, èr, sān, sì
    yī, èr, sān, sì, wǔ
    yī, èr, sān, sì, wǔ, liù

07 yī, èr, sān
    yī, èr, sān, sì, wǔ
    yī, èr, sān, sì, wǔ, liù, qī
    yī, èr, sān, sì, wǔ, liù, qī, bā

08 èr
    yī, èr, sān, sì, wǔ, liù, qī, bā, jiǔ, líng
    sān
    wǔ

09 jiǔ
    wǔ
    shí
    sān

10 shí
    liù
    qī
    yī

数词和量词及名词的单复数

01 一个女孩儿
女孩儿们
一个男孩儿
男孩儿们

02 一朵花儿
许多花儿
一只眼睛
两只眼睛

03 一个女人
女人们
一个男人
男人们

04 一个孩子
孩子们
一只狗
几只狗

05 一个婴儿
两个婴儿
一个鸡蛋
几个鸡蛋

06 一个男孩儿在跳。
男孩儿们在跳。
一个女孩儿在跑。
女孩儿们在跑。

07 一个男人在跳舞。
男人们在跳舞。
一个女人在唱歌。
女人们在唱歌。

08 一个骑自行车的男孩儿
骑自行车的男人们
一只鸟在飞。
一群鸟在飞。

09 那个孩子在坐着。
那两个孩子在坐着。
一辆自行车
几辆自行车

10 那匹马在走。
那些马在走。
那辆汽车是白色的。
那两辆汽车是白色的。

1-05

數詞和量詞及名詞的單復數

01 一個女孩兒
女孩兒們
一個男孩兒
男孩兒們

02 一朵花兒
許多花兒
一隻眼睛
兩隻眼睛

03 一個女人
女人們
一個男人
男人們

04 一個孩子
孩子們
一隻狗
幾隻狗

05 一個嬰兒
兩個嬰兒
一個雞蛋
幾個雞蛋

06 一個男孩兒在跳。
男孩兒們在跳。
一個女孩兒在跑。
女孩兒們在跑。

07 一個男人在跳舞。
男人們在跳舞。
一個女人在唱歌。
女人們在唱歌。

08 一個騎自行車的男孩兒
騎自行車的男人們
一隻鳥在飛。
一群鳥在飛。

09 那個孩子在坐著。
那兩個孩子在坐著。
一輛自行車
幾輛自行車

10 那匹馬在走。
那些馬在走。
那輛汽車是白色的。
那兩輛汽車是白色的。

1-05

shù cí hé liàng cí jí míng cí de dān fù shù

01 yī gè nǚ háir
   nǚ háir men
   yī gè nán háir
   nán háir men

02 yī duǒ huār
   xǔ duō huār
   yī zhī yǎn jīng
   liǎng zhī yǎn jīng

03 yī gè nǚ rén
   nǚ rén men
   yī gè nán rén
   nán rén men

04 yī gè hái zi
   hái zi men
   yī zhī gǒu
   jǐ zhī gǒu

05 yī gè yīng ér
   liǎng gè yīng ér
   yī gè jī dàn
   jǐ gè jī dàn

06 yī gè nán háir zài tiào.
   nán háir men zài tiào.
   yī gè nǚ háir zài pǎo.
   nǚ háir men zài pǎo.

07 yī gè nán rén zài tiào wǔ.
   nán rén men zài tiào wǔ.
   yī gè nǚ rén zài chàng gē.
   nǚ rén men zài chàng gē.

08 yī gè qí zì xíng chē de nán háir
   qí zì xíng chē de nán rén men
   yī zhī niǎo zài fēi.
   yī qún niǎo zài fēi.

09 nà gè hái zi zài zuò zhe.
   nà liǎng gè hái zi zài zuò zhe.
   yī liàng zì xíng chē
   jǐ liàng zì xíng chē

10 nà pǐ mǎ zài zǒu.
   nà xiē mǎ zài zǒu.
   nà liàng qì chē shì bái sè de.
   nà liǎng liàng qì chē shì bái sè de.

数字和时间表达法

01　一个女孩儿在骑马。
　　两个男人在骑马。
　　一个男人在骑摩托车。
　　两个男孩儿在跳。

02　一个女孩儿在跳。
　　两个女孩儿在跳。
　　四个孩子
　　四个球

03　这个数字是三。
　　这个数字是四。
　　这个数字是一。
　　这个数字是二。

04　这个数字是二。
　　这个数字是四。
　　这个数字是五。
　　这个数字是六。

05　现在是两点。
　　现在是四点。
　　现在是六点。
　　现在是三点。

06　一扇窗户
　　三扇窗户
　　四扇窗户
　　五扇窗户

07　一个蓝色的盘子
　　一个黄色的盘子
　　这儿有两个盘子。一个盘子是蓝色的，一个盘子是黄
　　　色的。
　　这儿有三个盘子。一个盘子是桔黄色的；一个盘子是
　　　蓝色的；一个盘子是黄色的。

08　一个盘子
　　两个盘子
　　三个盘子
　　十个盘子

09　十个手指
　　十五个手指
　　二十个手指
　　三十个手指

10　现在是四点。
　　现在是五点。
　　现在是六点。
　　现在是七点。

數字和時間表達法

01　一個女孩兒在騎馬。
　　兩個男人在騎馬。
　　一個男人在騎摩托車。
　　兩個男孩兒在跳。

02　一個女孩兒在跳。
　　兩個女孩兒在跳。
　　四個孩子
　　四個球

03　這個數字是三。
　　這個數字是四。
　　這個數字是一。
　　這個數字是二。

04　這個數字是二。
　　這個數字是四。
　　這個數字是五。
　　這個數字是六。

05　現在是兩點。
　　現在是四點。
　　現在是六點。
　　現在是三點。

06　一扇窗戶
　　三扇窗戶
　　四扇窗戶
　　五扇窗戶

07　一個藍色的盤子
　　一個黃色的盤子
　　這兒有兩個盤子。一個盤子是藍色的，一個盤子是黃
　　　色的。
　　這兒有三個盤子。一個盤子是桔黃色的；一個盤子是
　　　藍色的；一個盤子是黃色的。

08　一個盤子
　　兩個盤子
　　三個盤子
　　十個盤子

09　十個手指
　　十五個手指
　　二十個手指
　　三十個手指

10　現在是四點。
　　現在是五點。
　　現在是六點。
　　現在是七點。

shù zì hé shí jiān biǎo dá fǎ

01 yī gè nǚ háir zài qí mǎ.
liǎng gè nán rén zài qí mǎ.
yī gè nán rén zài qí mó tuō chē.
liǎng gè nán háir zài tiào.

02 yī gè nǚ háir zài tiào.
liǎng gè nǚ háir zài tiào.
sì gè hái zi
sì gè qiú

03 zhè gè shù zì shì sān.
zhè gè shù zì shì sì.
zhè gè shù zì shì yī.
zhè gè shù zì shì èr.

04 zhè gè shù zì shì èr.
zhè gè shù zì shì sì.
zhè gè shù zì shì wǔ.
zhè gè shù zì shì liù.

05 xiàn zài shì liǎng diǎn.
xiàn zài shì sì diǎn.
xiàn zài shì liù diǎn.
xiàn zài shì sān diǎn.

06 yī shàn chuāng hù
sān shàn chuāng hù
sì shàn chuāng hù
wǔ shàn chuāng hù

07 yī gè lán sè de pán zi
yī gè huáng sè de pán zi
zhèr yǒu liǎng gè pán zi. yī gè pán zi shì lán sè de, yī gè pán zi shì huáng sè de.
zhèr yǒu sān gè pán zi. yī gè pán zi shì jú huáng sè de; yī gè pán zi shì lán sè de; yī gè pán zi shì huáng
    sè de.

08 yī gè pán zi
liǎng gè pán zi
sān gè pán zi
shí gè pán zi

09 shí gè shǒu zhǐ
shí wǔ gè shǒu zhǐ
èr shí gè shǒu zhǐ
sān shí gè shǒu zhǐ

10 xiàn zài shì sì diǎn.
xiàn zài shì wǔ diǎn.
xiàn zài shì liù diǎn.
xiàn zài shì qī diǎn.

1-07

提问和回答；人称代词：他、她；物指代词：它

01 那条鱼是白色的吗？
对，它是白色的。

那辆汽车是白色的吗？
对，它是白色的。

那辆汽车是红色的吗？
对，它是红色的。

那只鸟是红色的吗？
对，它是红色的。

02 那架飞机是白色的吗？
对，它是白色的。

那架飞机是白色的吗？
不是，它是黄色的。

那辆汽车是黄色的吗？
不是，它是白色的。

那辆汽车是黄色的吗？
对，它是黄色的。

03 那辆汽车是红色的吗？
对，它是红色的。

那辆汽车是红色的吗？
不对，那辆汽车不是红色的，是黄色的。

那辆汽车是白色的吗？
对，它是白色的。

那辆汽车是白色的吗？
不对，那辆汽车不是白色的，是蓝色的。

04 那辆汽车是蓝色的吗？
对，它是蓝色的。

那辆汽车是蓝色的吗？
不对，它不是蓝色的，是黄色的。

那只猫是白色的吗？
不对，它不是白色的，是黑色的。

那辆汽车是黑色的吗？
不对，那辆汽车不是黑色的，是粉红色的。

05 那辆绿色的汽车是旧的吗？
对，那辆绿色的汽车是旧的。

那辆粉红色的汽车是新的吗？
不对，它不是新的。

那辆黑色的汽车是旧的吗？
不对，它不是旧的，是新的。

那辆红色的汽车是旧的吗？
不对，它不是旧的。

1-07

提問和回答；人稱代詞：他、她；物指代詞：它

01 那條魚是白色的嗎？
對，它是白色的。

那輛汽車是白色的嗎？
對，它是白色的。

那輛汽車是紅色的嗎？
對，它是紅色的。

那隻鳥是紅色的嗎？
對，它是紅色的。

02 那架飛機是白色的嗎？
對，它是白色的。

那架飛機是白色的嗎？
不是，它是黃色的。

那輛汽車是黃色的嗎？
不是，它是白色的。

那輛汽車是黃色的嗎？
對，它是黃色的。

03 那輛汽車是紅色的嗎？
對，它是紅色的。

那輛汽車是紅色的嗎？
不對，那輛汽車不是紅色的，是黃色的。

那輛汽車是白色的嗎？
對，它是白色的。

那輛汽車是白色的嗎？
不對，那輛汽車不是白色的，是藍色的。

04 那輛汽車是藍色的嗎？
對，它是藍色的。

那輛汽車是藍色的嗎？
不對，它不是藍色的，是黃色的。

那隻貓是白色的嗎？
不對，它不是白色的，是黑色的。

那輛汽車是黑色的嗎？
不對，那輛汽車不是黑色的，是粉紅色的。

05 那輛綠色的汽車是舊的嗎？
對，那輛綠色的汽車是舊的。

那輛粉紅色的汽車是新的嗎？
不對，它不是新的。

那輛黑色的汽車是舊的嗎？
不對，它不是舊的，是新的。

那輛紅色的汽車是舊的嗎？
不對，它不是舊的。

（继续）

1-07

tí wèn hé huí dá; rén chēng dài cí: tā, tā; wù zhǐ dài cí: tā

01　nà tiáo yú shì bái sè de ma?
　　duì, tā shì bái sè de.

　　nà liàng qì chē shì bái sè de ma?
　　duì, tā shì bái sè de.

　　nà liàng qì chē shì hóng sè de ma?
　　duì, tā shì hóng sè de.

　　nà zhī niǎo shì hóng sè de ma?
　　duì, tā shì hóng sè de.

02　nà jià fēi jī shì bái sè de ma?
　　duì, tā shì bái sè de.

　　nà jià fēi jī shì bái sè de ma?
　　bú shì, tā shì huáng sè de.

　　nà liàng qì chē shì huáng sè de ma?
　　bú shì, tā shì bái sè de.

　　nà liàng qì chē shì huáng sè de ma?
　　duì, tā shì huáng sè de.

03　nà liàng qì chē shì hóng sè de ma?
　　duì, tā shì hóng sè de.

　　nà liàng qì chē shì hóng sè de ma?
　　bú duì, nà liàng qì chē bú shì hóng sè de, shì huáng sè de.

　　nà liàng qì chē shì bái sè de ma?
　　duì, tā shì bái sè de.

　　nà liàng qì chē shì bái sè de ma?
　　bú dùi, nà liàng qì chē bú shì bái sè de, shì lán sè de.

04　nà liàng qì chē shì lán sè de ma?
　　duì, tā shì lán sè de.

　　nà liàng qì chē shì lán sè de ma?
　　bú duì, tā bú shì lán sè de, shì huáng sè de.

　　nà zhī māo shì bái sè de ma?
　　bú duì, tā bú shì bái sè de, shì hēi sè de.

　　nà liàng qì chē shì hēi sè de ma?
　　bú duì, nà liàng qì chē bú shì hēi sè de, shì fěn hóng sè de.

05　nà liàng lǜ sè de qì chē shì jiù de ma?
　　duì, nà liàng lǜ sè de qì chē shì jiù de.

　　nà liàng fěn hóng sè de qì chē shì xīn de ma?
　　bú duì, tā bú shì xīn de.

　　nà liàng hēi sè de qì chē shì jiù de ma?
　　bú duì, tā bú shì jiù de, shì xīn de.

　　nà liàng hóng sè de qì chē shì jiù de ma?
　　bú duì, tā bú shì jiù de.

(jì xù)

06　那辆汽车是旧的吗？
　　对，是旧的。

　　那辆汽车是旧的吗？
　　不对，它不是旧的。

　　房子上有一个男人吗？
　　对，有一个男人。

　　房子上有一个男人吗？
　　没有，房子上没人。

07　那个女人在跑吗？
　　对，她在跑。

　　那个女人在跑吗？
　　没有，她不在跑。

　　那两个女人在跑吗？
　　对，她们在跑。

　　那两个女人在跑吗？
　　没有，她们不在跑。

08　那个男孩儿在跳吗？
　　对，他在跳。

　　那些男孩儿在跳吗？
　　对，他们在跳。

　　那个男孩儿在跳吗？
　　没有，他不在跳。

　　那些男孩儿在跳吗？
　　没有，他们不在跳。

09　那个女人在坐着吗？
　　对，她在坐着。

　　那两个女人在坐着吗？
　　没有，她们没坐着。

　　那两个女人在坐着吗？
　　对，她们在坐着。

　　那个女人在坐着吗？
　　没有，她没坐着。

10　那个男人在吃东西吗？
　　对，他在吃东西。

　　那个女人在吃东西吗？
　　对，她在吃东西。

　　那个男人在吃东西吗？
　　没有，他不在吃东西。

　　那个女人在吃东西吗？
　　没有，她不在吃东西。

06　那輛汽車是舊的嗎？
　　對，是舊的。

　　那輛汽車是舊的嗎？
　　不對，它不是舊的。

　　房子上有一個男人嗎？
　　對，有一個男人。

　　房子上有一個男人嗎？
　　沒有，房子上沒人。

07　那個女人在跑嗎？
　　對，她在跑。

　　那個女人在跑嗎？
　　沒有，她不在跑。

　　那兩個女人在跑嗎？
　　對，她們在跑。

　　那兩個女人在跑嗎？
　　沒有，她們不在跑。

08　那個男孩兒在跳嗎？
　　對，他在跳。

　　那些男孩兒在跳嗎？
　　對，他們在跳。

　　那個男孩兒在跳嗎？
　　沒有，他不在跳。

　　那些男孩兒在跳嗎？
　　沒有，他們不在跳。

09　那個女人在坐著嗎？
　　對，她在坐著。

　　那兩個女人在坐著嗎？
　　沒有，她們沒坐著。

　　那兩個女人在坐著嗎？
　　對，她們在坐著。

　　那個女人在坐著嗎？
　　沒有，她沒坐著。

10　那個男人在吃東西嗎？
　　對，他在吃東西。

　　那個女人在吃東西嗎？
　　對，她在吃東西。

　　那個男人在吃東西嗎？
　　沒有，他不在吃東西。

　　那個女人在吃東西嗎？
　　沒有，她不在吃東西。

06 nà liàng qì chē shì jiù de ma?
     duì, shì jiù de.

     nà liàng qì chē shì jiù de ma?
     bú duì, tā bú shì jiù de.

     fáng zi shàng yǒu yī gè nán rén ma?
     duì, yǒu yī gè nán rén.

     fáng zi shàng yǒu yī gè nán rén ma?
     méi yǒu, fáng zi shàng méi rén.

07 nà gè nǚ rén zài pǎo ma?
     duì, tā zài pǎo.

     nà gè nǚ rén zài pǎo ma?
     méi yǒu, tā bú zài pǎo.

     nà liǎng gè nǚ rén zài pǎo ma?
     duì, tā men zài pǎo.

     nà liǎng gè nǚ rén zài pǎo ma?
     méi yǒu, tā men bú zài pǎo.

08 nà gè nán háir zài tiào ma?
     duì, tā zài tiào.

     nà xiē nán háir zài tiào ma?
     duì, tā men zài tiào.

     nà gè nán háir zài tiào ma?
     méi yǒu, tā bú zài tiào.

     nà xiē nán háir zài tiào ma?
     méi yǒu, tā men bú zài tiào.

09 nà gè nǚ rén zài zuò zhe ma?
     duì, tā zài zuò zhe.

     nà liǎng gè nǚ rén zài zuò zhe ma?
     méi yǒu, tā men méi zuò zhe.

     nà liǎng gè nǚ rén zài zuò zhe ma?
     duì, tā men zài zuò zhe.

     nà gè nǚ rén zài zuò zhe ma?
     méi yǒu, tā méi zuò zhe.

10 nà gè nán rén zài chī dōng xī ma?
     duì, tā zài chī dōng xī.

     nà gè nǚ rén zài chī dōng xī ma?
     duì, tā zài chī dōng xī.

     nà gè nán rén zài chī dōng xī ma?
     méi yǒu, tā bú zài chī dōng xī.

     nà gè nǚ rén zài chī dōng xī ma?
     méi yǒu, tā bú zài chī dōng xī.

食物、吃、喝；直接宾语

01 水果
　　牛奶
　　肉
　　面包

02 那个男人在吃东西。
　　那个男人在喝东西。
　　那个女人在吃东西。
　　那个女人在喝东西。

03 那个女人和那个女孩儿在喝牛奶。
　　那个男人在喝水。
　　那个女孩儿在喝牛奶。
　　那个女人在喝牛奶。

04 那个男孩儿在吃面包。
　　那匹马在吃胡萝卜。
　　那个男人在吃东西。
　　那个男人在喝东西。

05 那个男人在喝桔子汁。
　　那个男人在喝牛奶。
　　那个男人在喝水。
　　那个男孩儿在吃面包，那个小姑娘在喝牛奶。

06 黄色的香蕉
　　绿色的苹果和红色的苹果
　　红色的西红柿
　　黄色的奶酪

07 红色的草莓
　　红色的葡萄
　　绿色的梨
　　黄色的苹果

08 草莓是食物。
　　面包是食物。
　　球不是食物。
　　帽子不是食物。

09 篮子里的香蕉
　　袋子里的面包
　　箱子里的苹果
　　篮子里的西红柿

10 上面放着食物的桌子
　　上面没放食物的桌子
　　上面放着食物的盘子
　　上面没放食物的盘子

1-08

食物、吃、喝；直接賓語

01 水果
　　牛奶
　　肉
　　面包

02 那個男人在吃東西。
　　那個男人在喝東西。
　　那個女人在吃東西。
　　那個女人在喝東西。

03 那個女人和那個女孩兒在喝牛奶。
　　那個男人在喝水。
　　那個女孩兒在喝牛奶。
　　那個女人在喝牛奶。

04 那個男孩兒在吃面包。
　　那匹馬在吃胡蘿卜。
　　那個男人在吃東西。
　　那個男人在喝東西。

05 那個男人在喝桔子汁。
　　那個男人在喝牛奶。
　　那個男人在喝水。
　　那個男孩兒在吃面包，那個小姑娘在喝牛奶。

06 黃色的香蕉
　　綠色的苹果和红色的苹果
　　紅色的西紅柿
　　黃色的奶酪

07 紅色的草莓
　　紅色的葡萄
　　綠色的梨
　　黃色的苹果

08 草莓是食物。
　　面包是食物。
　　球不是食物。
　　帽子不是食物。

09 籃子裡的香蕉
　　袋子裡的面包
　　箱子裡的苹果
　　籃子裡的西紅柿

10 上面放著食物的桌子
　　上面沒放食物的桌子
　　上面放著食物的盤子
　　上面沒放食物的盤子

1-08

shí wù, chī, hē; zhí jiē bīn yǔ

01 shuǐ guǒ
   niú nǎi
   ròu
   miàn bāo

02 nà gè nán rén zài chī dōng xī.
   nà gè nán rén zài hē dōng xī.
   nà gè nǚ rén zài chī dōng xī.
   nà gè nǚ rén zài hē dōng xī.

03 nà gè nǚ rén hé nà gè nǚ háir zài hē niú nǎi.
   nà gè nán rén zài hē shuǐ.
   nà gè nǚ háir zài hē niú nǎi.
   nà gè nǚ rén zài hē niú nǎi.

04 nà gè nán háir zài chī miàn bāo.
   nà pǐ mǎ zài chī hú luó bo.
   nà gè nán rén zài chī dōng xī.
   nà gè nán rén zài hē dōng xī.

05 nà gè nán rén zài hē jú zi zhī.
   nà gè nán rén zài hē niú nǎi.
   nà gè nán rén zài hē shuǐ.
   nà gè nán háir zài chī miàn bāo, nà gè xiǎo gū niang zài hē niú nǎi.

06 huáng sè de xiāng jiāo
   lǜ sè de píng guǒ hé hóng sè de píng guǒ
   hóng sè de xī hóng shì
   huáng sè de nǎi lào

07 hóng sè de cǎo méi
   hóng sè de pú táo
   lǜ sè de lí
   huáng sè de píng guǒ

08 cǎo méi shì shí wù.
   miàn bāo shì shí wù.
   qiú bú shì shí wù.
   mào zi bú shì shí wù.

09 lán zi lǐ de xiāng jiāo
   dài zi lǐ de miàn bāo
   xiāng zi lǐ de píng guǒ
   lán zi lǐ de xī hóng shì

10 shàng miàn fàng zhe shí wù de zhuō zi
   shàng miàn méi fàng shí wù de zhuō zi
   shàng miàn fàng zhe shí wù de pán zi
   shàng miàn méi fàng shí wù de pán zi

1-09

服装和穿戴；动词的肯定和否定形式；直接宾语

01　一顶白色的帽子
　　一顶黑色的帽子
　　一些黑色的帽子
　　一些白色的帽子

02　一顶黑色的帽子和一顶褐色的帽子
　　一些灰色的帽子
　　一顶紫色的帽子
　　一顶白色的帽子

03　那个女孩儿穿白衬衣。
　　那个女人穿着蓝衬衣。
　　那个女人穿着白衬衣。
　　那个女人戴着一顶黑帽子。

04　那个男孩儿穿着白裤子。
　　那几个男人穿着蓝牛仔裤。
　　那几个男人穿着深色的衬衫和裤子。
　　那个女人穿着白衬衫和蓝牛仔裤。

05　那个女人没有穿外衣。
　　一个女人穿着红色的雨衣，一个女人穿着紫色的雨衣。
　　一个女人穿着黄色的雨衣，一个女人穿着蓝色的雨衣。
　　那个女人穿着黑外衣。

06　一个男孩儿穿着蓝 T 恤衫，一个男孩儿穿着红 T 恤衫。
　　两个女人都穿着蓝衬衫。
　　那个女人穿着白衬衫和黑裙子。
　　那个女人穿着白衬衫和蓝牛仔裤。

07　那个男人和那个女人都穿着游泳衣。
　　那个男人和那个女人都没穿游泳衣。
　　那个女人戴眼镜。
　　那个女人没戴眼镜。

08　那个女孩儿穿着一只鞋。
　　那个女孩儿穿着两只鞋。
　　那个男孩儿戴着一顶帽子。
　　那个男孩儿戴着两顶帽子。

09　那些女孩儿穿着白衬衫，黑裙子。
　　一个女孩儿穿着白连衣裙，一个女孩儿穿着红白相间的连衣裙。
　　那两个女孩儿穿着连衣裙，戴着帽子。
　　那两个女孩儿穿着黑裤子。

10　那个女孩儿没穿袜子。
　　那个女孩儿穿着白袜子。
　　那个男孩儿没穿鞋。
　　那个男孩儿穿着鞋。

1-09

服裝和穿戴；動詞的肯定和否定形式；直接賓語

01　一頂白色的帽子
　　一頂黑色的帽子
　　一些黑色的帽子
　　一些白色的帽子

02　一頂黑色的帽子和一頂褐色的帽子
　　一些灰色的帽子
　　一頂紫色的帽子
　　一頂白色的帽子

03　那個女孩兒穿著白襯衣。
　　那個女人穿著藍襯衣。
　　那個女人穿著白襯衣。
　　那個女人戴著一頂黑帽子。

04　那個男孩兒穿著白褲子。
　　那幾個男人穿著藍牛仔褲。
　　那幾個男人穿著深色的襯衫和褲子。
　　那個女人穿著白襯衫和藍牛仔褲。

05　那個女人沒有穿外衣。
　　一個女人穿著紅色的雨衣，一個女人穿著紫色的雨衣。
　　一個女人穿著黃色的雨衣，一個女人穿著藍色的雨衣。
　　那個女人穿著黑外衣。

06　一個男孩兒穿著藍 T 恤衫，一個男孩兒穿著紅 T 恤衫。
　　兩個女人都穿著藍襯衫。
　　那個女人穿著白襯衫和黑裙子。
　　那個女人穿著白襯衫和藍牛仔褲。

07　那個男人和那個女人都穿著游泳衣。
　　那個男人和那個女人都沒穿游泳衣。
　　那個女人戴眼鏡。
　　那個女人沒戴眼鏡。

08　那個女孩兒穿著一隻鞋。
　　那個女孩兒穿著兩隻鞋。
　　那個男孩兒戴著一頂帽子。
　　那個男孩兒戴著兩頂帽子。

09　那些女孩兒穿著白襯衫，黑裙子。
　　一個女孩兒穿著白連衣裙，一個女孩兒穿著紅白相間的連衣裙。
　　那兩個女孩兒穿著連衣裙，戴著帽子。
　　那兩個女孩兒穿著黑褲子。

10　那個女孩兒沒穿襪子。
　　那個女孩兒穿著白襪子。
　　那個男孩兒沒穿鞋。
　　那個男孩兒穿著鞋。

1-09

fú zhuāng hé chuān dài; dòng cí de kěn dìng hé fǒu dìng xíng shì; zhí jiē bīn yǔ

01 yī dǐng bái sè de mào zi
    yī dǐng hēi sè de mào zi
    yī xiē hēi sè de mào zi
    yī xiē bái sè de mào zi

02 yī dǐng hēi sè de mào zi hé yī dǐng hè sè de mào zi
    yī xiē huī sè de mào zi
    yī dǐng zǐ sè de mào zi
    yī dǐng bái sè de mào zi

03 nà gè nǚ háir chuān zhe bái chèn yī.
    nà gè nǚ rén chuān zhe lán chèn yī.
    nà gè nǚ rén chuān zhe bái chèn yī.
    nà gè nǚ rén dài zhe yī dǐng hēi mào zi.

04 nà gè nán háir chuān zhe bái kù zi.
    nà jǐ gè nán rén chuān zhe lán niú zǎi kù.
    nà jǐ gè nán rén chuān zhe shēn sè de chèn shān hé kù zi.
    nà gè nǚ rén chuān zhe bái chèn shān hé lán niú zǎi kù.

05 nà gè nǚ rén méi yǒu chuān wài yī.
    yī gè nǚ rén chuān zhe hóng sè de yǔ yī, yī gè nǚ rén chuān zhe zǐ sè de yǔ yī.
    yī gè nǚ rén chuān zhe huáng sè de yǔ yī, yī gè nǚ rén chuān zhe lán sè de yǔ yī.
    nà gè nǚ rén chuān zhe hēi wài yī.

06 yī gè nán háir chuān zhe lán tì xù shān, yī gè nán háir chuān zhe hóng tì xù shān.
    liǎng gè nǚ rén dōu chuān zhe lán chèn shān.
    nà gè nǚ rén chuān zhe bái chèn shān hé hēi qún zi.
    nà gè nǚ rén chuān zhe bái chèn shān hé lán niú zǎi kù.

07 nà gè nán rén hé nà gè nǚ rén dōu chuān zhe yóu yǒng yī.
    nà gè nán rén hé nà gè nǚ rén dōu méi chuān yóu yǒng yī.
    nà gè nǚ rén dài yǎn jìng.
    nà gè nǚ rén méi dài yǎn jìng.

08 nà gè nǚ háir chuān zhe yī zhī xié.
    nà gè nǚ háir chuān zhe liǎng zhī xié.
    nà gè nán háir dài zhe yī dǐng mào zi.
    nà gè nán háir dài zhe liǎng dǐng mào zi.

09 nà xiē nǚ háir chuān zhe bái chèn shān, hēi qún zi.
    yī gè nǚ háir chuān zhe bái lián yī qún, yī gè nǚ háir chuān zhe hóng bái xiāng jiàn de lián yī qún.
    nà liǎng gè nǚ háir chuān zhe lián yī qún, dài zhe mào zi.
    nà liǎng gè nǚ háir chuān zhe hēi kù zi.

10 nà gè nǚ háir méi chuān wà zi.
    nà gè nǚ háir chuān zhe bái wà zi.
    nà gè nán háir méi chuān xié.
    nà gè nán háir chuān zhe xié.

1-10

疑问代词的使用：谁、什么、在哪儿、哪个（些）

01　谁在看书？
　　那个女人在看书。

　　谁在跳舞？
　　那个男人在跳舞。

　　谁在游泳？
　　那个男孩儿在游泳。

　　谁在跑？
　　那匹马在跑。

02　谁在坐着？
　　那个小孩儿在坐着。

　　谁在吃东西？
　　那个男人在吃东西。

　　谁在喝牛奶？
　　那个女孩儿在喝牛奶。

　　谁在桌子下面？
　　那个男孩儿在桌子下面。

03　谁在吃胡萝卜？
　　那匹马在吃胡萝卜。

　　谁在吃面包？
　　那个男孩儿在吃面包。

　　什么在飞？
　　那架飞机在飞。

　　什么在飞？
　　那只鸟在飞。

04　那两个女人穿着什么？
　　她们穿着蓝衬衫。

　　那些女人穿着什么？
　　她们穿着白衬衫。

　　这是什么食物？
　　这是草莓。

　　这是什么食物？
　　这是面包。

05　那个男孩儿在哪儿？
　　那个男孩儿在桌子下面。

　　那个男孩儿在哪儿？
　　那个男孩儿在桌子上面。

　　那个男人在哪儿？
　　那个男人在那座老房子上。

　　那个男人在哪儿？
　　那个男人在自行车上。

1-10

疑問代詞的使用：誰、什麼、在哪兒、哪個（些）

01　誰在看書？
　　那個女人在看書。

　　誰在跳舞？
　　那個男人在跳舞。

　　誰在游泳？
　　那個男孩兒在游泳。

　　誰在跑？
　　那匹馬在跑。

02　誰在坐著？
　　那個小孩兒在坐著。

　　誰在吃東西？
　　那個男人在吃東西。

　　誰在喝牛奶？
　　那個女孩兒在喝牛奶。

　　誰在桌子下面？
　　那個男孩兒在桌子下面。

03　誰在吃胡蘿蔔？
　　那匹馬在吃胡蘿蔔。

　　誰在吃面包？
　　那個男孩兒在吃面包。

　　什麼在飛？
　　那架飛機在飛。

　　什麼在飛？
　　那隻鳥在飛。

04　那兩個女人穿著什麼？
　　她們穿著藍襯衫。

　　那些女人穿著什麼？
　　她們穿著白襯衫。

　　這是什麼食物？
　　這是草莓。

　　這是什麼食物？
　　這是面包。

05　那個男孩兒在哪兒？
　　那個男孩兒在桌子下面。

　　那個男孩兒在哪兒？
　　那個男孩兒在桌子上面。

　　那個男人在哪兒？
　　那個男人在那座老房子上。

　　那個男人在哪兒？
　　那個男人在自行車上。

（继续）

1-10

yí wèn dài cí de shǐ yòng:shéi, shén me, zài nǎr, nǎ gè(xiē)

01 shéi zài kàn shū?
nà gè nǚ rén zài kàn shū.

shéi zài tiào wǔ?
nà gè nán rén zài tiào wǔ.

shéi zài yóu yǒng?
nà gè nán háir zài yóu yǒng.

shéi zài pǎo?
nà pǐ mǎ zài pǎo.

02 shéi zài zuò zhe?
nà gè xiǎo háir zài zuò zhe.

shéi zài chī dōng xī?
nà gè nán rén zài chī dōng xī.

shéi zài hē niú nǎi?
nà gè nǚ háir zài hē niú nǎi.

shéi zài zhuō zi xià miàn?
nà gè nán háir zài zhuō zi xià miàn.

03 shéi zài chī hú luó bo?
nà pǐ mǎ zài chī hú luó bo.

shéi zài chī miàn bāo?
nà gè nán háir zài chī miàn bāo.

shén me zài fēi?
nà jià fēi jī zài fēi.

shén me zài fēi?
nà zhī niǎo zài fēi.

04 nà liǎng gè nǚ rén chuān zhe shén me?
tā men chuān zhe lán chèn shān.

nà xiē nǚ rén chuān zhe shén me?
tā men chuān zhe bái chèn shān.

zhè shì shén me shí wù?
zhè shì cǎo méi.

zhè shì shén me shí wù?
zhè shì miàn bāo.

05 nà gè nán háir zài nǎr?
nà gè nán háir zài zhuō zi xià miàn.

nà gè nán háir zài nǎr?
nà gè nán háir zài zhuō zi shàng miàn.

nà gè nán rén zài nǎr?
nà gè nán rén zài nà zuò lǎo fáng zi shàng.

nà gè nán rén zài nǎr?
nà gè nán rén zài zì xíng chē shàng.

(jì xù)

06　这辆汽车是什么颜色的？
　　这辆汽车是红色的。

　　这辆汽车是什么颜色的？
　　这辆汽车是黄色的。

　　那辆蓝色的汽车在哪儿？
　　那辆蓝色的汽车在这儿。

　　那辆白色的汽车在哪儿？
　　那辆白色的汽车在这儿。

07　那些香蕉在哪儿？

　　奶酪在哪儿？

　　哪匹马在跑？
　　这匹马在跑。

　　哪匹马在跳？
　　这匹马在跳。

08　哪辆汽车是蓝色的？

　　哪辆汽车是红色的？

　　哪两个女人穿着蓝衬衫？
　　这两个女人都穿着蓝衬衫。

　　哪个孩子在喝牛奶？
　　那个女孩儿在喝牛奶。

09　谁留着长发？
　　那个男人留着长发。

　　那个男孩儿在干什么？
　　他在游泳。

　　那个男孩儿在哪儿？
　　那个男孩儿在马上。

　　哪个孩子在吃面包？
　　那个男孩儿在吃面包。

10　那个女人和那个女孩儿在干什么？
　　她们在喝牛奶。

　　那两个孩子在哪儿？
　　他们在船上。

　　哪个男人的头发是蓝色的？

　　哪个男人的头发是红色的？

06　這輛汽車是什麼顏色的？
　　這輛汽車是紅色的。

　　這輛汽車是什麼顏色的？
　　這輛汽車是黃色的。

　　那輛藍色的汽車在哪兒？
　　那輛藍色的汽車在這兒。

　　那輛白色的汽車在哪兒？
　　那輛白色的汽車在這兒。

07　那些香蕉在哪兒？

　　奶酪在哪兒？

　　哪匹馬在跑？
　　這匹馬在跑。

　　哪匹馬在跳？
　　這匹馬在跳。

08　哪輛汽車是藍色的？

　　哪輛汽車是紅色的？

　　哪兩個女人穿著藍襯衫？
　　這兩個女人都穿著藍襯衫。

　　哪個孩子在喝牛奶？
　　那個女孩兒在喝牛奶。

09　誰留著長髮？
　　那個男人留著長髮。

　　那個男孩兒在干什麼？
　　他在游泳。

　　那個男孩兒在哪兒？
　　那個男孩兒在馬上。

　　哪個孩子在吃面包？
　　那個男孩兒在吃面包。

10　那個女人和那個女孩兒在干什麼？
　　她們在喝牛奶。

　　那兩個孩子在哪兒？
　　他們在船上。

　　哪個男人的頭髮是藍色的？

　　哪個男人的頭髮是紅色的？

06 zhè liàng qì chē shì shén me yán sè de?
zhè liàng qì chē shì hóng sè de.

zhè liàng qì chē shì shén me yán sè de?
zhè liàng qì chē shì huáng sè de.

nà liàng lán sè de qì chē zài nǎr?
nà liàng lán sè de qì chē zài zhèr.

nà liàng bái sè de qì chē zài nǎr?
nà liàng bái sè de qì chē zài zhèr.

07 nà xiē xiāng jiāo zài nǎr?

nǎi lào zài nǎr?

nǎ pǐ mǎ zài pǎo?
zhè pǐ mǎ zài pǎo.

nǎ pǐ mǎ zài tiào?
zhè pǐ mǎ zài tiào.

08 nǎ liàng qì chē shì lán sè de?

nǎ liàng qì chē shì hóng sè de?

nǎ liǎng gè nǚ rén chuān zhe lán chèn shān?
zhè liǎng gè nǚ rén dōu chuān zhe lán chèn shān.

nǎ gè hái zi zài hē niú nǎi?
nà gè nǚ háir zài hē niú nǎi.

09 shéi liú zhe cháng fà?
nà gè nán rén liú zhe cháng fà.

nà gè nán háir zài gàn shén me?
tā zài yóu yǒng.

nà gè nán háir zài nǎr?
nà gè nán háir zài mǎ shàng.

nǎ gè hái zi zài chī miàn bāo?
nà gè nán háir zài chī miàn bāo.

10 nà gè nǚ rén hé nà gè nǚ háir zài gàn shén me?
tā men zài hē niú nǎi.

nà liǎng gè hái zi zài nǎr?
tā men zài chuán shàng.

nǎ gè nán rén de tóu fà shì lán sè de?

nǎ gè nán rén de tóu fà shì hóng sè de?

1-11

复习第一部分

01　在飞机上面的一个男孩儿
　　在飞机下面的一个男孩儿
　　在桌子上面的一个男孩儿
　　在桌子下面的一个男孩儿

02　那两个女孩儿在走。
　　那两个女孩儿在跑。
　　那个男孩儿在跳。
　　那个男孩儿在走。

03　那个女人留着长发。
　　那个男人留着长发。
　　那个女人留着短发。
　　那个男人留着短发。

04　四、五、六
　　五、六、七
　　六、七、八
　　一、二、三

05　那匹马在走。
　　那些马在走。
　　那辆汽车是白色的。
　　那两辆汽车是白色的。

06　现在是两点。
　　现在是四点。
　　现在是六点。
　　现在是三点。

07　那辆绿色的汽车是旧的吗？
　　对，那辆绿色的汽车是旧的。

　　那辆粉红色的汽车是新的吗？
　　不对，它不是新的。

　　那辆黑色的汽车是旧的吗？
　　不对，它不是旧的，是新的。

　　那辆红色的汽车是旧的吗？
　　不对，它不是旧的。

08　篮子里的香蕉
　　袋子里的面包
　　箱子里的苹果
　　篮子里的西红柿

1-11

復習第一部分

01　在飛機上面的一個男孩兒
　　在飛機下面的一個男孩兒
　　在桌子上面的一個男孩兒
　　在桌子下面的一個男孩兒

02　那兩個女孩兒在走。
　　那兩個女孩兒在跑。
　　那個男孩兒在跳。
　　那個男孩兒在走。

03　那個女人留著長髮。
　　那個男人留著長髮。
　　那個女人留著短髮。
　　那個男人留著短髮。

04　四、五、六
　　五、六、七
　　六、七、八
　　一、二、三

05　那匹馬在走。
　　那些馬在走。
　　那輛汽車是白色的。
　　那兩輛汽車是白色的。

06　現在是兩點。
　　現在是四點。
　　現在是六點。
　　現在是三點。

07　那輛綠色的汽車是舊的嗎？
　　對，那輛綠色的汽車是舊的。

　　那輛粉紅色的汽車是新的嗎？
　　不對，它不是新的。

　　那輛黑色的汽車是舊的嗎？
　　不對，它不是舊的，是新的。

　　那輛紅色的汽車是舊的嗎？
　　不對，它不是舊的。

08　籃子裡的香蕉
　　袋子裡的面包
　　箱子裡的苹果
　　籃子裡的西紅柿

（继续）

fù xí dì yī bù fen

01 zài fēi jī shàng miàn de yī gè nán háir
   zài fēi jī xià miàn de yī gè nán háir
   zài zhuō zi shàng miàn de yī gè nán háir
   zài zhuō zi xià miàn de yī gè nán háir

02 nà liǎng gè nǚ háir zài zǒu.
   nà liǎng gè nǚ háir zài pǎo.
   nà gè nán háir zài tiào.
   nà gè nán háir zài zǒu.

03 nà gè nǚ rén liú zhe cháng fà.
   nà gè nán rén liú zhe cháng fà.
   nà gè nǚ rén liú zhe duǎn fà.
   nà gè nán rén liú zhe duǎn fà.

04 sì, wǔ, liù
   wǔ, liù, qī
   liù, qī, bā
   yī, èr, sān

05 nà pǐ mǎ zài zǒu.
   nà xiē mǎ zài zǒu.
   nà liàng qì chē shì bái sè de.
   nà liǎng liàng qì chē shì bái sè de.

06 xiàn zài shì liǎng diǎn.
   xiàn zài shì sì diǎn.
   xiàn zài shì liù diǎn.
   xiàn zài shì sān diǎn.

07 nà liàng lǜ sè de qì chē shì jiù de ma?
   duì, nà liàng lǜ sè de qì chē shì jiù de.

   nà liàng fěn hóng sè de qì chē shì xīn de ma?
   bú duì, tā bú shì xīn de.

   nà liàng hēi sè de qì chē shì jiù de ma?
   bú duì, tā bú shì jiù de, shì xīn de.

   nà liàng hóng sè de qì chē shì jiù de ma?
   bú duì, tā bú shì jiù de.

08 lán zi lǐ de xiāng jiāo
   dài zi lǐ de miàn bāo
   xiāng zi lǐ de píng guǒ
   lán zi lǐ de xī hóng shì

(jì xù)

09 那些女孩儿穿着白衬衫，黑裙子。
一个女孩儿穿着白连衣裙，一个女孩儿穿着红白相间
的连衣裙。
那两个女孩儿穿着连衣裙，戴着帽子。
那两个女孩儿穿着黑裤子。

10 那两个女人穿着什么？
她们穿着蓝衬衫。

那些女人穿着什么？
她们穿着白衬衫。

这是什么食物？
这是草莓。

这是什么食物？
这是面包。

09 那些女孩兒穿著白襯衫，黑裙子。
一個女孩兒穿著白連衣裙，一個女孩兒穿著紅白相間
的連衣裙。
那兩個女孩兒穿著連衣裙，戴著帽子。
那兩個女孩兒穿著黑褲子。

10 那兩個女人穿著什麼？
她們穿著藍襯衫。

那些女人穿著什麼？
她們穿著白襯衫。

這是什麼食物？
這是草莓。

這是什麼食物？
這是面包。

09 nà xiē nǚ háir chuān zhe bái chèn shān, hēi qún zi.
yī gè nǚ háir chuān zhe bái lián yī qún, yī gè nǚ háir chuān zhe hóng bái xiāng jiàn de lián yī qún.
nà liǎng gè nǚ háir chuān zhe lián yī qún, dài zhe mào zi.
nà liǎng gè nǚ háir chuān zhe hēi kù zi.

10 nà liǎng gè nǚ rén chuān zhe shén me?
tā men chuān zhe lán chèn shān.

nà xiē nǚ rén chuān zhe shén me?
tā men chuān zhe bái chèn shān.

zhè shì shén me shí wù?
zhè shì cǎo méi.

zhè shì shén me shí wù?
zhè shì miàn bāo.

2-01

更多的动词：跑、跳、掷、微笑等；现在
进行时

01 那个男孩儿在扔球。
那个女人在扔球。
那个男人在扔球。
那个男人在把那个男孩儿抛起来。

02 那个女人在接那个黄色的球。
那个男人在扔球。
那个女人在接那个白色的球。
那个男孩儿在接耙子。

03 那个男孩儿在扔球。
那个男孩儿在接球。
那个穿白衣服的男孩儿在踢球。
那个穿红衣服的男孩儿在踢球。

04 那个女孩儿在骑马。
那个男孩儿在骑自行车。
那个女孩儿在跳。
那个男孩儿在跑。

05 那个男孩儿在笑。
那个男孩儿在喝东西。
那个女人在坐着。
那个女人在跑。

06 那个女人在笑。
那个女人在指着什么东西。
那个女人在看报纸。
那个女人在打电话。

07 那个小女孩儿在大笑。
那个男人在大笑。
那个女孩儿在写字。
那个男人在骑自行车。

08 那个男孩儿在踢。
那头牛在踢。
那个男孩儿在笑。
那头牛在跑。

09 那个女孩儿在躺着。
那个女孩儿在跑。
那个女孩儿在大笑。
那个女孩儿在笑。

10 那些鸟在飞。
那两只鸭子在游。
那两只鹅在走。
那只鸟在飞。

2-01

更多的動詞：跑、跳、擲、微笑等；現在
進行時

01 那個男孩兒在扔球。
那個女人在扔球。
那個男人在扔球。
那個男人在把那個男孩兒拋起來。

02 那個女人在接那個黃色的球。
那個男人在扔球。
那個女人在接那個白色的球。
那個男孩兒在接耙子。

03 那個男孩兒在扔球。
那個男孩兒在接球。
那個穿白衣服的男孩兒在踢球。
那個穿紅衣服的男孩兒在踢球。

04 那個女孩兒在騎馬。
那個男孩兒在騎自行車。
那個女孩兒在跳。
那個男孩兒在跑。

05 那個男孩兒在笑。
那個男孩兒在喝東西。
那個女人在坐著。
那個女人在跑。

06 那個女人在笑。
那個女人在指著甚麼東西。
那個女人在看報紙。
那個女人在打電話。

07 那個小女孩兒在大笑。
那個男人在大笑。
那個女孩兒在寫字。
那個男人在騎自行車。

08 那個男孩兒在踢。
那頭牛在踢。
那個男孩兒在笑。
那頭牛在跑。

09 那個女孩兒在躺著。
那個女孩兒在跑。
那個女孩兒在大笑。
那個女孩兒在笑。

10 那些鳥在飛。
那兩只鴨子在游。
那兩只鵝在走。
那只鳥在飛。

2-01

gèng duō de dòng cí: pǎo, tiào, zhì, wēi xiào děng; xiàn zài jìn xíng shí

01 nà gè nán háir zài rēng qiú.
nà gè nǚ rén zài rēng qiú.
nà gè nán rén zài rēng qiú.
nà gè nán rén zài bǎ nà gè nán háir pāo qǐ lái.

02 nà gè nǚ rén zài jiē nà gè huáng sè de qiú.
nà gè nán rén zài rēng qiú.
nà gè nǚ rén zài jiē nà gè bái sè de qiú.
nà gè nán háir zài jiē pá zi.

03 nà gè nán háir zài rēng qiú.
nà gè nán háir zài jiē qiú.
nà gè chuān bái yī fú de nán háir zài tī qiú.
nà gè chuān hóng yī fú de nán háir zài tī qiú.

04 nà gè nǚ háir zài qí mǎ.
nà gè nán háir zài qí zì xíng chē.
nà gè nǚ háir zài tiào.
nà gè nán háir zài pǎo.

05 nà gè nán háir zài xiào.
nà gè nán háir zài hē dōng xi.
nà gè nǚ rén zài zuò zhe.
nà gè nǚ rén zài pǎo.

06 nà gè nǚ rén zài xiào.
nà gè nǚ rén zài zhǐ zhe shén me dōng xi.
nà gè nǚ rén zài kàn bào zhǐ.
nà gè nǚ rén zài dǎ diàn huà.

07 nà gè xiǎo nǚ háir zài dà xiào.
nà gè nán rén zài dà xiào.
nà gè nǚ háir zài xiě zì.
nà gè nán rén zài qí zì xíng chē.

08 nà gè nán háir zài tī.
nà tóu niú zài tī.
nà gè nán háir zài xiào.
nà tóu niú zài pǎo.

09 nà gè nǚ háir zài tǎng zhe.
nà gè nǚ háir zài pǎo.
nà gè nǚ háir zài dà xiào.
nà gè nǚ háir zài xiào.

10 nà xiē niǎo zài fēi.
nà liǎng zhī yā zi zài yóu.
nà liǎng zhī é zài zǒu.
nà zhī niǎo zài fēi.

人和动物、指示代词：这

01 他是一个男孩儿。
她是一个女孩儿。
他是一个男人。
她是一个女人。

02 那个男孩儿是一个儿童。
那个女孩儿是一个儿童。
那个男人是一个成年人。
那个女人是一个成年人。

03 两个成年人
一个成年人和一个孩子
两个孩子
三个孩子

04 一个成年人和两个孩子
两个成年人
三个成年人
两个孩子

05 狗是动物。
鱼是动物。
女孩儿是人。
女人是人。

06 狗不是人。狗是动物。
鱼不是人。鱼是动物。
女孩儿不是成年人。女孩儿是儿童。
女人不是儿童。女人是成年人。

07 一个孩子和一只动物
两个成年人和一个孩子
两个成年人和两只动物
一只动物

08 一个人和一只动物
三个人
两个人和两只动物
一只动物

09 这个人不是男的。
这个人不是女的。
这只动物不是马。
这只动物不是大象。

10 这个人已经成年。
这个人还未成年。
这只动物不是猫。
这只动物不是狗。

2-02

人和動物；指示代詞：這

01 他是一個男孩兒。
她是一個女孩兒。
他是一個男人。
她是一個女人。

02 那個男孩兒是一個兒童。
那個女孩兒是一個兒童。
那個男人是一個成年人。
那個女人是一個成年人。

03 兩個成年人
一個成年人和一個孩子
兩個孩子
三個孩子

04 一個成年人和兩個孩子
兩個成年人
三個成年人
兩個孩子

05 狗是動物。
魚是動物。
女孩兒是人。
女人是人。

06 狗不是人。狗是動物。
魚不是人。魚是動物。
女孩兒不是成年人。女孩兒是兒童。
女人不是兒童，女人是成年人。

07 一個孩子和一隻動物
兩個成年人和一個孩子
兩個成年人和兩隻動物
一隻動物

08 一個人和一隻動物
三個人
兩個人和兩隻動物
一隻動物

09 這個人不是男的。
這個人不是女的。
這隻動物不是馬。
這隻動物不是大象。

10 這個人已經成年。
這個人还未成年。
這隻動物不是貓。
這隻動物不是狗。

2-02

rén hé dòng wù, zhǐ shì dài cí: zhè

01 tā shì yī gè nán háir.
   tā shì yī gè nǚ háir.
   tā shì yī gè nán rén.
   tā shì yī gè nǚ rén.

02 nà gè nán háir shì yī gè ér tóng.
   nà gè nǚ háir shì yī gè ér tóng.
   nà gè nán rén shì yī gè chéng nián rén.
   nà gè nǚ rén shì yī gè chéng nián rén.

03 liǎng gè chéng nián rén
   yī gè chéng nián rén hé yī gè hái zi
   liǎng gè hái zi
   sān gè hái zi

04 yī gè chéng nián rén hé liǎng gè hái zi
   liǎng gè chéng nián rén
   sān gè chéng nián rén
   liǎng gè hái zi

05 gǒu shì dòng wù.
   yú shì dòng wù.
   nǚ háir shì rén.
   nǚ rén shì rén.

06 gǒu bú shì rén. gǒu shì dòng wù.
   yú bú shì rén. yú shì dòng wù.
   nǚ háir bú shì chéng nián rén. nǚ háir shì ér tóng.
   nǚ rén bú shì ér tóng. nǚ rén shì chéng nián rén.

07 yī gè hái zi hé yī zhī dòng wù
   liǎng gè chéng nián rén hé yī gè hái zi
   liǎng gè chéng nián rén hé liǎng zhī dòng wù
   yī zhī dòng wù

08 yī gè rén hé yī zhī dòng wù
   sān gè rén
   liǎng gè rén hé liǎng zhī dòng wù
   yī zhī dòng wù

09 zhè gè rén bú shì nán de.
   zhè gè rén bú shì nǚ de.
   zhè zhī dòng wù bú shì mǎ.
   zhè zhī dòng wù bú shì dà xiàng.

10 zhè gè rén yǐ jīng chéng nián.
   zhè gè rén hái wèi chéng nián.
   zhè zhī dòng wù bú shì māo.
   zhè zhī dòng wù bú shì gǒu.

名词；描述性形容词：大、小

01 一辆大轿车
  一个拿着一条大鱼的男人
  一个戴着一顶大帽子的男人
  一个拿着一把大工具的男人

02 一辆小轿车
  一匹小马
  一顶小帐篷
  一个大球和一个小球

03 大号的二
  小号的二
  大号的一
  小号的一

04 一匹大马
  一匹小马
  一把大伞
  一把小伞

05 一只小动物
  一只大动物
  一个小孩儿
  一个大人

06 一只大箱子
  一艘大船
  一只小箱子
  一只小船

07 一台大电视
  一辆大卡车
  一顶小帽子
  一顶大帽子

08 一个大沙发
  一个小沙发
  一辆小轿车
  一辆大轿车

09 一只大球
  一只大车轮和一只小车轮
  一只大车轮
  一只小球

10 一只白色的大车轮
  一只黑色的大车轮
  一只蓝色的大车轮
  一只大车轮和一只小车轮

2-03

名詞；描述性形容詞：大、小

01 一輛大轎車
  一個拿著一條大魚的男人
  一個戴著一頂大帽子的男人
  一個拿著一把大工具的男人

02 一輛小轎車
  一匹小馬
  一頂小帳篷
  一個大球和一個小球

03 大號的二
  小號的二
  大號的一
  小號的一

04 一匹大馬
  一匹小馬
  一把大傘
  一把小傘

05 一隻小動物
  一隻大動物
  一個小孩兒
  一個大人

06 一隻大箱子
  一艘大船
  一隻小箱子
  一隻小船

07 一臺大電視
  一輛大卡車
  一頂小帽子
  一頂大帽子

08 一個大沙發
  一個小沙發
  一輛小轎車
  一輛大轎車

09 一隻大球
  一隻大車輪和一隻小車輪
  一隻大車輪
  一隻小球

10 一隻白色的大車輪
  一隻黑色的大車輪
  一隻藍色的大車輪
  一隻大車輪和一隻小車輪

2-03

míng cí; miáo shù xìng xíng róng cí: dà, xiǎo

01 yī liàng dà jiào chē
yī gè ná zhe yī tiáo dà yú de nán rén
yī gè dài zhe yī dǐng dà mào zi de nán rén
yī gè ná zhe yī bǎ dà gōng jù de nán rén

02 yī liàng xiǎo jiào chē
yī pǐ xiǎo mǎ
yī dǐng xiǎo zhàng péng
yī gè dà qiú hé yī gè xiǎo qiú

03 dà hào de èr
xiǎo hào de èr
dà hào de yī
xiǎo hào de yī

04 yī pǐ dà mǎ
yī pǐ xiǎo mǎ
yī bǎ dà sǎn
yī bǎ xiǎo sǎn

05 yī zhī xiǎo dòng wù
yī zhī dà dòng wù
yī gè xiǎo háir
yī gè dà rén

06 yī zhī dà xiāng zi
yī sōu dà chuán
yī zhī xiǎo xiāng zi
yī zhī xiǎo chuán

07 yī tái dà diàn shì
yī liàng dà kǎ chē
yī dǐng xiǎo mào zi
yī dǐng dà mào zi

08 yī gè dà shā fā
yī gè xiǎo shā fā
yī liàng xiǎo jiào chē
yī liàng dà jiào chē

09 yī zhī dà qiú
yī zhī dà chē lún hé yī zhī xiǎo chē lún
yī zhī dà chē lún
yī zhī xiǎo qiú

10 yī zhī bái sè de dà chē lún
yī zhī hēi sè de dà chē lún
yī zhī lán sè de dà chē lún
yī zhī dà chē lún hé yī zhī xiǎo chē lún

形状和颜色；形容词及其比较级

01 一个大圆
一个小圆
一个大正方形
一个小正方形

02 那个红色的圆比那个蓝色的圆大。
那个蓝色的圆比那个红色的圆大。
那个正方形比那个圆大。
那个圆比那个正方形大。

03 那个蓝色的圆比那个红色的圆小。
那个红色的圆比那个蓝色的圆小。
那个圆比那个正方形小。
那个正方形比那个圆小。

04 那个最大的圆是红色的。
那个最大的圆是蓝色的。
那个最大的圆是黄色的。
那个最大的圆是黑色的。

05 那个最小的正方形是红色的。
那个最小的正方形是蓝色的。
那个最小的正方形是黄色的。
那个最小的正方形是白色的。

06 一个蓝色的长方形
一个红色的长方形
一个黄色的长方形
一个白色的长方形

07 一个大长方形
一个小长方形
一个红色的圆
一个绿色的圆

08 一个长的长方形
一个短的长方形
一个留长发的女人
一个留短发的女人

09 那个绿色的长方形比那个黄色的长方形长。
那个黄色的长方形比那个绿色的长方形长。
那个红色的圆比那个红色的正方形大。
那个红色的正方形比那个红色的圆大。

10 那个黄色的长方形比那个绿色的长方形短。
那个绿色的长方形比那个黄色的长方形短。
那个黄色的三角形比那个绿色的三角形小。
那个绿色的三角形比那个黄色的三角形小。

2-04

形狀和顏色；形容詞及其比較級

01 一個大圓
一個小圓
一個大正方形
一個小正方形

02 那個紅色的圓比那個藍色的圓大。
那個藍色的圓比那個紅色的圓大。
那個正方形比那個圓大。
那個圓比那個正方形大。

03 那個藍色的圓比那個紅色的圓小。
那個紅色的圓比那個藍色的圓小。
那個圓比那個正方形小。
那個正方形比那個圓小。

04 那個最大的圓是紅色的。
那個最大的圓是藍色的。
那個最大的圓是黃色的。
那個最大的圓是黑色的。

05 那個最小的正方形是紅色的。
那個最小的正方形是藍色的。
那個最小的正方形是黃色的。
那個最小的正方形是白色的。

06 一個藍色的長方形
一個紅色的長方形
一個黃色的長方形
一個白色的長方形

07 一個大長方形
一個小長方形
一個紅色的圓
一個綠色的圓

08 一個長的長方形
一個短的長方形
一個留長髮的女人
一個留短髮的女人

09 那個綠色的長方形比那個黃色的長方形長。
那個黃色的長方形比那個綠色的長方形長。
那個紅色的圓比那個紅色的正方形大。
那個紅色的正方形比那個紅色的圓大。

10 那個黃色的長方形比那個綠色的長方形短。
那個綠色的長方形比那個黃色的長方形短。
那個黃色的三角形比那個綠色的三角形小。
那個綠色的三角形比那個黃色的三角形小。

2-04

xíng zhuàng hé yán sè; xíng róng cí jí qí bǐ jiào jí

01   yī gè dà yuán
      yī gè xiǎo yuán
      yī gè dà zhèng fāng xíng
      yī gè xiǎo zhèng fāng xíng

02   nà gè hóng sè de yuán bǐ nà gè lán sè de yuán dà.
      nà gè lán sè de yuán bǐ nà gè hóng sè de yuán dà.
      nà gè zhèng fāng xíng bǐ nà gè yuán dà.
      nà gè yuán bǐ nà gè zhèng fāng xíng dà.

03   nà gè lán sè de yuán bǐ nà gè hóng sè de yuán xiǎo.
      nà gè hóng sè de yuán bǐ nà gè lán sè de yuán xiǎo.
      nà gè yuán bǐ nà gè zhèng fāng xíng xiǎo.
      nà gè zhèng fāng xíng bǐ nà gè yuán xiǎo.

04   nà gè zuì dà de yuán shì hóng sè de.
      nà gè zuì dà de yuán shì lán sè de.
      nà gè zuì dà de yuán shì huáng sè de.
      nà gè zuì dà de yuán shì hēi sè de.

05   nà gè zuì xiǎo de zhèng fāng xíng shì hóng sè de.
      nà gè zuì xiǎo de zhèng fāng xíng shì lán sè de.
      nà gè zuì xiǎo de zhèng fāng xíng shì huáng sè de.
      nà gè zuì xiǎo de zhèng fāng xíng shì bái sè de.

06   yī gè lán sè de cháng fāng xíng
      yī gè hóng sè de cháng fāng xíng
      yī gè huáng sè de cháng fāng xíng
      yī gè bái sè de cháng fāng xíng

07   yī gè dà cháng fāng xíng
      yī gè xiǎo cháng fāng xíng
      yī gè hóng sè de yuán
      yī gè lǜ sè de yuán

08   yī gè cháng de cháng fāng xíng
      yī gè duǎn de cháng fāng xíng
      yī gè liú cháng fà de nǚ rén
      yī gè liú duǎn fà de nǚ rén

09   nà gè lǜ sè de cháng fāng xíng bǐ nà gè huáng sè de cháng fāng xíng cháng.
      nà gè huáng sè de cháng fāng xíng bǐ nà gè lǜ sè de cháng fāng xíng cháng.
      nà gè hóng sè dc yuán bǐ nà gè hóng sè de zhèng fāng xíng dà.
      nà gè hóng sè de zhèng fāng xíng bǐ nà gè hóng sè de yuán dà.

10   nà gè huáng sè de cháng fāng xíng bǐ nà gè lǜ sè de cháng fāng xíng duǎn.
      nà gè lǜ sè de cháng fāng xíng bǐ nà gè huáng sè de cháng fāng xíng duǎn.
      nà gè huáng sè de sān jiǎo xíng bǐ nà gè lǜ sè de sān jiǎo xíng xiǎo.
      nà gè lǜ sè de sān jiǎo xíng bǐ nà gè huáng sè de sān jiǎo xíng xiǎo.

左、右；他的、她的；如何使用所有格

01 她的右手里有两个黄色的球。
她的左手里有一个黄色的球。
她的右手里有一个黄色的球。
她的左手里有两个黄色的球。

02 那只杯子在那个女人的右手里。
那支笔在那个女人的右手里，那张纸在她的左手里。
那个女人左手里有两个球，右手里也有两个球。
那个球在那个女人的右手里。

03 那个球在哪儿？那个球在她的左手里。
那个球在哪儿？那个球在她的右手里。
那顶帽子在哪儿？那个女孩儿把帽子拿在她的右手里。
那顶帽子在哪儿？那个女孩儿把帽子拿在她的左手里。

04 那个女人左手拿着电话。
那个女人右手拿着电话。
那个女孩儿右手拿着东西。
那个女孩儿左手拿着东西。

05 一个女人在指着什么东西。她在用右手指着。
一个女人在指着什么东西。她在用左手指着。
两个女人都在指着什么东西。一个在用右手指着，另一个在用左手指着。
两个女人什么东西也没有指。

06 麦克风在那个歌手的右手里。
麦克风在那个歌手的左手里。
那个男人右手里有一把吉他，左手里也有一把吉他。
那个男人在弹吉他。

07 不准左转弯。
不准右转弯。
不准停车。
不准转 U 形弯。

08 这只钟是圆形的。
这只钟是正方形的。
这扇窗户是正方形的。
这扇窗户是圆形的。

09 这块路牌是长方形的。
这块路牌是圆形的。
这块路牌是正方形的。
这块路牌不是长方形的，也不是圆形的和正方形的。

10 请小心袋鼠。
请小心牛。
请小心儿童。
请小心鹿。

2-05

左、右；他的、她的；如何使用所有格

01 她的右手裡有兩個黃色的球。
她的左手裡有一個黃色的球。
她的右手裡有一個黃色的球。
她的左手裡有兩個黃色的球。

02 那隻杯子在那個女人的右手裡。
那支筆在那個女人的右手裡，那張紙在她的左手裡。
那個女人左手裡有兩個球，右手裡也有兩個球。
那個球在那個女人的右手裡。

03 那個球在哪兒？那個球在她的左手裡。
那個球在哪兒？那個球在她的右手裡。
那頂帽子在哪兒？那個女孩兒把帽子拿在她的右手裡。
那頂帽子在哪兒？那個女孩兒把帽子拿在她的左手裡。

04 那個女人左手拿著電話。
那個女人右手拿著電話。
那個女孩兒右手拿著東西。
那個女孩兒左手拿著東西。

05 一個女人在指著甚麼東西。她在用右手指著。
一個女人在指著甚麼東西。她在用左手指著。
兩個女人都在指著甚麼東西。一個在用右手指著，另一個在用左手指著。
兩個女人甚麼東西也沒有指。

06 麥克風在那個歌手的右手裡。
麥克風在那個歌手的左手裡。
那個男人右手裡有一把吉他，左手裡也有一把吉他。
那個男人在彈吉他。

07 不准左轉彎。
不准右轉彎。
不准停車。
不准轉 U 形彎。

08 這隻鐘是圓形的。
這隻鐘是正方形的。
這扇窗戶是正方形的。
這扇窗戶是圓形的。

09 這塊路牌是長方形的。
這塊路牌是圓形的。
這塊路牌是正方形的。
這塊路牌不是長方形的，也不是圓形的和正方形的。

10 請小心袋鼠。
請小心牛。
請小心兒童。
請小心鹿。

2-05

zuǒ, yòu; tā de, tā de; rú hé shǐ yòng suǒ yoǔ gé

01 tā de yòu shǒu lǐ yǒu liǎng gè huáng sè de qiú.
   tā de zuǒ shǒu lǐ yǒu yī gè huáng sè de qiú.
   tā de yòu shǒu lǐ yǒu yī gè huáng sè de qiú.
   tā de zuǒ shǒu lǐ yǒu liǎng gè huáng sè de qiú.

02 nà zhī bēi zi zài nà gè nǚ rén de yòu shǒu lǐ.
   nà zhī bǐ zài nà gè nǚ rén de yòu shǒu lǐ. nà zhāng zhǐ zài tā de zuǒ shǒu lǐ.
   nà gè nǚ rén zuǒ shǒu lǐ yǒu liǎng gè qiú, yòu shǒu lǐ yě yǒu liǎng gè qiú.
   nà gè qiú zài nà gè nǚ rén de yòu shǒu lǐ.

03 nà gè qiú zài nǎr? nà gè qiú zài tā de zuǒ shǒu lǐ.
   nà gè qiú zài nǎr? nà gè qiú zài tā de yòu shǒu lǐ.
   nà dǐng mào zi zài nǎr? nà gè nǚ háir bǎ mào zi ná zài tā de yòu shǒu lǐ.
   nà dǐng mào zi zài nǎr? nà gè nǚ háir bǎ mào zi ná zài tā de zuǒ shǒu lǐ.

04 nà gè nǚ rén zuǒ shǒu ná zhe diàn huà.
   nà gè nǚ rén yòu shǒu ná zhe diàn huà.
   nà gè nǚ háir yòu shǒu ná zhe dōng xi.
   nà gè nǚ háir zuǒ shǒu ná zhe dōng xi.

05 yī gè nǚ rén zài zhǐ zhe shén mo dōng xi. tā zài yòng yòu shǒu zhǐ zhe.
   yī gè nǚ rén zài zhǐ zhe shén mo dōng xi. tā zài yòng zuǒ shǒu zhǐ zhe.
   liǎng gè nǚ rén dōu zài zhǐ zhe shén mo dōng xi. yī gè zài yòng yòu shǒu zhǐ zhe, lìng yī gè zài yòng zuǒ
      shǒu zhǐ zhe.
   liǎng gè nǚ rén shén mo dōng xi yě méi yǒu zhǐ.

06 mài kè fēng zài nà gè gē shǒu de yòu shǒu lǐ.
   mài kè fēng zài nà gè gē shǒu de zuǒ shǒu lǐ.
   nà gè nán rén yòu shǒu lǐ yǒu yī bǎ jí tā, zuǒ shǒu lǐ yě yǒu yī bǎ jí tā.
   nà gè nán rén zài tán jí tā.

07 bù zhǔn zuǒ zhuǎn wān
   bù zhǔn yòu zhuǎn wān
   bù zhǔn tíng chē
   bù zhǔn zhuǎn yōu xíng wān

08 zhè zhī zhōng shì yuán xíng de.
   zhè zhī zhōng shì zhèng fāng xíng de.
   zhè shàn chuāng hù shì zhèng fāng xíng de.
   zhè shàn chuāng hù shì yuán xíng de.

09 zhè kuài lù pái shì cháng fāng xíng de.
   zhè kuài lù pái shì yuán xíng de.
   zhè kuài lù pái shì zhèng fāng xíng de.
   zhè kuài lù pái bú shì cháng fāng xíng de, yě bú shì yuán xíng de hé zhèng fāng xíng de.

10 qǐng xiǎo xīn dài shǔ
   qǐng xiǎo xīn niú
   qǐng xiǎo xīn ér tóng
   qǐng xiǎo xīn lù

运用更多的动词；正在…、不在…

01 那个女人在跑。
那个女人没有跑。
这个男人有头发。
这个男人没有头发。

02 那个女孩儿在喝东西。
那个女孩儿没有喝东西。
这个男人戴着一顶安全帽。
这个男人没有戴安全帽。

03 这个女人戴着一顶白帽子。
这个女人戴着一顶黑帽子。
那个男孩儿戴着一顶白帽子。
那个男孩儿戴着一顶黑帽子。

04 这个女人没有戴黑帽子。她戴着一顶白帽子。
这个女人没有戴白帽子。她戴着一顶黑帽子。
那个男孩儿没有戴黑帽子。他戴着一顶白帽子。
那个男孩儿没有戴白帽子。他戴着一顶黑帽子。

05 这个女人没有戴黑帽子。
这个女人没有戴白帽子。
那个男孩儿没有戴黑帽子。
那个男孩儿没有戴白帽子。

06 这架飞机在飞。
这架飞机没有飞。
那些男孩儿在跳。
那些男孩儿没有跳。

07 这个男孩儿没有游泳。他正坐在那架飞机里。
这个男孩儿没有坐在那架飞机里。他在游泳。
这个女孩儿没有走。她在骑马。
这个女孩儿没有骑马。她在走。

08 这个男孩儿没有游泳。
这个男孩儿没有坐在那架飞机里。
这个女孩儿没有走。
这个女孩儿没有骑马。

09 那个女人在打电话。
那个女孩儿在打电话。
那个女人在指着什么东西。
那个女人没有打电话，她也没指什么东西。

10 那个女人没有打电话。
那个女人什么东西也没指。
那个男人在骑自行车。
那个男人没有骑自行车。

2-06

運用更多的動詞；正在…、不在…

01 那個女人在跑。
那個女人沒有跑。
這個男人有頭髮。
這個男人沒有頭髮。

02 那個女孩兒在喝東西。
那個女孩兒沒有喝東西。
這個男人戴著一頂安全帽。
這個男人沒有戴安全帽。

03 這個女人戴著一頂白帽子。
這個女人戴著一頂黑帽子。
那個男孩兒戴著一頂白帽子。
那個男孩兒戴著一頂黑帽子。

04 這個女人沒有戴黑帽子。她戴著一頂白帽子。
這個女人沒有戴白帽子。她戴著一頂黑帽子。
那個男孩兒沒有戴黑帽子。他戴著一頂白帽子。
那個男孩兒沒有戴白帽子，他戴著一頂黑帽子。

05 這個女人沒有戴黑帽子。
這個女人沒有戴白帽子。
那個男孩兒沒有戴黑帽子。
那個男孩兒沒有戴白帽子。

06 這架飛機在飛。
這架飛機沒有飛。
那些男孩兒在跳。
那些男孩兒沒有跳。

07 這個男孩兒沒有游泳。他正坐在那架飛機裡。
這個男孩兒沒有坐在那架飛機裡。他在游泳。
這個女孩兒沒有走。她在騎馬。
這個女孩兒沒有騎馬。她在走。

08 這個男孩兒沒有游泳。
這個男孩兒沒有坐在那架飛機裡。
這個女孩兒沒有走。
這個女孩兒沒有騎馬。

09 那個女人在打電話。
那個女孩兒在打電話。
那個女人在指著甚麼東西。
那個女人沒有打電話，她也沒指甚麼東西。

10 那個女人沒有打電話。
那個女人甚麼東西也沒指。
那個男人在騎自行車。
那個男人沒有騎自行車。

2-06

yùn yòng gèng duō de dòng cí; zhèng zài..., bú zài...

01 nà gè nǚ rén zài pǎo.
   nà gè nǚ rén méi yǒu pǎo.
   zhè gè nán rén yǒu tóu fà.
   zhè gè nán rén méi yǒu tóu fà.

02 nà gè nǚ háir zài hē dōng xi.
   nà gè nǚ háir méi yǒu hē dōng xī.
   zhè gè nán rén dài zhe yī dǐng ān quán mào.
   zhè gè nán rén méi yǒu dài ān quán mào.

03 zhè gè nǚ rén dài zhe yī dǐng bái mào zi.
   zhè gè nǚ rén dài zhe yī dǐng hēi mào zi.
   nà gè nán háir dài zhe yī dǐng bái mào zi.
   nà gè nán háir dài zhe yī dǐng hēi mào zi.

04 zhè gè nǚ rén méi yǒu dài hēi mào zi. tā dài zhe yī dǐng bái mào zi.
   zhè gè nǚ rén méi yǒu dài bái mào zi. tā dài zhe yī dǐng hēi mào zi.
   nà gè nán háir méi yǒu dài hēi mào zi. tā dài zhe yī dǐng bái mào zi.
   nà gè nán háir méi yǒu dài bái mào zi. tā dài zhe yī dǐng hēi mào zi.

05 zhè gè nǚ rén méi yǒu dài hēi mào zi.
   zhè gè nǚ rén méi yǒu dài bái mào zi.
   nà gè nán háir méi yǒu dài hēi mào zi.
   nà gè nán háir méi yǒu dài bái mào zi.

06 zhè jià fēi jī zài fēi.
   zhè jià fēi jī méi yǒu fēi.
   nà xiē nán háir zài tiào.
   nà xiē nán háir méi yǒu tiào.

07 zhè gè nán háir méi yǒu yóu yǒng. tā zhèng zuò zài nà jià fēi jī lǐ.
   zhè gè nán háir méi yǒu zuò zài nà jià fēi jī lǐ. tā zài yóu yǒng.
   zhè gè nǚ háir méi yǒu zǒu. tā zài qí mǎ.
   zhè gè nǚ háir méi yǒu qí mǎ. tā zài zǒu.

08 zhè gè nán háir méi yǒu yóu yǒng.
   zhè gè nán háir méi yǒu zuò zài nà jià fēi jī lǐ.
   zhè gè nǚ háir méi yǒu zǒu.
   zhè gè nǚ háir méi yǒu qí mǎ.

09 nà gè nǚ rén zài dǎ diàn huà.
   nà gè nǚ háir zài dǎ diàn huà.
   nà gè nǚ rén zài zhǐ zhe shén me dōng xi.
   nà gè nǚ rén méi yǒu dǎ diàn huà, tā yě méi zhǐ shén me dōng xi.

10 nà gè nǚ rén méi yǒu dǎ diàn huà.
   nà gè nǚ rén shén me dōng xi yě méi zhǐ.
   nà gè nán rén zài qí zì xíng chē.
   nà gè nán rén méi yǒu qí zì xíng chē.

复合主语；男孩儿和女孩儿等

01　那个男人和那个女人正在跳舞。
　　那些男人和女人正在跳舞。
　　那些男人正在跳舞。
　　那些女人正在跳舞。

02　那个男人正坐在自行车上，那个男孩儿正坐在栅栏
　　上。
　　那个男人和男孩儿正坐在自行车上，但是他们没有骑
　　自行车。
　　那个男人和男孩儿正在骑自行车。
　　那个男人和那个女人正在骑自行车。

03　那个男孩儿正坐在地上。
　　那个男孩儿和那个女孩儿正坐在地上。
　　那个男孩儿正躺在地上。
　　那个女人正躺在地上。

04　那两个女孩儿和那个男孩儿正在跑。
　　那两个女孩儿正站在桌子上面，那两个男孩儿正站在
　　地上。
　　那些男孩儿和女孩儿正站在桌子上。
　　一个女孩儿和一个男孩儿在地上，还有一个女孩儿正
　　站在桌子上面。

05　那个女人在牵着狗走。
　　那个男人和那个女人都在坐着。
　　那个男人和那个女人在走。
　　那个男人和那两个孩子在走。

06　那个男人和男孩儿正在那架飞机里面。
　　那个女人在走，那个男人在骑自行车。
　　那些男孩儿和女孩儿正从桌子上跳下来。
　　那些男孩儿和女孩儿正站在桌子上面。

07　那个女人和那个男孩儿头上顶着球。
　　那个男人和那个男孩儿头上顶着球。
　　那个女人和那个男孩儿正坐在椅子上面。
　　那个男人和那个男孩儿正坐着。

08　那些男人和那个女人正坐在轿车里面。
　　那个男人和那个女人正坐在轿车里面。
　　那个男人和那个女孩儿，还有那个婴儿正坐在拖拉机
　　上面。
　　那个男人和那个男孩儿正坐在拖拉机上面。

09　那些男人和女人正站着。
　　那两个女人正站着，那两个男人正坐着。
　　那两个女人和一个男人正站着，还有一个男人正坐
　　着。
　　那两个男人和一个女人正坐着，还有一个女人正站
　　着。

10　那个男人和那个女人正站在墙上面。
　　那个男人和那两个女人正站在墙前面。
　　那两个女人正站在墙上面。
　　那两个女人正站在墙前面。

2-07

復合主語；男孩兒和女孩兒等

01　那個男人和那個女人正在跳舞。
　　那些男人和女人正在跳舞。
　　那些男人正在跳舞。
　　那些女人正在跳舞。

02　那個男人正坐在自行車上，那個男孩兒正坐在柵欄
　　上。
　　那個男人和男孩兒正坐在自行車上，但是他們沒有騎
　　自行車。
　　那個男人和男孩兒正在騎自行車。
　　那個男人和那個女人正在騎自行車。

03　那個男孩兒正坐在地上。
　　那個男孩兒和那個女孩兒正坐在地上。
　　那個男孩兒正躺在地上。
　　那個女人正躺在地上。

04　那兩個女孩兒和那個男孩兒正在跑。
　　那兩個女孩兒正站在桌子上面，那兩個男孩兒正站在
　　地上。
　　那些男孩兒和女孩兒正站在桌子上。
　　一個女孩兒和一個男孩兒在地上，還有一個女孩兒正
　　站在桌子上面。

05　那個女人在牽著狗走。
　　那個男人和那個女人都在坐著。
　　那個男人和那個女人在走。
　　那個男人和那兩個孩子在走。

06　那個男人和男孩兒正在那架飛機裡面。
　　那個女人在走，那個男人在騎自行車。
　　那些男孩兒和女孩兒正從桌子上跳下來。
　　那些男孩兒和女孩兒正站在桌子上面。

07　那個女人和那個男孩兒頭上頂著球。
　　那個男人和那個男孩兒頭上頂著球。
　　那個女人和那個男孩兒正坐在椅子上面。
　　那個男人和那個男孩兒正坐著。

08　那些男人和那個女人正坐在轎車裡面。
　　那個男人和那個女人正坐在轎車裡面。
　　那個男人和那個女孩兒，還有那個嬰兒正坐在拖拉機
　　上面。
　　那個男人和那個男孩兒正坐在拖拉機上面。

09　那些男人和女人正站著。
　　那兩個女人正站著，那兩個男人正坐著。
　　那兩個女人和一個男人正站著，還有一個男人正坐
　　著。
　　那兩個男人和一個女人正坐著，還有一個女人正站
　　著。

10　那個男人和那個女人正站在牆上面。
　　那個男人和那兩個女人正站在牆前面。
　　那兩個女人正站在牆上面。
　　那兩個女人正站在牆前面。

2-07

01 nà gè nán rén hé nà gè nǚ rén zhèng zài tiào wǔ.
    nà xiē nán rén hé nǚ rén zhèng zài tiào wǔ.
    nà xiē nán rén zhèng zài tiào wǔ.
    nà xiē nǚ rén zhèng zài tiào wǔ.

02 nà gè nán rén zhèng zuò zài zì xíng chē shàng, nà gè nán háir zhèng zuò zài zhà lán shàng.
    nà gè nán rén hé nán háir zhèng zuò zài zì xíng chē shàng, dàn shì tā men méi yǒu qí zì xíng chē.
    nà gè nán rén hé nán háir zhèng zài qí zì xíng chē.
    nà gè nán rén hé nà gè nǚ rén zhèng zài qí zì xíng chē.

03 nà gè nán háir zhèng zuò zài dì shàng.
    nà gè nán háir hé nà gè nǚ háir zhèng zuò zài dì shàng.
    nà gè nán háir zhèng tǎng zài dì shàng.
    nà gè nǚ rén zhèng tǎng zài dì shàng.

04 nà liǎng gè nǚ háir hé nà gè nán háir zhèng zài pǎo.
    nà liǎng gè nǚ háir zhèng zhàn zài zhuō zi shàng miàn, nà liǎng gè nán háir zhèng zhàn zài dì shàng.
    nà xiē nán háir hé nǚ háir zhèng zhàn zài zhuō zi shàng.
    yī gè nǚ háir hé yī gè nán háir zài dì shàng, hái yǒu yī gè nǚ háir zhèng zhàn zài zhuō zi shàng miàn.

05 nà gè nǚ rén zài qiān zhe gǒu zǒu.
    nà gè nán rén hé nà gè nǚ rén dōu zài zuò zhe.
    nà gè nán rén hé nà gè nǚ rén zài zǒu.
    nà gè nán rén hé nà liǎng gè hái zi zài zǒu.

06 nà gè nán rén hé nán háir zhèng zài nà jià fēi jī lǐ miàn.
    nà gè nǚ rén zài zǒu, nà gè nán rén zài qí zì xíng chē.
    nà xiē nán háir hé nǚ háir zhèng cóng zhuō zi shàng tiào xià lái.
    nà xiē nán háir hé nǚ háir zhèng zhàn zài zhuō zi shàng miàn.

07 nà gè nǚ rén hé nà gè nán háir tóu shàng dǐng zhe qiú.
    nà gè nán rén hé nà gè nán háir tóu shàng dǐng zhe qiú.
    nà gè nǚ rén hé nà gè nán háir zhèng zuò zài yǐ zi shàng miàn.
    nà gè nán rén hé nà gè nán háir zhèng zuò zhe.

08 nà xiē nán rén hé nà gè nǚ rén zhèng zuò zài jiào chē lǐ miàn.
    nà gè nán rén hé nà gè nǚ rén zhèng zuò zài jiào chē lǐ miàn.
    nà gè nán rén hé nà gè nǚ háir, hái yǒu nà gè yīng ér zhèng zuò zài tuō lā jī shàng miàn.
    nà gè nán rén hé nà gè nán háir zhèng zuò zài tuō lā jī shàng miàn.

09 nà xiē nán rén hé nǚ rén zhèng zhàn zhe.
    nà liǎng gè nǚ rén zhèng zhàn zhe, nà liǎng gè nán rén zhèng zuò zhe.
    nà liǎng gè nǚ rén hé yī gè nán rén zhèng zhàn zhe, hái yǒu yī gè nán rén zhèng zuò zhe.
    nà liǎng gè nán rén hé yī gè nǚ rén zhèng zuò zhe, hái yǒu yī gè nǚ rén zhèng zhàn zhe.

10 nà gè nán rén hé nà gè nǚ rén zhèng zhàn zài qiáng shàng miàn.
    nà gè nán rén hé nà liǎng gè nǚ rén zhèng zhàn zài qiáng qián miàn.
    nà liǎng gè nǚ rén zhèng zhàn zài qiáng shàng miàn.
    nà liǎng gè nǚ rén zhèng zhàn zài qiáng qián miàn.

使用更多的介词: 在…之间、在…上面、在…后面等

01　那个男人在卡车里面。
　　那些香蕉在筐里面。
　　那些人在船上面。
　　那些人没在船上面。

02　那个男孩儿在栅栏上，那个男人在自行车上。
　　那顶帽子在男孩儿头上。
　　那些孩子在桌子上面。
　　那个球在男孩儿身上。

03　那个男孩儿在自行车上。
　　那个男孩儿在自行车旁边。
　　这个男人在马上。
　　这个男人在马旁边。

04　那头驴在那个男人的身下。
　　那头驴没在那个男人的身下。
　　那块儿糖在货架下面。
　　那些糖在那个男人的手里。

05　这个男孩儿在树后面。
　　这个男孩儿在树前面。
　　这个男人在轿车后面。
　　这个男人在轿车前面。

06　那两只碗并排放着。
　　这只杯子在盘子上面。
　　五在一和零中间。
　　那只中号的碗在大碗和小碗中间。

07　那个男人在两个女人旁边。
　　那个男人在两个女人中间。
　　那只狗在两个人中间。
　　那只狗在两个人旁边。

08　两个戴眼镜的人
　　两个没戴眼镜的人
　　一个拿棍子的男孩儿
　　一个没拿棍子的男孩儿

09　那架飞机在地面上。
　　那架飞机在空中。
　　那些鱼在潜水人周围。
　　那些椅子在桌子周围。

10　那个男人在自行车后面。
　　那个男人在自行车旁边。
　　那辆自行车在轿车旁边。
　　那辆自行车在轿车后面。

2-08

使用更多的介詞：在…之間、在…上面、在…後面等

01　那個男人在卡車裡面。
　　那些香蕉在筐裡面。
　　那些人在船上面。
　　那些人沒在船上面。

02　那個男孩兒在柵欄上，那個男人在自行車上。
　　那頂帽子在男孩兒頭上。
　　那些孩子在桌子上面。
　　那個球在男孩兒身上。

03　那個男孩兒在自行車上。
　　那個男孩兒在自行車旁邊。
　　這個男人在馬上。
　　這個男人在馬旁邊。

04　那頭驢在那個男人的身下。
　　那頭驢沒在那個男人的身下。
　　那塊兒糖在貨架下面。
　　那些糖在那個男人的手裡。

05　這個男孩兒在樹後面。
　　這個男孩兒在樹前面。
　　這個男人在轎車後面。
　　這個男人在轎車前面。

06　那兩隻碗並排放著。
　　這隻杯子在盤子上面。
　　五在一和零中間。
　　那隻中號的碗在大碗和小碗中間。

07　那個男人在兩個女人旁邊。
　　那個男人在兩個女人中間。
　　那隻狗在兩個人中間。
　　那隻狗在兩個人旁邊。

08　兩個戴眼鏡的人
　　兩個沒戴眼鏡的人
　　一個拿棍子的男孩兒
　　一個沒拿棍子的男孩兒

09　那架飛機在地面上。
　　那架飛機在空中。
　　那些魚在潛水人週圍。
　　那些椅子在桌子週圍。

10　那個男人在自行車後面。
　　那個男人在自行車旁邊。
　　那輛自行車在轎車旁邊。
　　那輛自行車在轎車後面。

2-08

shǐ yòng gèng duō de jiè cí: zài... zhī jiān, zài... shàng miàn, zài... hòu miàn děng

01   nà gè nán rén zài kǎ chē lǐ miàn.
     nà xiē xiāng jiāo zài kuāng lǐ miàn.
     nà xiē rén zài chuán shàng miàn.
     nà xiē rén méi zài chuán shàng miàn.

02   nà gè nán háir zài zhà lán shàng, nà gè nán rén zài zì xíng chē shàng.
     nà dǐng mào zi zài nán háir tóu shàng.
     nà xiē hái zi zài zhuō zi shàng miàn.
     nà gè qiú zài nán háir shēn shàng.

03   nà gè nán háir zài zì xíng chē shàng.
     nà gè nán háir zài zì xíng chē páng biān.
     zhè gè nán rén zài mǎ shàng.
     zhè gè nán rén zài mǎ páng biān.

04   nà tóu lú zài nà gè nán rén de shēn xià.
     nà tóu lú méi zài nà gè nán rén de shēn xià.
     nà kuàir táng zài huò jià xià miàn.
     nà xiē táng zài nà gè nán rén de shǒu lǐ.

05   zhè gè nán háir zài shù hòu miàn.
     zhè gè nán háir zài shù qián miàn.
     zhè gè nán rén zài jiào chē hòu miàn.
     zhè gè nán rén zài jiào chē qián miàn.

06   nà liǎng zhī wǎn bìng pái fàng zhe.
     zhè zhī bēi zi zài pán zi shàng miàn.
     wǔ zài yī hé líng zhōng jiān.
     nà zhī zhōng hào de wǎn zài dà wǎn hé xiǎo wǎn zhōng jiān.

07   nà gè nán rén zài liǎng gè nǚ rén páng biān.
     nà gè nán rén zài liǎng gè nǚ rén zhōng jiān.
     nà zhī gǒu zài liǎng gè rén zhōng jiān.
     nà zhī gǒu zài liǎng gè rén páng biān.

08   liǎng gè dài yǎn jìng de rén
     liǎng gè méi dài yǎn jìng de rén
     yī gè ná gùn zi de nán háir
     yī gè méi ná gùn zi de nán háir

09   nà jià fēi jī zài dì miàn shàng.
     nà jià fēi jī zài kōng zhōng.
     nà xiē yú zài qián shuǐ rén zhōu wéi.
     nà xiē yǐ zi zài zhuō zi zhōu wéi.

10   nà gè nán rén zài zì xíng chē hòu miàn.
     nà gè nán rén zài zì xíng chē páng biān.
     nà liàng zì xíng chē zài jiào chē páng biān.
     nà liàng zì xíng chē zài jiào chē hòu miàn.

头部、脸、手和脚；物主名词与代词

01　一只眼睛
　　一只鼻子
　　一张嘴
　　一张脸

02　人的脚
　　一只耳朵
　　那个男人在摸马的耳朵。
　　象的脚

03　女人的头
　　一只手
　　男人的头
　　一双手和一双脚

04　三只手
　　四只手
　　四只胳膊
　　三只胳膊

05　那个男人的双手放在膝上。
　　那个男人的双手抱着头。
　　那个男人的双手放在桌子上。
　　那个男人一只手放在脸上，另一只手放在臂肘上。

06　那个女人的胳膊放在膝上。
　　那个男人的手放在头上。
　　那个小伙子的臂肘放在桌子上。
　　那个男人的双手放在桌子上。

07　一双眼睛和一只鼻子
　　一只鼻子和一张嘴
　　一张脸
　　一只耳朵

08　那个孩子正把杯子拿到嘴边。
　　那个女人正把杯子拿到嘴边。
　　这个小伙子嘴里有食物。
　　这个小伙子嘴里没有食物。

09　他在摸自己的鼻子。
　　他在摸自己的嘴。
　　她在摸自己的眼睛。
　　她在摸自己的下巴。

10　那个女人在用发刷儿梳头。
　　那个女人在用发刷儿梳女孩儿的头。
　　那个女人在用梳子梳头。
　　那个女人在用梳子梳女孩儿的头。

2-09

頭部、臉、手和腳；物主名詞與代詞

01　一隻眼睛
　　一隻鼻子
　　一張嘴
　　一張臉

02　人的腳
　　一隻耳朵
　　那個男人在摸馬的耳朵。
　　象的腳

03　女人的頭
　　一隻手
　　男人的頭
　　一雙手和一雙腳

04　三隻手
　　四隻手
　　四隻胳膊
　　三隻胳膊

05　那個男人的雙手放在膝上。
　　那個男人的雙手抱著頭。
　　那個男人的雙手放在桌子上。
　　那個男人一隻手放在臉上，另一隻手放在臂肘上。

06　那個女人的胳膊放在膝上。
　　那個男人的手放在頭上。
　　那個小夥子的臂肘放在桌子上。
　　那個男人的雙手放在桌子上。

07　一雙眼睛和一隻鼻子
　　一隻鼻子和一張嘴
　　一張臉
　　一隻耳朵

08　那個孩子正把杯子拿到嘴邊。
　　那個女人正把杯子拿到嘴邊。
　　這個小夥子嘴裡有食物。
　　這個小夥子嘴裡沒有食物。

09　他在摸自己的鼻子。
　　他在摸自己的嘴。
　　她在摸自己的眼睛。
　　她在摸自己的下巴。

10　那個女人在用髮刷兒梳頭。
　　那個女人在用髮刷兒梳女孩兒的頭。
　　那個女人在用梳子梳頭。
　　那個女人在用梳子梳女孩兒的頭。

2-09

tóu bù, liǎn, shǒu hé jiǎo; wù zhǔ míng cí yǔ dài cí

01 yī zhī yǎn jīng
   yī zhī bí zi
   yī zhāng zuǐ
   yī zhāng liǎn

02 rén de jiǎo
   yī zhī ěr duo
   nà gè nán rén zài mō mǎ de ěr duō.
   xiàng de jiǎo

03 nǚ rén de tóu
   yī zhī shǒu
   nán rén de tóu
   yī shuāng shǒu hé yī shuāng jiǎo

04 sān zhī shǒu
   sì zhī shǒu
   sì zhī gē bo
   sān zhī gē bo

05 nà gè nán rén de shuāng shǒu fàng zài xī shàng.
   nà gè nán rén de shuāng shǒu bào zhe tóu.
   nà gè nán rén de shuāng shǒu fàng zài zhuō zi shàng.
   nà gè nán rén yī zhī shǒu fàng zài liǎn shàng, lìng yī zhī shǒu fàng zài bì zhǒu shàng.

06 nà gè nǚ rén de gē bo fàng zài xī shàng.
   nà gè nán rén de shǒu fàng zài tóu shàng.
   nà gè xiǎo huǒ zi de bì zhǒu fàng zài zhuō zi shàng.
   nà gè nán rén de shuāng shǒu fàng zài zhuō zi shàng.

07 yī shuāng yǎn jīng hé yī zhī bí zi
   yī zhī bí zi hé yī zhāng zuǐ
   yī zhāng liǎn
   yī zhī ěr duo

08 nà gè hái zi zhèng bǎ bēi zi ná dào zuǐ biān.
   nà gè nǚ rén zhèng bǎ bēi zi ná dào zuǐ biān.
   zhè gè xiǎo huǒ zi zuǐ lǐ yǒu shí wù.
   zhè gè xiǎo huǒ zi zuǐ lǐ méi yǒu shí wù.

09 tā zài mō zì jǐ de bí zi.
   tā zài mō zì jǐ de zuǐ.
   tā zài mō zì jǐ de yǎn jīng.
   tā zài mō zì jǐ de xià ba.

10 nà gè nǚ rén zài yòng fà shuār shū tóu.
   nà gè nǚ rén zài yòng fà shuār shū nǚ háir de tóu.
   nà gè nǚ rén zài yòng shū zi shū tóu.
   nà gè nǚ rén zài yòng shū zi shū nǚ háir de tóu.

2-10

各种时态：现在进行时；现在完成时； 用 "正要"、"想" 表示的一般将来时

01 那个女人在跳。
    那个女人已经跳完了。
    那匹马在跳。
    那匹马已经跳过去了。

02 那个男孩儿正摔下来。
    那个男孩儿已经摔下来了。
    那个牛仔正摔下来。
    那个牛仔已经摔下来了。

03 那个女孩儿在剪纸。
    那个女孩儿已经把纸剪完了。
    那个男孩儿正往水里跳。
    那个男孩儿已经跳进水里了。

04 那匹马正要跳。
    那个孩子正要跳。
    那匹马在跳。
    那匹马已经跳过去了。

05 那个女孩儿正要剪纸。
    那个女孩儿在剪纸。
    那个女孩儿已经把纸剪完了。
    那个女孩儿在跳。

06 那个男孩儿正要往水里跳。
    那个男孩儿正往水里跳。
    那个男孩儿已经跳进水里了。
    那些男孩儿正往水里跳。

07 那个骑马的人要摔下来了。
    那个骑马的人正摔下来。
    那个骑马的人已经摔下来了。
    那个男孩儿正摔下来。

08 那两个女孩儿不想跳。那个男孩儿想跳。
    那两个女孩儿不在跳。那个男孩儿在跳。
    那两个女孩儿没有跳。那个男孩儿已经跳下去了。
    那个男孩儿和那两个女孩儿都在跳。

09 那个男人正要喝牛奶。
    那个男人在喝牛奶。
    那个男人已经把牛奶喝了。
    那个男孩儿正要吃面包。

10 那个男孩儿正要吃面包。
    那个男孩儿在吃面包。
    那个男孩儿已经吃了一点儿面包。
    那个男孩儿在戴帽子。

2-10

各種時態：現在進行時；現在完成時；用 "正要"、"想" 表示的一般將來時

01 那個女人在跳。
    那個女人已經跳完了。
    那匹馬在跳。
    那匹馬已經跳過去了。

02 那個男孩兒正摔下來。
    那個男孩兒已經摔下來了。
    那個牛仔正摔下來。
    那個牛仔已經摔下來了。

03 那個女孩兒在剪紙。
    那個女孩兒已經把紙剪完了。
    那個男孩兒正往水裡跳。
    那個男孩兒已經跳進水裡了。

04 那匹馬正要跳。
    那個孩子正要跳。
    那匹馬在跳。
    那匹馬已經跳過去了。

05 那個女孩兒正要剪紙。
    那個女孩兒在剪紙。
    那個女孩兒已經把紙剪完了。
    那個女孩兒在跳。

06 那個男孩兒正要往水裡跳。
    那個男孩兒正往水裡跳。
    那個男孩兒已經跳進水裡了。
    那些男孩兒正往水裡跳。

07 那個騎馬的人要摔下來了。
    那個騎馬的人正摔下來。
    那個騎馬的人已經摔下來了。
    那個男孩兒正摔下來。

08 那兩個女孩兒不想跳。那個男孩兒想跳。
    那兩個女孩兒不在跳。那個男孩兒在跳。
    那兩個女孩兒沒有跳。那個男孩兒已經跳下去了。
    那個男孩兒和那兩個女孩兒都在跳。

09 那個男人正要喝牛奶。
    那個男人在喝牛奶。
    那個男人已經把牛奶喝了。
    那個男孩兒正要吃面包。

10 那個男孩兒正要吃面包。
    那個男孩兒在吃面包。
    那個男孩兒已經吃了一點兒面包。
    那個男孩兒在戴帽子。

2-10

gè zhǒng shí tài: xiàn zài jìn xíng shí; xiàn zài wán chéng shí; yòng "zhèng yào", "xiǎng" biǎo shì de yī bān jiāng lái shí

01 nà gè nǚ rén zài tiào.
nà gè nǚ rén yǐ jīng tiào wán le.
nà pǐ mǎ zài tiào.
nà pǐ mǎ yǐ jīng tiào guò qù le.

02 nà gè nán háir zhèng shuāi xià lái.
nà gè nán háir yǐ jīng shuāi xià lái le.
nà gè niú zǎi zhèng shuāi xià lái.
nà gè niú zǎi yǐ jīng shuāi xià lái le.

03 nà gè nǚ háir zài jiǎn zhǐ.
nà gè nǚ háir yǐ jīng bǎ zhǐ jiǎn wán le.
nà gè nán háir zhèng wǎng shuǐ lǐ tiào.
nà gè nán háir yǐ jīng tiào jìn shuǐ lǐ le.

04 nà pǐ mǎ zhèng yào tiào.
nà gè hái zi zhèng yào tiào.
nà pǐ mǎ zài tiào.
nà pǐ mǎ yǐ jīng tiào guò qù le.

05 nà gè nǚ háir zhèng yào jiǎn zhǐ.
nà gè nǚ hái zài jiǎn zhǐ.
nà gè nǚ háir yǐ jīng bǎ zhǐ jiǎn wán le.
nà gè nǚ háir zài tiào.

06 nà gè nán háir zhèng yào wǎng shuǐ lǐ tiào.
nà gè nán háir zhèng wǎng shuǐ lǐ tiào.
nà gè nán háir yǐ jīng tiào jìn shuǐ lǐ le.
nà xiē nán háir zhèng wǎng shuǐ lǐ tiào.

07 nà gè qí mǎ de rén yào shuāi xià lái le.
nà gè qí mǎ de rén zhèng shuāi xià lái.
nà gè qí mǎ de rén yǐ jīng shuāi xià lái le.
nà gè nán háir zhèng shuāi xià lái.

08 nà liǎng gè nǚ háir bù xiǎng tiào. nà gè nán háir xiǎng tiào.
nà liǎng gè nǚ háir bú zài tiào. nà gè nán háir zài tiào.
nà liǎng gè nǚ háir méi yǒu tiào. nà gè nán háir yǐ jīng tiào xià qù le.
nà gè nán háir hé nà liǎng gè nǚ háir dōu zài tiào.

09 nà gè nán rén zhèng yào hē niú nǎi.
nà gè nán rén zài hē niú nǎi.
nà gè nán rén yǐ jīng bǎ niú nǎi hē le.
nà gè nán háir zhèng yào chī miàn bāo.

10 nà gè nán háir zhèng yào chī miàn bāo.
nà gè nán háir zài chī miàn bāo.
nà gè nán háir yǐ jīng chī le yī diǎnr miàn bāo.
nà gè nán háir zài dài mào zi.

2-11

复习第二部分

01 那个女人在笑。
那个女人在指着什么东西。
那个女人在看报纸。
那个女人在打电话。

02 这个人已经成年。
这个人还未成年。
这只动物不是猫。
这只动物不是狗。

03 一只大箱子
一艘大船
一只小箱子
一只小船

04 那个蓝色的圆比那个红色的圆小。
那个红色的圆比那个蓝色的圆小。
那个圆比那个正方形小。
那个正方形比那个圆小。

05 一个女人在指着什么东西。她在用右手指着。
一个女人在指着什么东西。她在用左手指着。
两个女人都在指着什么东西。一个在用右手指着，另
    一个在用左手指着。
两个女人什么东西也没有指。

06 那个女人在打电话。
那个女孩儿在打电话。
那个女人在指着什么东西。
那个女人没有打电话，她也没指什么东西。

07 那些男人和女人正站着。
那两个女人正站着，那两个男人正坐着。
那两个女人和一个男人正站着，还有一个男人正坐
    着。
那两个男人和一个女人正坐着，还有一个女人正站
    着。

08 那个男人在两个女人旁边。
那个男人在两个女人中间。
那只狗在两个人中间。
那只狗在两个人旁边。

09 他在摸自己的鼻子。
他在摸自己的嘴。
她在摸自己的眼睛。
她在摸自己的下巴。

10 那两个女孩儿不想跳。那个男孩儿想跳。
那两个女孩儿不在跳。那个男孩儿在跳。
那两个女孩儿没有跳。那个男孩儿已经跳下去了。
那个男孩儿和那两个女孩儿都在跳。

2-11

復習第二部分

01 那個女人在笑。
那個女人在指著甚麼東西。
那個女人在看報紙。
那個女人在打電話。

02 這個人已經成年。
這個人还未成年。
這隻動物不是貓。
這隻動物不是狗。

03 一隻大箱子
一艘大船
一隻小箱子
一隻小船

04 那個藍色的圓比那個紅色的圓小。
那個紅色的圓比那個藍色的圓小。
那個圓比那個正方形小。
那個正方形比那個圓小。

05 一個女人在指著甚麼東西。她在用右手指著。
一個女人在指著甚麼東西。她在用左手指著。
兩個女人都在指著甚麼東西。一個在用右手指著，另
    一個在用左手指著。
兩個女人甚麼東西也沒有指。

06 那個女人在打電話。
那個女孩兒在打電話。
那個女人在指著甚麼東西。
那個女人沒有打電話，她也沒指甚麼東西。

07 那些男人和女人正站著。
那兩個女人正站著，那兩個男人正坐著。
那兩個女人和一個男人正站著，還有一個男人正坐
    著。
那兩個男人和一個女人正坐著，還有一個女人正站
    著。

08 那個男人在兩個女人旁邊。
那個男人在兩個女人中間。
那隻狗在兩個人中間。
那隻狗在兩個人旁邊。

09 他在摸自己的鼻子。
他在摸自己的嘴。
她在摸自己的眼睛。
她在摸自己的下巴。

10 那兩個女孩兒不想跳。那個男孩兒想跳。
那兩個女孩兒不在跳。那個男孩兒在跳。
那兩個女孩兒沒有跳。那個男孩兒已經跳下去了。
那個男孩兒和那兩個女孩兒都在跳。

2-11

fù xí dì èr bù fen

01　nà gè nǚ rén zài xiào.
　　nà gè nǚ rén zài zhǐ zhe shén me dōng xi.
　　nà gè nǚ rén zài kàn bào zhǐ.
　　nà gè nǚ rén zài dǎ diàn huà.

02　zhè gè rén yǐ jīng chéng nián.
　　zhè gè rén haí wèi chéng nián.
　　zhè zhī dòng wù bú shì māo.
　　zhè zhī dòng wù bú shì gǒu.

03　yī zhī dà xiāng zi
　　yī sōu dà chuán
　　yī zhī xiǎo xiāng zi
　　yī zhī xiǎo chuán

04　nà gè lán sè de yuán bǐ nà gè hóng sè de yuán xiǎo.
　　nà gè hóng sè de yuán bǐ nà gè lán sè de yuán xiǎo.
　　nà gè yuán bǐ nà gè zhèng fāng xíng xiǎo.
　　nà gè zhèng fāng xíng bǐ nà gè yuán xiǎo.

05　yī gè nǚ rén zài zhǐ zhe shén mo dōng xi. tā zài yòng yòu shǒu zhǐ zhe.
　　yī gè nǚ rén zài zhǐ zhe shén mo dōng xi. tā zài yòng zuǒ shǒu zhǐ zhe.
　　liǎng gè nǚ rén dōu zài zhǐ zhe shén mo dōng xi. yī gè zài yòng yòu shǒu zhǐ zhe, lìng yī gè zài yòng zuǒ
　　　shǒu zhǐ zhe.
　　liǎng gè nǚ rén shén mo dōng xi yě méi yǒu zhǐ.

06　nà gè nǚ rén zài dǎ diàn huà.
　　nà gè nǚ háir zài dǎ diàn huà.
　　nà gè nǚ rén zài zhǐ zhe shén mo dōng xi.
　　nà gè nǚ rén méi yǒu dǎ diàn huà, tā yě méi zhǐ shén mo dōng xi.

07　nà xiē nán rén hé nǚ rén zhèng zhàn zhe.
　　nà liǎng gè nǚ rén zhèng zhàn zhe, nà liǎng gè nán rén zhèng zuò zhe.
　　nà liǎng gè nǚ rén hé yī gè nán rén zhèng zhàn zhe, hái yǒu yī gè nán rén zhèng zuò zhe.
　　nà liǎng gè nán rén hé yī gè nǚ rén zhèng zuò zhe, hái yǒu yī gè nǚ rén zhèng zhàn zhe.

08　nà gè nán rén zài liǎng gè nǚ rén páng biān.
　　nà gè nán rén zài liǎng gè nǚ rén zhōng jiān.
　　nà zhī gǒu zài liǎng gè rén zhōng jiān.
　　nà zhī gǒu zài liǎng gè rén páng biān.

09　tā zài mō zì jǐ de bí zi.
　　tā zài mō zì jǐ de zuǐ.
　　tā zài mō zì jǐ de yǎn jīng.
　　tā zài mō zì jǐ de xià ba.

10　nà liǎng gè nǚ háir bù xiǎng tiào. nà gè nán háir xiǎng tiào.
　　nà liǎng gè nǚ háir bú zài tiào. nà gè nán háir zài tiào.
　　nà liǎng gè nǚ háir méi yǒu tiào. nà gè nán háir yǐ jīng tiào xià qù le.
　　nà gè nán háir hé nà liǎng gè nǚ háir dōu zài tiào.

用形容词描述人

01 一位年纪较大的女人
一位年纪较轻的女人
一位年纪较轻的男人
一位年纪较大的男人

02 一群跳舞的人
两个跳舞的人
一群赛跑的人
两个赛跑的人

03 这个小伙子留着短发。
这个小伙子留着长发。
那两位年轻女人留着长发。
一位年轻女人留着长发，另一位年轻女人留着短发。

04 谁长着黑色短发？
谁长着金色长发？
谁长着棕色长发？
谁秃发？

05 这个年轻女人长着卷发。
这个小伙子长着卷发。
这个年轻女人长着直发。
这个小伙子长着直发。

06 谁长着又短又直的黑发？
谁长着又长又卷的黑发？
谁长着又短又卷的黑发？
谁长着又长又直的黑发？

07 右边的那个男人胖。左边的那个男人瘦。
那三个女人瘦。
那两个女人很胖。
左边的那个男人胖。右边的那个男人瘦。

08 左边的那个小丑儿矮。右边的那个小丑儿高。
左边的那个小丑儿高。右边的那个小丑儿矮。
穿红衣服的那个女人矮。
穿红衣服的那个女人高。

09 哪个高的男人戴着眼镜？
哪个高的男人没戴眼镜？
哪个小孩儿没戴眼镜？
哪个小孩儿戴着眼镜？

10 那个女人长着黑发。
那个女人长着金色直发。
那个女人长着金色卷发。
那个女人长着白发。

3-01

用形容詞描述人

01 一位年紀較大的女人
一位年紀較輕的女人
一位年紀較輕的男人
一位年紀較大的男人

02 一群跳舞的人
兩個跳舞的人
一群賽跑的人
兩個賽跑的人

03 這個小夥子留著短髮。
這個小夥子留著長髮。
那兩位年輕女人留著長髮。
一位年輕女人留著長髮，另一位年輕女人留著短髮。

04 誰長著黑色短髮？
誰長著金色長髮？
誰長著棕色長髮？
誰禿髮？

05 這個年輕女人長著卷髮。
這個小夥子長著卷髮。
這個年輕女人長著直髮。
這個小夥子長著直髮。

06 誰長著又短又直的黑髮？
誰長著又長又卷的黑髮？
誰長著又短又卷的黑髮？
誰長著又長又直的黑髮？

07 右邊的那個男人胖。左邊的那個男人瘦。
那三個女人瘦。
那兩個女人很胖。
左邊的那個男人胖。右邊的那個男人瘦。

08 左邊的那個小醜兒矮。右邊的那個小醜兒高。
左邊的那個小醜兒高。右邊的那個小醜兒矮。
穿紅衣服的那個女人矮。
穿紅衣服的那個女人高。

09 哪個高的男人戴著眼鏡？
哪個高的男人沒戴眼鏡？
哪個小孩兒沒戴眼鏡？
哪個小孩兒戴著眼鏡？

10 那個女人長著黑髮。
那個女人長著金色直髮。
那個女人長著金色卷髮。
那個女人長著白髮。

3-01

yòng xíng róng cí miáo shù rén

01 yī wèi nián jì jiào dà de nǚ rén
    yī wèi nián jì jiào qīng de nǚ rén
    yī wèi nián jì jiào qīng de nán rén
    yī wèi nián jì jiào dà de nán rén

02 yī qún tiào wǔ de rén
    liǎng gè tiào wǔ de rén
    yī qún sài pǎo de rén
    liǎng gè sài pǎo de rén

03 zhè gè xiǎo huǒ zi liú zhe duǎn fà.
    zhè gè xiǎo huǒ zi liú zhe cháng fà.
    nà liǎng wèi nián qīng nǚ rén liú zhe cháng fà.
    yī wèi nián qīng nǚ rén liú zhe cháng fà, lìng yī wèi nián qīng nǚ rén liú zhe duǎn fà.

04 shéi zhǎng zhe hēi sè duǎn fà?
    shéi zhǎng zhe jīn sè cháng fà?
    shéi zhǎng zhe zōng sè cháng fà?
    shéi tū fà?

05 zhè gè nián qīng nǚ rén zhǎng zhe juǎn fà.
    zhè gè xiǎo huǒ zi zhǎng zhe juǎn fà.
    zhè gè nián qīng nǚ rén zhǎng zhe zhí fà.
    zhè gè xiǎo huǒ zi zhǎng zhe zhí fà.

06 shéi zhǎng zhe yòu duǎn yòu zhí de hēi fà?
    shéi zhǎng zhe yòu cháng yòu juǎn de hēi fà?
    shéi zhǎng zhe yòu duǎn yòu juǎn de hēi fà?
    shéi zhǎng zhe yòu cháng yòu zhí de hēi fà?

07 yòu biān de nà gè nán rén pàng, zuǒ biān de nà gè nán rén shòu.
    nà sān gè nǚ rén shòu.
    nà liǎng gè nǚ rén hěn pàng.
    zuǒ biān de nà gè nán rén pàng. yòu biān de nà gè nán rén shòu.

08 zuǒ biān de nà gè xiǎo chǒu ǎi. yòu biān de nà gè xiǎo chǒu gāo.
    zuǒ biān de nà gè xiǎo chǒu gāo. yòu biān de nà gè xiǎo chǒu ǎi.
    chuān hóng yī fu de nà gè nǚ rén ǎi.
    chuān hóng yī fu de nà gè nǚ rén gāo.

09 nǎ gè gāo de nán rén dài zhe yǎn jìng?
    nǎ gè gāo de nán rén méi dài yǎn jìng?
    nǎ gè xiǎo háir méi dài yǎn jìng?
    nǎ gè xiǎo háir dài zhe yǎn jìng?

10 nà gè nǚ rén zhǎng zhe hēi fà.
    nà gè nǚ rén zhǎng zhe jīn sè zhí fà.
    nà gè nǚ rén zhǎng zhe jīng sè juǎn fà.
    nà gè nǚ rén zhǎng zhe bái fà.

数词和量词：比较多少

01 许多男孩儿
一个男孩儿
许多气球
几个气球

02 许多帽子
一顶帽子
许多伞
一把伞

03 一块面包
许多面包
两块面包
没有面包

04 一个牛仔和一匹马
一个牛仔，但没有马
两个牛仔和几匹马
许多牛仔帽，但没有牛仔

05 有多少枚硬币？有许多硬币。
有多少个玻璃球？有一个。
有多少个玻璃球？有几个。
有多少个玻璃球？有许多玻璃球。

06 许多西红柿和几只香蕉
许多苹果，但没有香蕉
许多西红柿，但没有香蕉
许多香蕉，但没有苹果

07 椅子比桌子多。
公共汽车比轿车多。
西红柿比香蕉多。
男人和女人一样多。

08 人比马多。
马比人多。
伞和人一样多。
人比伞多。

09 马比人少。
人比马少。
伞比人少。
马和人一样多。

10 女孩儿和男孩儿一样多。
女孩儿比男孩儿少。
女孩儿比男孩儿多。
没有女孩儿，也没有男孩儿。

3-02

數詞和量詞：比較多少

01 許多男孩兒
一個男孩兒
許多氣球
幾個氣球

02 許多帽子
一頂帽子
許多傘
一把傘

03 一塊面包
許多面包
兩塊面包
沒有面包

04 一個牛仔和一匹馬
一個牛仔，但沒有馬
兩個牛仔和幾匹馬
許多牛仔帽，但沒有牛仔

05 有多少枚硬幣？有許多硬幣。
有多少個玻璃球？有一個。
有多少個玻璃球？有幾個。
有多少個玻璃球？有許多玻璃球。

06 許多西紅柿和幾只香蕉
許多苹果，但沒有香蕉
許多西紅柿，但沒有香蕉
許多香蕉，但沒有苹果

07 椅子比桌子多。
公共汽車比轎車多。
西紅柿比香蕉多。
男人和女人一樣多。

08 人比馬多。
馬比人多。
傘和人一樣多。
人比傘多。

09 馬比人少。
人比馬少。
傘比人少。
馬和人一樣多。

10 女孩兒和男孩兒一樣多。
女孩兒比男孩兒少。
女孩兒比男孩兒多。
沒有女孩兒，也沒有男孩兒。

3-02

shù cí hé liàng cí, bǐ jiào duō shǎo

01 xǔ duō nán háir
   yī gè nán háir
   xǔ duō qì qiú
   jǐ gè qì qiú

02 xǔ duō mào zi
   yī dǐng mào zi
   xǔ duō sǎn
   yī bǎ sǎn

03 yī kuài miàn bāo
   xǔ duō miàn bāo
   liǎng kuài miàn bāo
   méi yǒu miàn bāo

04 yī gè niú zǎi hé yī pǐ mǎ
   yī gè niú zǎi, dàn méi yǒu mǎ
   liǎng gè niú zǎi hé jǐ pǐ mǎ
   xǔ duō niú zǎi mào, dàn méi yǒu niú zǎi

05 yǒu duō shǎo méi yìng bì? yǒu xǔ duō yìng bì.
   yǒu duō shǎo gè bō li qiú? yǒu yī gè.
   yǒu duō shǎo gè bō li qiú? yǒu jǐ gè.
   yǒu duō shǎo gè bō li qiú? yǒu xǔ duō bō li qiú.

06 xǔ duō xī hóng shì hé jǐ zhī xiāng jiāo
   xǔ duō píng guǒ, dàn méi yǒu xiāng jiāo
   xǔ duō xī hóng shì, dàn méi yǒu xiāng jiāo
   xǔ duō xiāng jiāo, dàn méi yǒu píng guǒ

07 yǐ zi bǐ zhuō zi duō.
   gōng gòng qì chē bǐ jiào chē duō.
   xī hóng shì bǐ xiāng jiāo duō.
   nán rén hé nǚ rén yī yàng duō.

08 rén bǐ mǎ duō.
   mǎ bǐ rén duō.
   sǎn hé rén yī yàng duō.
   rén bǐ sǎn duō.

09 mǎ bǐ rén shǎo.
   rén bǐ mǎ shǎo.
   sǎn bǐ rén shǎo.
   mǎ hé rén yī yàng duō.

10 nǚ háir hé nán háir yī yàng duō.
   nǚ háir bǐ nán háir shǎo.
   nǚ háir bǐ nán háir duō.
   méi yǒu nǚ háir, yě méi yǒu nán háir.

服装

01 那个男人穿着蓝毛衣。
那两个女孩儿穿着连衣裙。
那个男孩儿穿着红毛衣。
那个女人穿着紫毛衣。

02 那个女人穿着黑衬衫。
那个女人穿着黑裤子。
那个男孩儿穿着蓝 T 恤衫。
那个男孩儿穿着蓝裤子。

03 两只鞋
一只鞋
两只袜子
一只袜子

04 她穿着红白花儿的毛衣。
她穿着紫色的衬衫。
他穿着毛衣。
他没穿毛衣。

05 她穿着红白花儿的毛衣和牛仔裤。
那个女人穿着红连衣裙。
那个女人穿着红风衣。
那个女人穿着红裙子。

06 他穿着黑短裤和白运动衫。
一个人穿着黄色的无袖衫，另一个人穿着红色的 T 恤
衫。
一个女人穿着黄连衣裙，另一个女人穿着红连衣裙。
她什么都没穿。

07 她穿着连衣裙。
她穿着裤子。
她穿着短裤。
她穿着裙子。

08 他穿着蓝 T 恤衫。
他穿着蓝牛仔裤。
他穿着蓝毛衣。
他穿着蓝夹克衫。

09 他在穿袜子。
他在穿鞋。
他在穿衬衫。
他在穿裤子。

10 那个小丑儿穿着裤子。
那个小丑儿在穿裤子。
那个戴眼镜的男人穿着毛衣。
那个戴眼镜的男人在穿毛衣。

3-03

服装

01 那個男人穿著藍毛衣。
那兩個女孩兒穿著連衣裙。
那個男孩兒穿著紅毛衣。
那個女人穿著紫毛衣。

02 那個女人穿著黑襯衫。
那個女人穿著黑褲子。
那個男孩兒穿著藍 T 恤衫。
那個男孩兒穿著藍褲子。

03 兩隻鞋
一隻鞋
兩隻襪子
一隻襪子

04 她穿著紅白花兒的毛衣。
她穿著紫色的襯衫。
他穿著毛衣。
他沒穿毛衣。

05 她穿著紅白花兒的毛衣和牛仔褲。
那個女人穿著紅連衣裙。
那個女人穿著紅風衣。
那個女人穿著紅裙子。

06 他穿著黑短褲和白運動衫。
一個人穿著黃色的無袖衫，另一個人穿著紅色的 T 恤
衫。
一個女人穿著黃連衣裙，另一個女人穿著紅連衣裙。
她什麼都沒穿。

07 她穿著連衣裙。
她穿著褲子。
她穿著短褲。
她穿著裙子。

08 他穿著藍 T 恤衫。
他穿著藍牛仔褲。
他穿著藍毛衣。
他穿著藍夾克衫。

09 他在穿襪子。
他在穿鞋。
他在穿襯衫。
他在穿褲子。

10 那個小醜兒穿著褲子。
那個小醜兒在穿褲子。
那個戴眼鏡的男人穿著毛衣。
那個戴眼鏡的男人在穿毛衣。

3-03

fú zhuāng

01 nà gè nán rén chuān zhe lán máo yī.
nà liǎng gè nǚ háir chuān zhe lián yī qún.
nà gè nán háir chuān zhe hóng máo yī.
nà gè nǚ rén chuān zhe zǐ máo yī.

02 nà gè nǚ rén chuān zhe hēi chèn shān.
nà gè nǚ rén chuān zhe hēi kù zi.
nà gè nán háir chuān zhe lán T xù shān.
nà gè nán háir chuān zhe lán kù zi.

03 liǎng zhī xié
yī zhī xié
liǎng zhī wà zi
yī zhī wà zi

04 tā chuān zhe hóng bái huār de máo yī.
tā chuān zhe zǐ sè de chèn shān.
tā chuān zhe máo yī.
tā méi chuān máo yī.

05 tā chuān zhe hóng bái huār de máo yī hé niú zǎi kù.
nà gè nǚ rén chuān zhe hóng lián yī qún.
nà gè nǚ rén chuān zhe hóng fēng yī.
nà gè nǚ rén chuān zhe hóng qún zi.

06 tā chuān zhe hēi duǎn kù hé bái yùn dòng shān.
yī gè rén chuān zhe huáng sè de wú xiù shān, lìng yī gè rén chuān zhe hóng sè de T xù shān.
yī gè nǚ rén chuān zhe huáng lián yī qún, lìng yī gè nǚ rén chuān zhe hóng lián yī qún.
tā shén me dōu méi chuān.

07 tā chuān zhe lián yī qún.
tā chuān zhe kù zi.
tā chuān zhe duǎn kù.
tā chuān zhe qún zi.

08 tā chuān zhe lán T xù shān.
tā chuān zhe lán niú zǎi kù.
tā chuān zhe lán máo yī.
tā chuān zhe lán jiá kè shān.

09 tā zài chuān wà zi.
tā zài chuān xié.
tā zài chuān chèn shān.
tā zài chuān kù zi.

10 nà gè xiǎo chǒur chuān zhe kù zi.
nà gè xiǎo chǒur zài chuān kù zi.
nà gè dài yǎn jìng de nán rén chuān zhe máo yī.
nà gè dài yǎn jìng de nán rén zài chuān máo yī.

运用更多的介词：里面、外面、上面

01 那个男孩儿正坐在桌旁。
那个男孩儿在桌子下面。
那些孩子正站在桌子上面。
那些孩子在跳绳。

02 谁在跑？那些男人在跑。
谁在坐着？那个男孩儿在坐着。
谁在跑？那两个女孩儿在跑。
谁在跳？那些孩子在跳。

03 有几个孩子在跳？有三个孩子在跳。
有几个孩子在站着？有三个孩子在站着。
有几个孩子在跳？有四个孩子在跳。
有几个孩子正站在桌子上面？有一个女孩儿正站在桌子上面。

04 有几个女孩儿穿着白衬衣？有一个。
有几个女孩儿穿着白衬衣？有两个。
有几个男孩儿在坐着？有一个。
有几个男孩儿在坐着？有两个。

05 那个女孩儿在桌子上面。她在跳绳。
有三个孩子在玩儿。他们在跳绳。
那些孩子在桌子上面。他们不在跳绳。
那个男孩儿在跑。他不在跳绳。

06 桌子上面的那个女孩儿在跳绳。
那个男孩儿在摇绳，那个女孩儿在跳绳。
没跳绳的那个男孩儿在跑。
没跑的那个男孩儿在跳绳。

07 这只猫在房子外面。
这只猫在房子里面。
这些花儿在房子外面。
这些花儿在房子里面。

08 这是一座房子的外面。
这是一座房子的里面。
这是一座教堂的外面。
这是一座教堂的里面。

09 那个男孩儿正躺在房子外面。
那个男孩儿正躺在房子里面。
这是那座建筑物的外面。
这是那座建筑物的里面。

10 哪个男孩儿在房子里面？
哪个男孩儿在房子外面？
哪些孩子在房子外面？
哪两个孩子在房子里面？

3-04

運用更多的介詞：裡面、外面、上面

01 那個男孩兒正坐在桌旁。
那個男孩兒在桌子下面。
那些孩子正站在桌子上面。
那些孩子在跳繩。

02 誰在跑？那些男人在跑。
誰在坐著？那個男孩兒在坐著。
誰在跑？那兩個女孩兒在跑。
誰在跳？那些孩子在跳。

03 有幾個孩子在跳？有三個孩子在跳。
有幾個孩子在站著？有三個孩子在站著。
有幾個孩子在跳？有四個孩子在跳。
有幾個孩子正站在桌子上面？有一個女孩兒正站在桌子上面。

04 有幾個女孩兒穿著白襯衣？有一個。
有幾個女孩兒穿著白襯衣？有兩個。
有幾個男孩兒在坐著？有一個。
有幾個男孩兒在坐著？有兩個。

05 那個女孩兒在桌子上面。她在跳繩。
有三個孩子在玩兒。他們在跳繩。
那些孩子在桌子上面。他們不在跳繩。
那個男孩兒在跑。他不在跳繩。

06 桌子上面的那個女孩兒在跳繩。
那個男孩兒在搖繩，那個女孩兒在跳繩。
沒跳繩的那個男孩兒在跑。
沒跑的那個男孩兒在跳繩。

07 這隻貓在房子外面。
這隻貓在房子裡面。
這些花兒在房子外面。
這些花兒在房子裡面。

08 這是一座房子的外面。
這是一座房子的裡面。
這是一座教堂的外面。
這是一座教堂的裡面。

09 那個男孩兒正躺在房子外面。
那個男孩兒正躺在房子裡面。
這是那座建築物的外面。
這是那座建築物的裡面。

10 哪個男孩兒在房子裡面？
哪個男孩兒在房子外面？
哪些孩子在房子外面？
哪兩個孩子在房子裡面？

yùn yòng gèng duō de jiè cí: lǐ miàn, wài miàn, shàng miàn

01 nà gè nán háir zhèng zuò zài zhuō páng.
   nà gè nán háir zài zhuō zi xià miàn.
   nà xiē hái zi zhèng zhàn zài zhuō zi shàng miàn.
   nà xiē hái zi zài tiào shéng.

02 shéi zài pǎo? nà xiē nán rén zài pǎo.
   shéi zài zuò zhe? nà gè nán háir zài zuò zhe.
   shéi zài pǎo? nà liǎng gè nǚ háir zài pǎo.
   shéi zài tiào? nà xiē hái zi zài tiào.

03 yǒu jǐ gè hái zi zài tiào? yǒu sān gè hái zi zài tiào.
   yǒu jǐ gè hái zi zài zhàn zhe? yǒu sān gè hái zi zài zhàn zhe.
   yǒu jǐ gè hái zi zài tiào? yǒu sì gè hái zi zài tiào.
   yǒu jǐ gè hái zi zhèng zhàn zài zhuō zi shàng miàn? yǒu yī gè nǚ háir zhèng zhàn zài zhuō zi shàng
      miàn.

04 yǒu jǐ gè nǚ háir chuān zhe bái chèn yī? yǒu yī gè.
   yǒu jǐ gè nǚ háir chuān zhe bái chèn yī? yǒu liǎng gè.
   yǒu jǐ gè nán háir zài zuò zhe? yǒu yī gè.
   yǒu jǐ gè nán háir zài zuò zhe? yǒu liǎng gè.

05 nà gè nǚ háir zài zhuō zi shàng miàn. tā zài tiào shéng.
   yǒu sān gè hái zi zài wánr. tā men zài tiào shéng.
   nà xiē hái zi zài zhuō zi shàng miàn. tā men bú zài tiào shéng.
   nà gè nán háir zài pǎo. tā bú zài tiào shéng.

06 zhuō zi shàng miàn de nà gè nǚ háir zài tiào shéng.
   nà gè nán háir zài yáo shéng, nà gè nǚ háir zài tiào shéng.
   méi tiào shéng de nà gè nán háir zài pǎo.
   méi pǎo de nà gè nán háir zài tiào shéng.

07 zhè zhī māo zài fáng zi wài miàn.
   zhè zhī māo zài fáng zi lǐ miàn.
   zhè xiē huār zài fáng zi wài miàn.
   zhè xiē huār zài fáng zi lǐ miàn.

08 zhè shì yī zuò fáng zi de wài miàn.
   zhè shì yī zuò fáng zi de lǐ miàn.
   zhè shì yī zuò jiào táng de wài miàn.
   zhè shì yī zuò jiào táng de lǐ miàn.

09 nà gè nán háir zhèng tǎng zài fáng zi wài miàn.
   nà gè nán háir zhèng tǎng zài fáng zi lǐ miàn.
   zhè shì nà zuò jiàn zhù wù de wài miàn.
   zhè shì nà zuò jiàn zhù wù de lǐ miàn.

10 nǎ gè nán háir zài fáng zi lǐ miàn?
   nǎ gè nán háir zài fáng zi wài miàn?
   nǎ xiē hái zi zài fáng zi wài miàn?
   nǎ liǎng gè hái zi zài fáng zi lǐ miàn?

3-05

颜色和数字

01 那个鸡蛋是什么颜色的？是蓝色的。
那个鸡蛋是什么颜色的？是黄色的。
那个鸡蛋是什么颜色的？是红色的。
那个鸡蛋是什么颜色的？是粉红色的。

02 那个姑娘在刷哪匹马？那匹棕色的马。
哪匹是白马？
哪匹马在吃草？那匹灰色的马在吃草。
哪匹是黑马？

03 一只黑白花狗
一只黑白花猫
一只棕色的狗
一只棕白花猫

04 绿草，一顶草绿色的帽子
黄花儿
一件红 T 恤衫
一座白色的建筑物

05 那匹木马的背景是黄色的。
那匹木马的背景是紫色的。
那匹木马的背景是蓝色的。
那匹木马的背景是红色的。

06 蓝色的水
桔黄色，黄色
黄色，黑色
绿草

07 两朵红花儿
两朵长着黄蕊的白花儿
一朵黄花儿，一朵红花儿，一朵粉红色的花儿
几朵粉红色的花儿

08 三
七
九
四

09 十
九
五个球
六个球

10 一个球
两个球
八个手指
五

3-05

顏色和數字

01 那個雞蛋是什麼顏色的？是藍色的。
那個雞蛋是什麼顏色的？是黃色的。
那個雞蛋是什麼顏色的？是紅色的。
那個雞蛋是什麼顏色的？ 是粉紅色的。

02 那個姑娘在刷哪匹馬？那匹棕色的馬。
哪匹是白馬？
哪匹馬在吃草？那匹灰色的馬在吃草。
哪匹是黑馬？

03 一隻黑白花狗
一隻黑白花貓
一隻棕色的狗
一隻棕白花貓

04 綠草，一頂草綠色的帽子
黃花兒
一件紅 T 恤衫
一座白色的建筑物

05 那匹木馬的背景是黃色的。
那匹木馬的背景是紫色的。
那匹木馬的背景是藍色的。
那匹木馬的背景是紅色的。

06 藍色的水
桔黃色，黃色
黃色，黑色
綠草

07 兩朵紅花兒
兩朵長著黃蕊的白花兒
一朵黃花兒，一朵紅花兒，一朵粉紅色的花兒
幾朵粉紅色的花兒

08 三
七
九
四

09 十
九
五個球
六個球

10 一個球
兩個球
八個手指
五

3-05

yán sè hé shù zì

01 nà gè jī dàn shì shén me yán sè de? shì lán sè de.
nà gè jī dàn shì shén me yán sè de? shì huáng sè de.
nà gè jī dàn shì shén me yán sè de? shì hóng sè de.
nà gè jī dàn shì shén me yán sè de? shì fěn hóng sè de.

02 nà gè gū niang zài shuā nǎ pǐ mǎ? nà pǐ zōng sè de mǎ.
nǎ pǐ shì bái mǎ?
nǎ pǐ mǎ zài chī cǎo? nà pǐ huī sè de mǎ zài chī cǎo.
nǎ pǐ shì hēi mǎ?

03 yī zhī hēi bái huā gǒu
yī zhī hēi bái huā māo
yī zhī zōng sè de gǒu
yī zhī zōng bái huā māo

04 lǜ cǎo, yī dǐng cǎo lǜ sè de mào zi
huáng huār
yī jiàn hóng T xù shān
yī zuò bái sè de jiàn zhù wù

05 nà pǐ mù mǎ de bèi jǐng shì huáng sè de.
nà pǐ mù mǎ de bèi jǐng shì zǐ sè de.
nà pǐ mù mǎ de bèi jǐng shì lán sè de.
nà pǐ mù mǎ de bèi jǐng shì hóng sè de.

06 lán sè de shuǐ
jú huáng sè, huáng sè
huáng sè, hēi sè
lǜ cǎo

07 liǎng duǒ hóng huār
liǎng duǒ zhǎng zhe huáng ruǐ de bái huār
yī duǒ huáng huār, yī duǒ hóng huār, yī duǒ fěn hóng sè de huār
jǐ duǒ fěn hóng sè de huār

08 sān
qī
jiǔ
sì

09 shí
jiǔ
wǔ gè qiú
liù gè qiú

10 yī gè qiú
liǎng gè qiú
bā gè shǒu zhǐ
wǔ

3-06

动物；真的，假的

01 两条灰色的鱼在游。
一条灰色的鱼在游。
一只白色的狗在走。
一只猫在走。

02 一只袋鼠
一群山羊
一群牛
两头牛在跑。

03 许多羊站着。
一只乌龟
一头狮子
一只黑天鹅

04 一只白天鹅
那只鸟在坐着。
一只长颈鹿
一只鸟在飞。

05 两头猪
一头熊
两头牛
一只虎

06 一只羊
一头象
那只骆驼三条腿站着。
那只骆驼四条腿站着。

07 这匹马不是真的。
这匹马是真的。
这只鸟不是真的。
这只鸟是真的。

08 这两头牛不是真的。
这两头牛是真的。
这匹马是真的。
木马不是真马。

09 哪只猫是真的？
哪只猫不是真的？
哪只羊不是真的？
哪只羊是真的？

10 那只白虎在走。
那只白虎在躺着。
那只白虎在爬。
一条龙

3-06

動物；真的、假的

01 兩條灰色的魚在游。
一條灰色的魚在游。
一隻白色的狗在走。
一隻貓在走。

02 一隻袋鼠
一群山羊
一群牛
兩頭牛在跑。

03 許多羊站著。
一隻烏龜
一頭獅子
一隻黑天鵝

04 一隻白天鵝
那隻鳥在坐著。
一隻長頸鹿
一隻鳥在飛。

05 兩頭豬
一頭熊
兩頭牛
一隻虎

06 一隻羊
一頭象
那隻駱駝三條腿站著。
那隻駱駝四條腿站著。

07 這匹馬不是真的。
這匹馬是真的。
這隻鳥不是真的。
這隻鳥是真的。

08 這兩頭牛不是真的。
這兩頭牛是真的。
這匹馬是真的。
木馬不是真馬。

09 哪隻貓是真的？
哪隻貓不是真的？
哪隻羊不是真的？
哪隻羊是真的？

10 那隻白虎在走。
那隻白虎在躺著。
那隻白虎在爬。
一條龍

3-06

dòng wù; zhēn de, jiǎ de

01 liǎng tiáo huī sè de yú zài yóu.
   yī tiáo huī sè de yú zài yóu.
   yī zhī bái sè de gǒu zài zǒu.
   yī zhī māo zài zǒu.

02 yī zhī dài shǔ
   yī qún shān yáng
   yī qún niú
   liǎng tóu niú zài pǎo.

03 xǔ duō yáng zhàn zhe.
   yī zhī wū guī
   yī tóu shī zi
   yī zhī hēi tiān é

04 yī zhī bái tiān é
   nà zhī niǎo zài zuò zhe.
   yī zhī cháng jǐng lù
   yī zhī niǎo zài fēi.

05 liǎng tóu zhū
   yī tóu xióng
   liǎng tóu niú
   yī zhī hǔ

06 yī zhī yáng
   yī tóu xiàng
   nà zhī luò tuó sān tiáo tuǐ zhàn zhe.
   nà zhī luò tuó sì tiáo tuǐ zhàn zhe.

07 zhè pǐ mǎ bú shì zhēn de.
   zhè pǐ mǎ shì zhēn de.
   zhè zhī niǎo bú shì zhēn de.
   zhè zhī niǎo shì zhēn de.

08 zhè liǎng tóu niú bú shì zhēn de.
   zhè liǎng tóu niú shì zhēn de.
   zhè pǐ mǎ shì zhēn de.
   mù mǎ bú shì zhēn mǎ.

09 nǎ zhī māo shì zhēn de?
   nǎ zhī māo bú shì zhēn de?
   nǎ zhī yáng bú shì zhēn de?
   nǎ zhī yáng shì zhēn de?

10 nà zhī bái hǔ zài zǒu.
   nà zhī bái hǔ zài tǎng zhe.
   nà zhī bái hǔ zài pá.
   yī tiáo lóng

用形容词描述人的感觉

01　那个女人饿了。
　　那个男人饿了。
　　那个女人吃饱了。
　　那个男人吃饱了。

02　他们很冷。
　　他们很热。
　　他很冷。
　　他很热。

03　她累了。
　　她不累。
　　他们累了。
　　他们不累。

04　他很壮。
　　他很弱。
　　他们不累。
　　他们又热又累。

05　那个男人病了。
　　那个男人很健康。
　　那只鸟漂亮。
　　那只鸟难看。

06　那个男人没吃饱。
　　那个男人不饿。
　　那个女人没吃饱。
　　那个女人不饿。

07　那个男孩儿和那只狗都很高兴。
　　那个男孩儿和那只狗都不高兴。
　　那个男人很高兴。
　　那个女人很不高兴。

08　他们累了。
　　那个女人累了。那个男孩儿不累。
　　他累了。他们不累。
　　那个男人累了。那个女人不累。

09　他病了。
　　他渴了。
　　他冷了。
　　他很有钱。

10　有人渴了。
　　有人饿了。
　　那两个人不热。
　　那两个人又热又累。

3-07

用形容詞描述人的感覺

01　那個女人餓了。
　　那個男人餓了。
　　那個女人吃飽了。
　　那個男人吃飽了。

02　他們很冷。
　　他們很熱。
　　他很冷。
　　他很熱。

03　她累了。
　　她不累。
　　他們累了。
　　他們不累。

04　他很壯。
　　他很弱。
　　他們不累。
　　他們又熱又累。

05　那個男人病了。
　　那個男人很健康。
　　那隻鳥漂亮。
　　那隻鳥難看。

06　那個男人沒吃飽。
　　那個男人不餓。
　　那個女人沒吃飽。
　　那個女人不餓。

07　那個男孩兒和那隻狗都很高興。
　　那個男孩兒和那隻狗都不高興。
　　那個男人很高興。
　　那個女人很不高興。

08　他們累了。
　　那個女人累了。那個男孩兒不累。
　　他累了。他們不累。
　　那個男人累了。那個女人不累。

09　他病了。
　　他渴了。
　　他冷了。
　　他很有錢。

10　有人渴了。
　　有人餓了。
　　那兩個人不熱。
　　那兩個人又熱又累。

3-07

yòng xíng róng cí miáo shù rén de găn jué

01 nà gè nǚ rén è le.
   nà gè nán rén è le.
   nà gè nǚ rén chī bǎo le.
   nà gè nán rén chī bǎo le.

02 tā men hěn lěng.
   tā men hěn rè.
   tā hěn lěng.
   tā hěn rè.

03 tā lèi le.
   tā bú lèi.
   tā men lèi le.
   tā men bú lèi.

04 tā hěn zhuàng.
   tā hěn ruò.
   tā men bú lèi.
   tā men yòu rè yòu lèi.

05 nà gè nán rén bìng le.
   nà gè nán rén hěn jiàn kāng.
   nà zhī niǎo piào liàng.
   nà zhī niǎo nán kàn.

06 nà gè nán rén méi chī bǎo.
   nà gè nán rén bú è.
   nà gè nǚ rén méi chī bǎo.
   nà gè nǚ rén bú è.

07 nà gè nán háir hé nà zhī gǒu dōu hěn gāo xìng.
   nà gè nán háir hé nà zhī gǒu dōu bù gāo xìng.
   nà gè nán rén hěn gāo xìng.
   nà gè nǚ rén hěn bù gāo xìng.

08 tā men lèi le.
   nà gè nǚ rén lèi le. nà gè nán háir bú lèi.
   tā lèi le. tā men bú lèi.
   nà gè nán rén lèi le. nà gè nǚ rén bú lèi.

09 tā bìng le.
   tā kě le.
   tā lěng le.
   tā hěn yǒu qián.

10 yǒu rén kě le.
   yǒu rén è le.
   nà liǎng gè rén bú rè.
   nà liǎng gè rén yòu rè yòu lèi.

3-08

各种职业；形容词：胖、瘦、冷、热等

01 一位医生
一位护士
一位机械工
一名学生

02 一位警察
一位牙医
一位木匠
一位科学家

03 一位秘书
一位厨师
一名教师
一位男招待

04 他很尴尬。
他很疼。
他很害怕。
他病了。

05 那个男人不热。
那个男人不冷。
那个男人很害怕。
那个男人是一位医生。

06 那个男人为他的儿子感到骄傲。
那个男人为他的轿车感到骄傲。
那个男人瘦。
那个男人胖。

07 一家银行
一所警察局
这个男人有钱。
这个男人正在银行取钱。

08 他很疼。
那个男人在做饭。
那个女人在做饭。
他很尴尬。

09 那位护士在照顾那个男人。
那位医生在为那个男人看病。
那位机械工在修理轿车。
那位牙医在为那个男人治牙。

10 那位面点师在烤面包。
那位秘书在打字。
那名教师在教书。
那两名学生在读书。

3-08

各種職業；形容詞：胖、瘦、冷、熱等

01 一位醫生
一位護士
一位機械工
一名學生

02 一位警察
一位牙醫
一位木匠
一位科學家

03 一位秘書
一位廚師
一名教師
一位男招待

04 他很尷尬。
他很疼。
他很害怕。
他病了。

05 那個男人不熱。
那個男人不冷。
那個男人很害怕。
那個男人是一位醫生。

06 那個男人為他的兒子感到驕傲。
那個男人為他的轎車感到驕傲。
那個男人瘦。
那個男人胖。

07 一家銀行
一所警察局
這個男人有錢。
這個男人正在銀行取錢。

08 他很疼。
那個男人在做飯。
那個女人在做飯。
他很尷尬。

09 那位護士在照顧那個男人。
那位醫生在為那個男人看病。
那位機械工在修理轎車。
那位牙醫在為那個男人治牙。

10 那位面點師在烤面包。
那位秘書在打字。
那名教師在教書。
那兩名學生在讀書。

3-08

gè zhǒng zhí yè; xíng róng cí: pàng, shòu, lěng, rè děng

01 yī wèi yī shēng
yī wèi hù shì
yī wèi jī xiè gōng
yī míng xué shēng

02 yī wèi jǐng chá
yī wèi yá yī
yī wèi mù jiàng
yī wèi kē xué jiā

03 yī wèi mì shū
yī wèi chú shī
yī míng jiào shī
yī wèi nán zhāo dài

04 tā hěn gān gà.
tā hěn téng.
tā hěn hài pà.
tā bìng le.

05 nà gè nán rén bú rè.
nà gè nán rén bù lěng.
nà gè nán rén hěn hài pà.
nà gè nán rén shì yī wèi yī shēng.

06 nà gè nán rén wèi tā de ér zi gǎn dào jiāo ào.
nà gè nán rén wèi tā de jiào chē gǎn dào jiāo ào.
nà gè nán rén shòu.
nà gè nán rén pàng.

07 yī jiā yín háng
yī suǒ jǐng chá jú
zhè gè nán rén yǒu qián.
zhè gè nán rén zhèng zài yín háng qǔ qián.

08 tā hěn téng.
nà gè nán rén zài zuò fàn.
nà gè nǚ rén zài zuò fàn.
tā hěn gān gà.

09 nà wèi hù shì zài zhào gù nà gè nán rén.
nà wèi yī shēng zài wèi nà gè nán rén kàn bìng.
nà wèi jī xiè gōng zài xiū lǐ jiào chē.
nà wèi yá yī zài wèi nà gè nán rén zhì yá.

10 nà wèi miàn diǎn shī zài kǎo miàn bāo.
nà wèi mì shū zài dǎ zì.
nà míng jiào shī zài jiāo shū.
nà liǎng míng xué shēng zài dú shū.

身体的各个部位；画（图案）

01 一只胳膊
两只胳膊
三只胳膊
四只胳膊

02 有六个手指吗？没有，有四个手指。
有三支胳膊吗？没有，有四支胳膊。
有四条腿吗？对，有四条。
有六个手指吗？没有，有五个。

03 马的腿
人的胳膊
象的腿
人的腿

04 他的头在胳膊上。
她的双手在膝上。
他的手在胳膊上。
她的双手蒙着眼睛。

05 那顶帽子在他的头上。
那顶帽子在马蹄上。
那顶帽子在他的手里。
那顶帽子在狗的嘴里。

06 这些花儿是真的。
这是一幅花儿的画。
这个女人是真的。
这是一幅女人的画。

07 一个真的男人
一幅男人的画
一座男人的塑像
一只真兔子

08 那些画挂在墙上。
那些画在地板上。
那幅画挂在墙上。
有幅画在地板上。

09 这件 T 恤衫上有一幅猫的图案。
这件 T 恤衫上有一幅熊的图案。
这件 T 恤衫上有一幅笑脸的图案。
这件 T 恤衫上没有图案。

10 哪个骑马的人是真的？
哪个骑马的人是塑像？
哪个头不是真的？
哪个头是真的？

身體的各個部位；畫（圖案）

01 一隻胳膊
兩隻胳膊
三隻胳膊
四隻胳膊

02 有六個手指嗎？沒有，有四個手指。
有三隻胳膊嗎？沒有，有四隻胳膊。
有四條腿嗎？對，有四條。
有六個手指嗎？沒有，有五個。

03 馬的腿
人的胳膊
象的腿
人的腿

04 他的頭在胳膊上。
她的雙手在膝上。
他的手在胳膊上。
她的雙手蒙著眼睛。

05 那頂帽子在他的頭上。
那頂帽子在馬蹄上。
那頂帽子在他的手裡。
那頂帽子在狗的嘴裡。

06 這些花兒是真的。
這是一幅花兒的畫。
這個女人是真的。
這是一幅女人的畫。

07 一個真的男人
一幅男人的畫
一座男人的塑像
一隻真兔子

08 那些畫挂在牆上。
那些畫在地板上。
那幅畫挂在牆上。
有幅畫在地板上。

09 這件 T 恤衫上有一幅貓的圖案。
這件 T 恤衫上有一幅熊的圖案。
這件 T 恤衫上有一幅笑臉的圖案。
這件 T 恤衫上沒有圖案。

10 哪個騎馬的人是真的？
哪個騎馬的人是塑像？
哪個頭不是真的？
哪個頭是真的？

3-09

shēn tǐ de gè ge bù wèi; huà(tú àn)

01 yī zhī gē bo
   liǎng zhī gē bo
   sān zhī gē bo
   sì zhī gē bo

02 yǒu liù gè shǒu zhǐ ma? méi yǒu, yǒu sì gè shǒu zhǐ.
   yǒu sān zhī gē bo ma? méi yǒu, yǒu sì zhī gē bo.
   yǒu sì tiáo tuǐ ma? duì, yǒu sì tiáo.
   yǒu liù gè shǒu zhǐ ma? méi yǒu, yǒu wǔ gè.

03 mǎ de tuǐ
   rén de gē bo
   xiàng de tuǐ
   rén de tuǐ

04 tā de tóu zài gē bo shàng.
   tā de shuāng shǒu zài xī shàng.
   tā de shǒu zài gē bo shàng.
   tā de shuāng shǒu méng zhe yǎn jīng.

05 nà dǐng mào zi zài tā de tóu shàng.
   nà dǐng mào zi zài mǎ tí shàng.
   nà dǐng mào zi zài tā de shǒu lǐ.
   nà dǐng mào zi zài gǒu de zuǐ lǐ.

06 zhè xiē huār shì zhēn de.
   zhè shì yī fú huār de huà.
   zhè gè nǚ rén shì zhēn de.
   zhè shì yī fú nǚ rén de huà.

07 yī gè zhēn de nán rén
   yī fú nán rén de huà
   yī zuò nán rén de sù xiàng
   yī zhī zhēn tù zi

08 nà xiē huà guà zài qiáng shàng.
   nà xiē huà zài dì bǎn shàng.
   nà fú huà guà zài qiáng shàng.
   yǒu fú huà zài dì bǎn shàng.

09 zhè jiàn T xù shān shàng yǒu yī fú māo de tú àn.
   zhè jiàn T xù shān shàng yǒu yī fú xióng de tú àn.
   zhè jiàn T xù shān shàng yǒu yī fú xiào liǎn de tú àn.
   zhè jiàn T xù shān shàng méi yǒu tú àn.

10 nǎ gè qí mǎ de rén shì zhēn de?
   nǎ gè qí mǎ de rén shì sù xiàng?
   nǎ gè tóu bú shì zhēn de?
   nǎ gè tóu shì zhēn de?

时间表达法；上午、下午、晚上

01　五
　　十
　　十五
　　二十

02　现在是两点。
　　现在是四点。
　　现在是六点。
　　现在是八点。

03　现在是三点半。
　　现在是五点半。
　　现在是七点半。
　　现在是九点半。

04　现在是六点。
　　现在是六点半。
　　现在是七点。
　　现在是七点半。

05　现在是两点。
　　现在是两点十五。
　　现在是两点半。
　　现在是三点差一刻。

06　现在是八点。
　　现在是八点过一刻。
　　现在是八点半。
　　现在八点差一刻。

07　现在是五点。
　　现在快五点了。
　　现在刚过五点。
　　现在是五点半。

08　现在是两点。
　　现在快两点了。
　　现在是两点半。
　　现在刚过两点。

09　现在是七点。
　　现在是七点过一刻。
　　现在是七点半。
　　现在是七点四十五。

10　现在快十点半了，是上午。
　　现在快上午十一点半了。
　　现在刚过五点，是下午。
　　现在九点差一刻，是晚上。

3-10

時間表達法；上午、下午、晚上

01　五
　　十
　　十五
　　二十

02　現在是兩點。
　　現在是四點。
　　現在是六點。
　　現在是八點。

03　現在是三點半。
　　現在是五點半。
　　現在是七點半。
　　現在是九點半。

04　現在是六點。
　　現在是六點半。
　　現在是七點。
　　現在是七點半。

05　現在是兩點。
　　現在是兩點十五。
　　現在是兩點半。
　　現在是三點差一刻。

06　現在是八點。
　　現在是八點過一刻。
　　現在是八點半。
　　現在八點差一刻。

07　現在是五點。
　　現在快五點了。
　　現在剛過五點。
　　現在是五點半。

08　現在是兩點。
　　現在快兩點了。
　　現在是兩點半。
　　現在剛過兩點。

09　現在是七點。
　　現在是七點過一刻。
　　現在是七點半。
　　現在是七點四十五。

10　現在快十點半了，是上午。
　　現在快上午十一點半了。
　　現在剛過五點，是下午。
　　現在九點差一刻，是晚上。

3-10

shí jiān biǎo dá fǎ; shàng wǔ, xià wǔ, wǎn shàng

01   wǔ
      shí
      shí wǔ
      èr shí

02   xiàn zài shì liǎng diǎn.
      xiàn zài shì sì diǎn.
      xiàn zài shì liù diǎn.
      xiàn zài shì bā diǎn.

03   xiàn zài shì sān diǎn bàn.
      xiàn zài shì wǔ diǎn bàn.
      xiàn zài shì qī diǎn bàn.
      xiàn zài shì jiǔ diǎn bàn.

04   xiàn zài shì liù diǎn.
      xiàn zài shì liù diǎn bàn.
      xiàn zài shì qī diǎn.
      xiàn zài shì qī diǎn bàn.

05   xiàn zài shì liǎng diǎn.
      xiàn zài shì liǎng diǎn shí wǔ.
      xiàn zài shì liǎng diǎn bàn.
      xiàn zài shì sān diǎn chà yī kè.

06   xiàn zài shì bā diǎn.
      xiàn zài shì bā diǎn guò yī kè.
      xiàn zài shì bā diǎn bàn.
      xiàn zài bā diǎn chà yī kè.

07   xiàn zài shì wǔ diǎn.
      xiàn zài kuài wǔ diǎn le.
      xiàn zài gāng guò wǔ diǎn.
      xiàn zài shì wǔ diǎn bàn.

08   xiàn zài shì liǎng diǎn.
      xiàn zài kuài liǎng diǎn le.
      xiàn zài shì liǎng diǎn bàn.
      xiàn zài gāng guò liǎng diǎn.

09   xiàn zài shì qī diǎn.
      xiàn zài shì qī diǎn guò yī kè.
      xiàn zài shì qī diǎn bàn.
      xiàn zài shì qī diǎn sì shí wǔ.

10   xiàn zài kuài shí diǎn bàn le, shì shàng wǔ.
      xiàn zài kuài shàng wǔ shí yī diǎn bàn le.
      xiàn zài gāng guò wǔ diǎn, shì xià wǔ.
      xiàn zài jiǔ diǎn chà yī kè, shì wǎn shàng.

3-11

复习第三部分

01 哪个高的男人戴着眼镜？
   哪个高的男人没戴眼镜？
   哪个小孩儿没戴眼镜？
   哪个小孩儿戴着眼镜？

02 人比马多。
   马比人多。
   伞和人一样多。
   人比伞多。

03 那个小丑儿穿着裤子。
   那个小丑儿在穿裤子。
   那个戴眼镜的男人穿着毛衣。
   那个戴眼镜的男人在穿毛衣。

04 那个男孩儿正躺在房子外面。
   那个男孩儿正躺在房子里面。
   这是那座建筑物的外面。
   这是那座建筑物的里面。

05 两朵红花儿
   两朵长着黄蕊的白花儿
   一朵黄花儿，一朵红花儿，一朵粉红色的花儿
   几朵粉红色的花儿

06 哪只猫是真的？
   哪只猫不是真的？
   哪只羊不是真的？
   哪只羊是真的？

07 他很壮。
   他很弱。
   他们不累。
   他们又热又累。

08 那位面点师在烤面包。
   那位秘书在打字。
   那名教师在教书。
   那两名学生在读书。

09 这些花儿是真的。
   这是一幅花儿的画。
   这个女人是真的。
   这是一幅女人的画。

10 现在是七点。
   现在是七点过一刻。
   现在是七点半。
   现在是七点四十五。

3-11

復習第三部分

01 哪個高的男人戴著眼鏡？
   哪個高的男人沒戴眼鏡？
   哪個小孩兒沒戴眼鏡？
   哪個小孩兒戴著眼鏡？

02 人比馬多。
   馬比人多。
   傘和人一樣多。
   人比傘多。

03 那個小醜兒穿著褲子。
   那個小醜兒在穿褲子。
   那個戴眼鏡的男人穿著毛衣。
   那個戴眼鏡的男人在穿毛衣。

04 那個男孩兒正躺在房子外面。
   那個男孩兒正躺在房子裡面。
   這是那座建筑物的外面。
   這是那座建筑物的裡面。

05 兩朵紅花兒
   兩朵長著黃蕊的白花兒
   一朵黃花兒，一朵紅花兒，一朵粉紅色的花兒
   幾朵粉紅色的花兒

06 哪隻貓是真的？
   哪隻貓不是真的？
   哪隻羊不是真的？
   哪隻羊是真的？

07 他很壯。
   他很弱。
   他們不累。
   他們又熱又累。

08 那位面點師在烤面包。
   那位秘書在打字。
   那名教師在教書。
   那兩名學生在讀書。

09 這些花兒是真的。
   這是一幅花兒的畫。
   這個女人是真的。
   這是一幅女人的畫。

10 現在是七點。
   現在是七點過一刻。
   現在是七點半。
   現在是七點四十五。

3-11

01 nǎ ge gāo de nán rén dài zhe yǎn jìng?
   nǎ ge gāo de nán rén méi dài yǎn jìng?
   nǎ ge xiǎo háir méi dài yǎn jìng?
   nǎ ge xiǎo háir dài zhe yǎn jìng?

02 rén bǐ mǎ duō.
   mǎ bǐ rén duō.
   sǎn hé rén yī yàng duō.
   rén bǐ sǎn duō.

03 nà ge xiǎo chǒur chuān zhe kù zi.
   nà ge xiǎo chǒur zài chuān kù zi.
   nà ge dài yǎn jìng de nán rén chuān zhe máo yī.
   nà ge dài yǎn jìng de nán rén zài chuān máo yī.

04 nà ge nán háir zhèng tǎng zài fáng zi wài miàn.
   nà ge nán háir zhèng tǎng zài fáng zi lǐ miàn.
   zhè shì nà zuò jiàn zhù wù de wài miàn.
   zhè shì nà zuò jiàn zhù wù de lǐ miàn.

05 liǎng duǒ hóng huār
   liǎng duǒ zhǎng zhe huáng ruǐ de bái huār
   yī duǒ huáng huār, yī duǒ hóng huār, yī duǒ fěn hóng sè de huār
   jǐ duǒ fěn hóng sè de huār

06 nǎ zhī māo shì zhēn de?
   nǎ zhī māo bú shì zhēn de?
   nǎ zhī yáng bú shì zhēn de?
   nǎ zhī yáng shì zhēn de?

07 tā hěn zhuàng.
   tā hěn ruò.
   tā men bú lèi.
   tā men yòu rè yòu lèi.

08 nà wèi miàn diǎn shī zài kǎo miàn bāo.
   nà wèi mì shū zài dǎ zì.
   nà míng jiào shī zài jiāo shū.
   nà liǎng míng xué shēng zài dú shū.

09 zhè xiē huār shì zhēn de.
   zhè shì yī fú huār de huà.
   zhè ge nǚ rén shì zhēn de.
   zhè shì yī fú nǚ rén de huà.

10 xiàn zài shì qī diǎn.
   xiàn zài shì qī diǎn guò yī kè.
   xiàn zài shì qī diǎn bàn.
   xiàn zài shì qī diǎn sì shí wǔ.

4-01

对于动作的提问和回答

01 那个女人在走吗？
对，她在走。

那个男孩儿在笑吗？
对，他在笑。

那些孩子在玩儿吗？
对，他们在玩儿。

那个女人在笑吗？
对，她在笑。

02 那些孩子在跳吗？
对，他们在跳。

那两个孩子在跳吗？
没有，他们在坐着。

那个男人在骑马吗？
对，他在骑马。

那个男人在骑马吗？
没有，他在走。

03 他在拉小提琴吗？
对，他在拉小提琴。

他在拉小提琴吗？
没有，他不在拉琴。

那辆自行车上下放反了吗？
没有，这样放是对的。

那辆自行车上下放反了吗？
对，是放反了。

04 那辆轿车是黄色的吗？
对，它是黄色的。

那辆轿车是黄色的吗？
不对，它不是黄色的。

那些男孩儿在跳吗？
对，他们在跳。

那两个男孩儿在跳吗？
没有，他们不在跳。

05 她在干什么？
她在跑。

她们在干什么？
她们在走。

他在干什么？
他在骑自行车。

他们在干什么？
他们在骑马。

4-01

對於動作的提問和回答

01 那個女人在走嗎？
對，她在走。

那個男孩兒在笑嗎？
對，他在笑。

那些孩子在玩兒嗎？
對，他們在玩兒。

那個女人在笑嗎？
對，她在笑。

02 那些孩子在跳嗎？
對，他們在跳。

那兩個孩子在跳嗎？
沒有，他們在坐著。

那個男人在騎馬嗎？
對，他在騎馬。

那個男人在騎馬嗎？
沒有，他在走。

03 他在拉小提琴嗎？
對，他在拉小提琴。

他在拉小提琴嗎？
沒有，他不在拉琴。

那輛自行車上下放反了嗎？
沒有，這樣放是對的。

那輛自行車上下放反了嗎？
對，是放反了。

04 那輛轎車是黃色的嗎？
對，它是黃色的。

那輛轎車是黃色的嗎？
不對，它不是黃色的。

那些男孩兒在跳嗎？
對，他們在跳。

那兩個男孩兒在跳嗎？
沒有，他們不在跳。

05 她在干什麼？
她在跑。

她們在干什麼？
她們在走。

他在干什麼？
他在騎自行車。

他們在干什麼？
他們在騎馬。

（继续）

4-01

duì yú dòng zuò de tí wèn hé huí dá

01 nà gè nǚ rén zài zǒu ma?
    duì, tā zài zǒu.

    nà gè nán háir zài xiào ma?
    duì, tā zài xiào.

    nà xiē hái zi zài wánr ma?
    duì, tā men zài wánr.

    nà gè nǚ rén zài xiào ma?
    duì, tā zài xiào.

02 nà xiē hái zi zài tiào ma?
    duì, tā men zài tiào.

    nà liǎng gè hái zi zài tiào ma?
    méi yǒu, tā men zài zuò zhe.

    nà gè nán rén zài qí mǎ ma?
    duì, tā zài qí mǎ.

    nà gè nán rén zài qí mǎ ma?
    méi yǒu, tā zài zǒu.

03 tā zài lā xiǎo tí qín ma?
    duì, tā zài lā xiǎo tí qín.

    tā zài lā xiǎo tí qín ma?
    méi yǒu, tā bú zài lā qín.

    nà liàng zì xíng chē shàng xià fàng fǎn le ma?
    méi yǒu, zhè yàng fàng shì duì de.

    nà liàng zì xíng chē shàng xià fàng fǎn le ma?
    duì, shì fàng fǎn le.

04 nà liàng jiào chē shì huáng sè de ma?
    duì, tā shì huáng sè de.

    nà liàng jiào chē shì huáng sè de ma?
    bú duì, tā bú shì huáng sè de.

    nà xiē nán háir zài tiào ma?
    duì, tā men zài tiào.

    nà liǎng gè nán háir zài tiào ma?
    méi yǒu, tā men bú zài tiào.

05 tā zài gàn shén me?
    tā zài pǎo.

    tā men zài gàn shén me?
    tā men zài zǒu.

    tā zài gàn shén me?
    tā zài qí zì xíng chē.

    tā men zài gàn shén me?
    tā men zài qí mǎ.

(jì xù)

06 那个男孩儿在干什么？
他在和他爸爸玩儿。

那个男孩儿在干什么？
他在走。

那个男孩儿在干什么？
他在躺着。

那个男孩儿在干什么？
他在逗狗玩儿。

07 那个男人在干什么？
他在喝水。

那个男人在干什么？
他在弹吉他。

那个男人在干什么？
他在穿毛衣。

那个男人在干什么？
他正和他儿子坐在一起。

08 他要摔倒了吗？
他可能要摔倒了。

他正摔下来吗？
对，他正摔下来。

那个男孩儿要摔倒了吗？
没有，他不会摔倒的。

她们要摔倒了吗？
没有，她们不会摔倒的。

09 那个男孩儿在笑吗？
对，他在笑。

那个男人在笑吗？
没有，他不在笑。

她在笑吗？
对，她在笑。

那只狗在笑吗？
狗会笑吗？

10 那是一匹小马吗？
对，它是一匹小马。

那是一只狗吗？
对，它是一只狗。

那是一只狗吗？
不是，那是一只猫。

那是一只狗吗？
不是，那是一条鱼。

06 那個男孩兒在干什麼？
他在和他爸爸玩兒。

那個男孩兒在干什麼？
他在走。

那個男孩兒在干什麼？
他在躺著。

那個男孩兒在干什麼？
他在逗狗玩兒。

07 那個男人在干什麼？
他在喝水。

那個男人在干什麼？
他在彈吉他。

那個男人在干什麼？
他在穿毛衣。

那個男人在干什麼？
他正和他兒子坐在一起。

08 他要摔倒了嗎？
他可能要摔倒了。

他正摔下來嗎？
對，他正摔下來。

那個男孩兒要摔倒了嗎？
沒有，他不會摔倒的。

她們要摔倒了嗎？
沒有，她們不會摔倒的。

09 那個男孩兒在笑嗎？
對，他在笑。

那個男人在笑嗎？
沒有，他不在笑。

她在笑嗎？
對，她在笑。

那隻狗在笑嗎？
狗會笑嗎？

10 那是一匹小馬嗎？
對，它是一匹小馬。

那是一隻狗嗎？
對，它是一隻狗。

那是一隻狗嗎？
不是，那是一隻貓。

那是一隻狗嗎？
不是，那是一條魚。

06   nà gè nán háir zài gàn shén me?
tā zài hé tā bà bà wánr.

nà gè nán háir zài gàn shén me?
tā zài zǒu.

nà gè nán háir zài gàn shén me?
tā zài tǎng zhe.

nà gè nán háir zài gàn shén me?
tā zài dòu gǒu wánr.

07   nà gè nán rén zài gàn shén me?
tā zài hē shuǐ.

nà gè nán rén zài gàn shén me?
tā zài tán jí tā.

nà gè nán rén zài gàn shén me?
tā zài chuān máo yī.

nà gè nán rén zài gàn shén me?
tā zhèng hé tā ér zi zuò zài yī qǐ.

08   tā yào shuāi dǎo le ma?
tā kě néng yào shuāi dǎo le.

tā zhèng shuāi xià lái ma?
duì, tā zhèng shuāi xià lái.

nà gè nán háir yào shuāi dǎo le ma?
méi yǒu, tā bú huì shuāi dǎo de.

tā men yào shuāi dǎo le ma?
méi yǒu, tā men bú huì shuāi dǎo de.

09   nà gè nán háir zài xiào ma?
duì, tā zài xiào.

nà gè nán rén zài xiào ma?
méi yǒu, tā bú zài xiào.

tā zài xiào ma?
duì, tā zài xiào.

nà zhī gǒu zài xiào ma?
gǒu huì xiào ma?

10   nà shì yī pǐ xiǎo mǎ ma?
duì, tā shì yī pǐ xiǎo mǎ.

nà shì yī zhī gǒu ma?
duì, tā shì yī zhī gǒu.

nà shì yī zhī gǒu ma?
bú shì, nà shì yī zhī māo.

nà shì yī zhī gǒu ma?
bú shì, nà shì yī tiáo yú.

开－关；睁／张－闭；一起－分开；直－弯

01 那辆轿车的门开着。
那辆轿车的门关着。
那个女人睁着眼睛。
那个女人闭着眼睛。

02 那双眼睛睁着。
那双眼睛闭着。
她张着嘴。
她闭着嘴。

03 那个男人闭着眼睛，张着嘴。
那个男人睁着眼睛，闭着嘴。
那个女人张着嘴，睁着眼睛。
那个女人闭着眼睛，也闭着嘴。

04 他的手攥着。
他的手张开着。
一只手张开着，一只手攥着。
她张着嘴。

05 四只胳膊
许多条腿
四个手指
五个脚趾

06 那双手并在一起。
那双手分开着。
那双脚并在一起。
那双脚分开着。

07 那个男人的腿并在一起。
那个男人的腿分开着。
那个男孩儿的腿并在一起。
那个男孩儿的腿分开着。

08 手分开着，脚也分开着。
手脚并在一起。
脚分开着，手并在一起。
脚并在一起，手分开着。

09 那个男人和那个女人在一起。
那些马在一起。
那个男人和那个女人没靠在一起。
那两匹马没在一起。

10 那个女人的胳膊是直的。
那个女人的胳膊是弯的。
那个男人的腿是弯的。
那个男人的腿是直的。

4-02

開－關；睜／張－閉；一起－分開；直－彎

01 那輛轎車的門開著。
那輛轎車的門關著。
那個女人睜著眼睛。
那個女人閉著眼睛。

02 那雙眼睛睜著。
那雙眼睛閉著。
她張著嘴。
她閉著嘴。

03 那個男人閉著眼睛，張著嘴。
那個男人睜著眼睛，閉著嘴。
那個女人張著嘴，睜著眼睛。
那個女人閉著眼睛，也閉著嘴。

04 他的手攥著。
他的手張開著。
一隻手張開著，一隻手攥著。
她張著嘴。

05 四隻胳膊
許多條腿
四個手指
五個腳趾

06 那雙手並在一起。
那雙手分開著。
那雙腳並在一起。
那雙腳分開著。

07 那個男人的腿並在一起。
那個男人的腿分開著。
那個男孩兒的腿並在一起。
那個男孩兒的腿分開著。

08 手分開著，腳也分開著。
手腳並在一起。
腳分開著，手並在一起。
腳並在一起，手分開著。

09 那個男人和那個女人在一起。
那些馬在一起。
那個男人和那個女人沒靠在一起。
那兩匹馬沒在一起。

10 那個女人的胳膊是直的。
那個女人的胳膊是彎的。
那個男人的腿是彎的。
那個男人的腿是直的。

4-02

kāi-guān; zhēng/zhāng-bì; yī qǐ-fēn kāi; zhí-wān

01 nà liàng jiào chē de mén kāi zhe.
    nà liàng jiào chē de mén guān zhe.
    nà gè nǚ rén zhēng zhe yǎn jīng.
    nà gè nǚ rén bì zhe yǎn jīng.

02 nà shuāng yǎn jīng zhēng zhe.
    nà shuāng yǎn jīng bì zhe.
    tā zhāng zhe zuǐ.
    tā bì zhe zuǐ.

03 nà gè nán rén bì zhe yǎn jīng, zhāng zhe zuǐ.
    nà gè nán rén zhēng zhe yǎn jīng, bì zhe zuǐ.
    nà gè nǚ rén zhāng zhe zuǐ, zhēng zhe yǎn jīng.
    nà gè nǚ rén bì zhe yǎn jīng, yě bì zhe zuǐ.

04 tā de shǒu zuàn zhe.
    tā de shǒu zhāng kāi zhe.
    yī zhī shǒu zhāng kāi zhe, yī zhī shǒu zuàn zhe.
    tā zhāng zhe zuǐ.

05 sì zhī gē bo
    xǔ duō tiáo tuǐ
    sì gè shǒu zhǐ
    wǔ gè jiǎo zhǐ

06 nà shuāng shǒu bìng zài yī qǐ.
    nà shuāng shǒu fēn kāi zhe.
    nà shuāng jiǎo bìng zài yī qǐ.
    nà shuāng jiǎo fēn kāi zhe.

07 nà gè nán rén de tuǐ bìng zài yī qǐ.
    nà gè nán rén de tuǐ fēn kāi zhe.
    nà gè nán háir de tuǐ bìng zài yī qǐ.
    nà gè nán háir de tuǐ fēn kāi zhe.

08 shǒu fēn kāi zhe, jiǎo yě fēn kāi zhe.
    shǒu jiǎo bìng zài yī qǐ.
    jiǎo fēn kāi zhe, shǒu bìng zài yī qǐ.
    jiǎo bìng zài yī qǐ, shǒu fēn kāi zhe.

09 nà gè nán rén hé nà gè nǚ rén zài yī qǐ.
    nà xiē mǎ zài yī qǐ.
    nà gè nán rén hé nà gè nǚ rén méi kào zài yī qǐ.
    nà liǎng pǐ mǎ méi zài yī qǐ.

10 nà gè nǚ rén de gē bo shì zhí de.
    nà gè nǚ rén de gē bo shì wān de.
    nà gè nán rén de tuǐ shì wān de.
    nà gè nán rén de tuǐ shì zhí de.

数字：一到一百

01 一 二 三 四

02 五 六 七 八

03 九 十 十一 十二

04 十三 十四 十五 十六

05 十七 十八 十九 二十

06 二十 三十 四十 五十

07 六十 七十 八十 九十

08 七十五 八十五 九十五 一百

09 二十二 三十二 四十二 五十二

10 四十六 六十六 八十六 一百

4-03

數字：一到一百

01 一 二 三 四

02 五 六 七 八

03 九 十 十一 十二

04 十三 十四 十五 十六

05 十七 十八 十九 二十

06 二十 三十 四十 五十

07 六十 七十 八十 九十

08 七十五 八十五 九十五 一百

09 二十二 三十二 四十二 五十二

10 四十六 六十六 八十六 一百

4-03

shù zì: yī dào yī bǎi

01 yī
    èr
    sān
    sì

02 wǔ
    liù
    qī
    bā

03 jiǔ
    shí
    shí yī
    shí èr

04 shí sān
    shí sì
    shí wǔ
    shí liù

05 shí qī
    shí bā
    shí jiǔ
    èr shí

06 èr shí
    sān shí
    sì shí
    wǔ shí

07 liù shí
    qī shí
    bā shí
    jiǔ shí

08 qī shí wǔ
    bā shí wǔ
    jiǔ shí wǔ
    yī bǎi

09 èr shí èr
    sān shí èr
    sì shí èr
    wǔ shí èr

10 sì shí liù
    liù shí liù
    bā shí liù
    yī bǎi

4-04

人物；讲话、交谈

01 戈尔巴乔夫在讲话。
那三个男人在交谈。
那个穿黄 T 恤衫的男人在讲话。
那个女人在讲话。

02 这个男人在讲话。
这个男人在下棋。
这个男孩儿在讲话。
这个男孩儿在躺着。

03 那个男孩儿在和那个男人讲话。
那个男人在和那个男孩儿讲话。
那个穿蓝衣服的女人在和那个穿红衣服的女人讲话。
那个女人在和那个男人讲话。

04 这个男孩儿在和这个男人谈论那架飞机。
这个男人在和这个男孩儿谈论那架飞机。
这个男人在用对讲机。
这个男人在打手提电话。

05 这个女人在和这个女孩儿谈论那本书。
这两个女人在谈论那棵植物。
这个女人没在讲话。她在笑。
这两个女孩儿根本没在讲话。

06 这个女人没在讲话。
这两个男人没在讲话。
这两个男人在讲话。
这个女人在讲话。

07 这个男人在打电话。
这个女人在打电话。
这个男人没在打电话。
这个女人没在打电话。

08 哪个男人能讲话？
这两个女人能讲话。
哪个男人不能讲话？
这两个女人不能讲话。它们是人体模型。

09 那个男人现在不能讲话，因为他在喝东西。
那个男人能讲话，因为他没有喝东西。
那个男孩儿不能讲话，因为他在水下。
那个男孩儿能讲话，因为他没有在水下。

10 哪个男人不能讲话？
哪个男人能讲话？
哪个男孩儿能讲话？
哪个男孩儿不能讲话？

4-04

人物：講話、交談

01 戈爾巴喬夫在講話。
那三個男人在交談。
那個穿黃 T 恤衫的男人在講話。
那個女人在講話。

02 這個男人在講話。
這個男人在下棋。
這個男孩兒在講話。
這個男孩兒在躺著。

03 那個男孩兒在和那個男人講話。
那個男人在和那個男孩兒講話。
那個穿藍衣服的女人在和那個穿紅衣服的女人講話。
那個女人在和那個男人講話。

04 這個男孩兒在和這個男人談論那架飛機。
這個男人在和這個男孩兒談論那架飛機。
這個男人在用對講機。
這個男人在打手提電話。

05 這個女人在和這個女孩兒談論那本書。
這兩個女人在談論那棵植物。
這個女人沒在講話。她在笑。
這兩個女孩兒根本沒在講話。

06 這個女人沒在講話。
這兩個男人沒在講話。
這兩個男人在講話。
這個女人在講話。

07 這個男人在打電話。
這個女人在打電話。
這個男人沒在打電話。
這個女人沒在打電話。

08 哪個男人能講話？
這兩個女人能講話。
哪個男人不能講話？
這兩個女人不能講話。它們是人體模型。

09 那個男人現在不能講話，因為他在喝東西。
那個男人能講話，因為他沒有喝東西。
那個男孩兒不能講話，因為他在水下。
那個男孩兒能講話，因為他沒有在水下。

10 哪個男人不能講話？
哪個男人能講話？
哪個男孩兒能講話？
哪個男孩兒不能講話？

4-04

rén wù; jiǎng huà, jiāo tán

01 gē ěr bā qiáo fū zài jiǎng huà.
   nà sān gè nán rén zài jiāo tán.
   nà gè chuān huáng T xù shān de nán rén zài jiǎng huà.
   nà gè nǚ rén zài jiǎng huà.

02 zhè gè nán rén zài jiǎng huà.
   zhè gè nán rén zài xià qí.
   zhè gè nán háir zài jiǎng huà.
   zhè gè nán háir zài tǎng zhe.

03 nà gè nán háir zài hé nà gè nán rén jiǎng huà.
   nà gè nán rén zài hé nà gè nán háir jiǎng huà.
   nà gè chuān lán yī fú de nǚ rén zài hé nà gè chuān hóng yī fú de nǚ rén jiǎng huà.
   nà gè nǚ rén zài hé nà gè nán rén jiǎng huà.

04 zhè gè nán háir zài hé zhè gè nán rén tán lùn nà jià fēi jī.
   zhè gè nán rén zài hé zhè gè nán háir tán lùn nà jià fēi jī.
   zhè gè nán rén zài yòng duì jiǎng jī.
   zhè gè nán rén zài dǎ shǒu tí diàn huà.

05 zhè gè nǚ rén zài hé zhè gè nǚ háir tán lùn nà běn shū.
   zhè liǎng gè nǚ rén zài tán lùn nà kē zhí wù.
   zhè gè nǚ rén méi zài jiǎng huà. tā zài xiào.
   zhè liǎng gè nǚ háir gēn běn méi zài jiǎng huà.

06 zhè gè nǚ rén méi zài jiǎng huà.
   zhè liǎng gè nán rén méi zài jiǎng huà.
   zhè liǎng gè nán rén zài jiǎng huà.
   zhè gè nǚ rén zài jiǎng huà.

07 zhè gè nán rén zài dǎ diàn huà.
   zhè gè nǚ rén zài dǎ diàn huà.
   zhè gè nán rén méi zài dǎ diàn huà.
   zhè gè nǚ rén méi zài dǎ diàn huà.

08 nǎ gè nán rén néng jiǎng huà?
   zhè liǎng gè nǚ rén néng jiǎng huà.
   nǎ gè nán rén bù néng jiǎng huà?
   zhè liǎng gè nǚ rén bù néng jiǎng huà. tā men shì rén tǐ mó xíng.

09 nà gè nán rén xiàn zài bù néng jiǎng huà, yīn wéi tā zài hē dōng xī.
   nà gè nán rén néng jiǎng huà, yīn wéi tā méi yǒu hē dōng xī.
   nà gè nán háir bù néng jiǎng huà, yīn wéi tā zài shuǐ xià.
   nà gè nán háir néng jiǎng huà, yīn wéi tā méi yǒu zài shuǐ xià.

10 nǎ gè nán rén bù néng jiǎng huà?
   nǎ gè nán rén néng jiǎng huà?
   nǎ gè nán háir néng jiǎng huà?
   nǎ gè nán háir bù néng jiǎng huà?

4-05

来和去；上和下；睡和醒

01 那两个女人正走过来。
那两个女人正离开。
那些马正跑过来。
那对男女正离开。

02 他在爬墙。
他在上楼梯。
他在下楼梯。
他在爬梯子。

03 那只猫在睡觉。
那只猫不在睡觉。
那个婴儿在睡觉。
那个婴儿不在睡觉。

04 那只猫睡着了。
那只猫醒着。
那个婴儿睡着了。
那个婴儿醒着。

05 那对男女正走过来。
那对男女正离开。
那对男女在亲吻。
那对男女不在亲吻。

06 那匹马正走进那辆大货车。
那匹马已经从那辆大货车里出来了。
这个男孩儿正往水里去。
这个男孩儿正从水里出来。

07 那个女人正乘着自动扶梯上楼。
那个女人正乘着自动扶梯下楼。
那个男人在上台阶。
那个男人在下台阶。

08 这些人正乘着自动扶梯上楼。
这两个在上台阶。
这两个人正乘着自动扶梯下楼。
这两个人在下台阶。

09 那个男人在上飞机。
那个男人在下飞机。
那个男人在下卡车。
那个男人在上卡车。

10 那对男女正走进那座房子。
那对男女正离开那座房子。
那个男人在上马车。
那个男人在下马车。

4-05

來和去；上和下；睡和醒

01 那兩個女人正走過來。
那兩個女人正離開。
那些馬正跑過來。
那對男女正離開。

02 他在爬牆。
他在上樓梯。
他在下樓梯。
他在爬梯子。

03 那隻貓在睡覺。
那隻貓不在睡覺。
那個嬰兒在睡覺。
那個嬰兒不在睡覺。

04 那隻貓睡著了。
那隻貓醒著。
那個嬰兒睡著了。
那個嬰兒醒著。

05 那對男女正走過來。
那對男女正離開。
那對男女在親吻。
那對男女不在親吻。

06 那匹馬正走進那輛大貨車。
那匹馬已經從那輛大貨車裡出來了。
這個男孩兒正往水裡去。
這個男孩兒正從水裡出來。

07 那個女人正乘著自動扶梯上樓。
那個女人正乘著自動扶梯下樓。
那個男人在上臺階。
那個男人在下臺階。

08 這些人正乘著自動扶梯上樓。
這兩個人在上臺階。
這兩個人正乘著自動扶梯下樓。
這兩個人在下臺階。

09 那個男人在上飛機。
那個男人在下飛機。
那個男人在下卡車。
那個男人在上卡車。

10 那對男女正走進那座房子。
那對男女正離開那座房子。
那個男人在上馬車。
那個男人在下馬車。

4-05

lái hé qù; shàng hé xià; shuì hé xǐng

01 nà liǎng gè nǚ rén zhèng zǒu guò lái.
    nà liǎng gè nǚ rén zhèng lí kāi.
    nà xiē mǎ zhèng pǎo guò lái.
    nà duì nán nǚ zhèng lí kāi.

02 tā zài pá qiáng.
    tā zài shàng lóu tī.
    tā zài xià lóu tī.
    tā zài pá tī zi.

03 nà zhī māo zài shuì jiào.
    nà zhī māo bú zài shuì jiào.
    nà gè yīng ér zài shuì jiào.
    nà gè yīng ér bú zài shuì jiào.

04 nà zhī māo shuì zháo le.
    nà zhī māo xǐng zhe.
    nà gè yīng ér shuì zháo le.
    nà gè yīng ér xǐng zhe.

05 nà duì nán nǚ zhèng zǒu guò lái.
    nà duì nán nǚ zhèng lí kāi.
    nà duì nán nǚ zài qīn wěn.
    nà duì nán nǚ bú zài qīn wěn.

06 nà pǐ mǎ zhèng zǒu jìn nà liàng dà huò chē.
    nà pǐ mǎ yǐ jīng cóng nà liàng dà huò chē lǐ chū lái le.
    zhè gè nán háir zhèng wǎng shuǐ lǐ qù.
    zhè gè nán háir zhèng cóng shuǐ lǐ chū lái.

07 nà gè nǚ rén zhèng chèng zhe zì dòng fú tī shàng lóu.
    nà gè nǚ rén zhèng chèng zhe zì dòng fú tī xià lóu.
    nà gè nán rén zài shàng tái jiē.
    nà gè nán rén zài xià tái jiē.

08 zhè xiē rén zhèng chèng zhe zì dòng fú tī shàng lóu.
    zhè liǎng ge rén zài shàng tái jiē.
    zhè liǎng gè rén zhèng chèng zhe zì dòng fú tī xià lóu.
    zhè liǎng ge rén zài xià tái jiē.

09 nà gè nán rén zài shàng fēi jī.
    nà gè nán rén zài xià fēi jī.
    nà gè nán rén zài xià kǎ chē.
    nà gè nán rén zài shàng kǎ chē.

10 nà duì nán nǚ zhèng zǒu jìn nà zuò fáng zi.
    nà duì nán nǚ zhèng lí kāi nà zuò fáng zi.
    nà gè nán rén zài shàng mǎ chē.
    nà gè nán rén zài xià mǎ chē.

4-06

描述两种动作同时发生：一边 ... 一边

描述兩種動作同時發生：一邊…一邊

01	那个女孩儿在闻花儿。 那个男孩儿在看电视。 那个男孩儿在闻花儿。 那个女孩儿在看电视。

01 那個女孩兒在聞花兒。
那個男孩兒在看電視。
那個男孩兒在聞花兒。
那個女孩兒在看電視。

02 那个女人要开车。
那个女人在骑马。
那个女人在亲那匹马。
那个女人在赶马车。

02 那個女人要開車。
那個女人在騎馬。
那個女人在親那匹馬。
那個女人在趕馬車。

03 那个男孩儿在闻花儿。
那个男孩儿没在闻花儿。
那个女孩儿在梳头。
那个女孩儿在跳舞。

03 那個男孩兒在聞花兒。
那個男孩兒沒在聞花兒。
那個女孩兒在梳頭。
那個女孩兒在跳舞。

04 那个女人戴着帽子。
那个男人正摸着马蹄子。
那个男人正摸着马耳朵。
那个男人在戴手套。

04 那個女人戴著帽子。
那個男人正摸著馬蹄子。
那個男人正摸著馬耳朵。
那個男人在戴手套。

05 那个男人在上马车。
那个男人在上卡车。
那个女人在亲那个男人。
那个女人在亲那匹马。

05 那個男人在上馬車。
那個男人在上卡車。
那個女人在親那個男人。
那個女人在親那匹馬。

06 那个女孩儿没在看电视。
那个女孩儿看电视时戴着帽子。
那个女孩儿一边看电视，一边梳头。
那个女孩儿一边看电视，一边跳舞。

06 那個女孩兒沒在看電視。
那個女孩兒看電視時戴著帽子。
那個女孩兒一邊看電視，一邊梳頭。
那個女孩兒一邊看電視，一邊跳舞。

07 那个女人一边弹着电子琴，一边在唱歌。
那个女人一边弹着电子琴，一边在喝东西。
那个女人一手拿着手提包，一手在梳头。
那个女人一边拿着手提包，一边在写字。

07 那個女人一邊彈著電子琴，一邊在唱歌。
那個女人一邊彈著電子琴，一邊在喝東西。
那個女人一手拿著手提包，一手在梳頭。
那個女人一邊拿著手提包，一邊在寫字。

08 那个男人一边拿着书，一边伸手去拿铁锹。
那个男人一手拿着铁锹，一手指着窗户。
那个男人在看书。那只狗站在他两腿之间。
那个男人在读书。那个男孩儿在听他读

08 那個男人一邊拿著書，一邊伸手去拿鐵鍬。
那個男人一手拿著鐵鍬，一手指著窗戶。
那個男人在看書，那只狗站在他兩腿之間。
那個男人在讀書。那個男孩兒在听他讀。

09 有个女孩儿在走，手里还拿着一顶帽子。
那个男人坐在马车上，喝着水。
那个男孩儿在爬栅栏，那个男人坐在自行车上。
那两个孩子在看那个男人写字。

09 有個女孩兒在走，手裡還拿著一頂帽子。
那個男人坐在馬車上，喝著水。
那個男孩兒在爬柵欄，那個男人坐在自行車上。
那兩個孩子在看那個男人寫字。

10 那个男人在看那个男孩儿上梯子。
没人在看那个男孩儿上梯子。
那些男人过河时，手里拿着枪。
那些男人列队行进时，手里拿着枪。

10 那個男人在看那個男孩兒上梯子。
沒人在看那個男孩兒上梯子。
那些男人過河時，手裡拿著槍。
那些男人列隊行進時，手裡拿著槍。

4-06

miáo shù liǎng zhǒng dòng zuò tóng shí fā shēng: yī biān... yī biān...

01 nà gè nǚ háir zài wén huār.
    nà gè nán háir zài kàn diàn shì.
    nà gè nán háir zài wén huār.
    nà gè nǚ háir zài kàn diàn shì.

02 nà gè nǚ rén yào kāi chē.
    nà gè nǚ rén zài qí mǎ.
    nà gè nǚ rén zài qīn nà pǐ mǎ.
    nà gè nǚ rén zài gǎn mǎ chē.

03 nà gè nán háir zài wén huār.
    nà gè nán háir méi zài wén huār.
    nà gè nǚ háir zài shū tóu.
    nà gè nǚ háir zài tiào wǔ.

04 nà gè nǚ rén dài zhe mào zi.
    nà gè nán rén zhèng mō zhe mǎ tí zi.
    nà gè nán rén zhèng mō zhe mǎ ěr duo.
    nà gè nán rén zài dài shǒu tào.

05 nà gè nán rén zài shàng mǎ chē.
    nà gè nán rén zài shàng kǎ chē.
    nà gè nǚ rén zài qīn nà gè nán rén.
    nà gè nǚ rén zài qīn nà pǐ mǎ.

06 nà gè nǚ háir méi zài kàn diàn shì.
    nà gè nǚ háir kàn diàn shì shí dài zhe mào zi.
    nà gè nǚ háir yī biān kàn diàn shì, yī biān shū tóu.
    nà gè nǚ háir yī biān kàn diàn shì, yī biān tiào wǔ.

07 nà gè nǚ rén yī biān tán zhe diàn zi qín, yī biān zài chàng gē.
    nà gè nǚ rén yī biān tán zhe diàn zi qín, yī biān zài hē dōng xi.
    nà gè nǚ rén yī shǒu ná zhe shǒu tí bāo, yī shǒu zài shū tóu.
    nà gè nǚ rén yī biān ná zhe shǒu tí bāo, yī biān zài xiě zì.

08 nà gè nán rén yī biān ná zhe shū, yī biān shēn shǒu qù ná tiě qiāo.
    nà gè nán rén yī shǒu ná zhe tiě qiāo, yī shǒu zhǐ zhe chuāng hù.
    nà gè nán rén zài kàn shū, nà zhī gǒu zhàn zài tā liǎng tuǐ zhī jiān.
    nà gè nán rén zài dú shū, nà gè nán háir zài tīng tā dú.

09 yǒu gè nǚ háir zài zǒu, shǒu lǐ hái ná zhe yī dǐng mào zi.
    nà gè nán rén zuò zài mǎ chē shàng, hē zhe shuǐ.
    nà gè nán háir zài pá zhà lán, nà gè nán rén zuò zài zì xíng chē shàng.
    nà liǎng gè hái zi zài kàn nà gè nán rén xiě zì.

10 nà gè nán rén zài kàn nà gè nán háir shàng tī zi.
    méi rén zài kàn nà gè nán háir shàng tī zi.
    nà xiē nán rén guò hé shí shǒu lǐ ná zhe qiāng.
    nà xiē nán rén liè duì xíng jìn shí shǒu lǐ ná zhe qiāng.

4-07

家庭关系

01 一个女孩儿和她的母亲
一个女孩儿和她的父亲
一个男孩儿和他的母亲
一个男孩儿和他的父亲

02 一个女孩儿和她的母亲
一个女孩儿和她的父亲
一个女孩儿和她的弟弟
一个女孩儿和她的家人

03 一个男孩儿和他的母亲
一个男孩儿和他的父亲
一个男孩儿和他的姐姐
一个男孩儿和他的家人

04 那个女人挨着她的丈夫坐在沙发上。
那个女人同她的丈夫和孩子们站在一起。
那个女人挨着她的丈夫坐在椅子上。
那个女人坐在她的丈夫身上。

05 那个男人挨着他的妻子坐在沙发上。
那个男人同他的妻子和孩子们站在一起。
那个男人挨着他的妻子坐在椅子上。
那个男人的妻子坐在他身上。

06 一位母亲和她的儿子
一位父亲和他的儿子
一位父亲和他的女儿
一位母亲和她的女儿

07 兄妹俩和他们的母亲
一对夫妇和他们的女儿
兄妹俩和他们的父母
哥哥和妹妹

08 这四个人是一家的。
这四个人不是一家的。
这三个人是一家的。
这三个人不是一家的。

09 父母和孩子们
父母
兄弟俩和他们的父亲
兄弟俩和他们的母亲

10 姐妹俩和她们的父亲
兄弟俩和他们的父亲
一个孩子和他的父母
这些人不是一家的。

4-07

家庭關系

01 一個女孩兒和她的母親
一個女孩兒和她的父親
一個男孩兒和他的母親
一個男孩兒和他的父親

02 一個女孩兒和她的母親
一個女孩兒和她的父親
一個女孩兒和她的弟弟
一個女孩兒和她的家人

03 一個男孩兒和他的母親
一個男孩兒和他的父親
一個男孩兒和他的姐姐
一個男孩兒和他的家人

04 那個女人挨著她的丈夫坐在沙發上。
那個女人同她的丈夫和孩子們站在一起。
那個女人挨著她的丈夫坐在椅子上。
那個女人坐在她的丈夫身上。

05 那個男人挨著他的妻子坐在沙發上。
那個男人同他的妻子和孩子們站在一起。
那個男人挨著他的妻子坐在椅子上。
那個男人的妻子坐在他身上。

06 一位母親和她的兒子
一位父親和他的兒子
一位父親和他的女兒
一位母親和她的女兒

07 兄妹倆和他們的母親
一對夫婦和他們的女兒
兄妹倆和他們的父母
哥哥和妹妹

08 這四個人是一家的。
這四個人不是一家的。
這三個人是一家的。
這三個人不是一家的。

09 父母和孩子們
父母
兄弟倆和他們的父親
兄弟倆和他們的母親

10 姐妹倆和她們的父親
兄弟倆和他們的父親
一個孩子和他的父母
這些人不是一家的。

4-07

jiā tíng guān xì

01 yī gè nǚ háir hé tā de mǔ qīn
   yī gè nǚ háir hé tā de fù qīn
   yī gè nán háir hé tā de mǔ qīn
   yī gè nán háir hé tā de fù qīn

02 yī gè nǚ háir hé tā de mǔ qīn
   yī gè nǚ háir hé tā de fù qīn
   yī gè nǚ háir hé tā de dì dì
   yī gè nǚ háir hé tā de jiā rén

03 yī gè nán háir hé tā de mǔ qīn
   yī gè nán háir hé tā de fù qīn
   yī gè nán háir hé tā de jiě jiě
   yī gè nán háir hé tā de jiā rén

04 nà gè nǚ rén āi zhe tā de zhàng fū zuò zài shā fā shàng.
   nà gè nǚ rén tóng tā de zhàng fū hé hái zi men zhàn zài yī qǐ.
   nà gè nǚ rén āi zhe tā de zhàng fū zuò zài yǐ zi shàng.
   nà gè nǚ rén zuò zài tā de zhàng fū shēn shàng.

05 nà gè nán rén āi zhe tā de qī zǐ zuò zài shā fā shàng.
   nà gè nán rén tóng tā de qī zǐ hé hái zi men zhàn zài yī qǐ.
   nà gè nán rén āi zhe tā de qī zǐ zuò zài yǐ zi shàng.
   nà gè nán rén de qī zǐ zuò zài tā shēn shàng.

06 yī wèi mǔ qīn hé tā de ér zi
   yī wèi fù qīn hé tā de ér zi
   yī wèi fù qīn hé tā de nǚ ér
   yī wèi mǔ qīn hé tā de nǚ ér

07 xiōng mèi liǎ hé tā men de mǔ qīn
   yī duì fū fù hé tā men de nǚ ér
   xiōng mèi liǎ hé tā men de fù mǔ
   gē ge hé mèi mei

08 zhè sì gè rén shì yī jiā de.
   zhè sì gè rén bú shì yī jiā de.
   zhè sān gè rén shì yī jiā de.
   zhè sān gè rén bú shì yī jiā de.

09 fù mǔ hé hái zi men
   fù mǔ
   xiōng dì liǎ hé tā men de fù qīn
   xiōng dì liǎ hé tā men de mǔ qīn

10 jiě mèi liǎ hé tā men de fù qīn
   xiōng dì liǎ hé tā men de fù qīn
   yī gè hái zi hé tā de fù mǔ
   zhè xiē rén bú shì yī jiā de.

每（个）人、有人、没（有）人

01　每个人都戴着黄帽子。
　　每个人都在跑。
　　每个人都在坐着。
　　每个人都在跳舞。

02　有人在树后。
　　有人在那个男人身后。
　　有人在照相。
　　有人穿着黄衣服。

03　每个人都戴着黄帽子。
　　没有人戴黄帽子。
　　有人在摸那只猫。
　　没有人在摸那只猫。

04　每个人都穿着白衣服。
　　没有人穿白衣服。
　　有人穿着白衣服，也有人没穿白衣服。
　　那个牛仔穿着白衣服。

05　每个人都在跳水。
　　三个男孩儿谁都没跳水。
　　有人在跳水，也有人没跳水。
　　有人在水里游泳。

06　有人在踢球。
　　没有人在踢球。
　　那架飞机里有人吗？没有，那架飞机是空的。
　　那架飞机里有人吗？有，那个男孩儿在那架飞机里。

07　有人在踢球吗？有，那个男孩儿在踢球。
　　有人在踢球吗？没有，没人踢球。
　　那架飞机里没人。
　　那架飞机里有人。

08　那个穿蓝衣服的男人在拿着什么东西。
　　那个穿蓝衣服的男人什么东西也没拿。
　　他们在指着什么东西。
　　他们没指什么东西。

09　有人在骑马。
　　没有人在骑马。
　　盘子上有东西。
　　盘子上没有东西。

10　桌子上有东西。
　　那些桌子上全都没有东西。
　　有人正躺在帐篷里。
　　帐篷里没有人。

4-08

每（個）人、有人、沒有人

01　每個人都戴著黃帽子。
　　每個人都在跑。
　　每個人都在坐著。
　　每個人都在跳舞。

02　有人在樹後。
　　有人在那個男人身後。
　　有人在照相。
　　有人穿著黃衣服。

03　每個人都戴著黃帽子。
　　沒有人戴黃帽子。
　　有人在摸那隻貓。
　　沒有人在摸那隻貓。

04　每個人都穿著白衣服。
　　沒有人穿白衣服。
　　有人穿著白衣服，也有人沒穿白衣服。
　　那個牛仔穿著白衣服。

05　每個人都在跳水。
　　三個男孩兒誰都沒跳水。
　　有人在跳水，也有人沒跳水。
　　有人在水裡游泳。

06　有人在踢球。
　　沒有人在踢球。
　　那架飛機裡有人嗎？沒有，那架飛機是空的。
　　那架飛機裡有人嗎？有，那個男孩兒在那架飛機裡。

07　有人在踢球嗎？有，那個男孩兒在踢球。
　　有人在踢球嗎？沒有，沒人踢球。
　　那架飛機裡沒人。
　　那架飛機裡有人。

08　那個穿藍衣服的男人在拿著甚麼東西。
　　那個穿藍衣服的男人甚麼東西也沒拿。
　　他們在指著甚麼東西。
　　他們沒指甚麼東西。

09　有人在騎馬。
　　沒有人在騎馬。
　　盤子上有東西。
　　盤子上沒有東西。

10　桌子上有東西。
　　那些桌子上全都沒有東西。
　　有人正躺在帳篷裡。
　　帳篷裡沒有人。

4-08

měi (gè)rén, yǒu rén, méi (yǒu) rén

01   měi gè rén dōu dài zhe huáng mào zi.
     měi gè rén dōu zài pǎo.
     měi gè rén dōu zài zuò zhe.
     měi gè rén dōu zài tiào wǔ.

02   yǒu rén zài shù hòu.
     yǒu rén zài nà gè nán rén shēn hòu.
     yǒu rén zài zhào xiàng.
     yǒu rén chuān zhe huáng yī fu.

03   měi gè rén dōu dài zhe huáng mào zi.
     méi yǒu rén dài huáng mào zi.
     yǒu rén zài mō nà zhī māo.
     méi yǒu rén zài mō nà zhī māo.

04   měi gè rén dōu chuān zhe bái yī fu.
     méi yǒu rén chuān bái yī fu.
     yǒu rén chuān zhe bái yī fu, yě yǒu rén méi chuān bái yī fu.
     nà gè niú zǎi chuān zhe bái yī fu.

05   měi gè rén dōu zài tiào shuǐ.
     sān gè nán háir shéi dōu méi tiào shuǐ.
     yǒu rén zài tiào shuǐ, yě yǒu rén méi tiào shuǐ.
     yǒu rén zài shuǐ lǐ yóu yǒng.

06   yǒu rén zài tī qiú.
     méi yǒu rén zài tī qiú.
     nà jià fēi jī lǐ yǒu rén ma? méi yǒu, nà jià fēi jī shì kōng de.
     nà jià fēi jī lǐ yǒu rén ma? yǒu, nà gè nán háir zài nà jià fēi jī lǐ.

07   yǒu rén zài tī qiú ma? yǒu, nà gè nán háir zài tī qiú.
     yǒu rén zài tī qiú ma? méi yǒu, méi rén tī qiú.
     nà jià fēi jī lǐ méi yǒu rén.
     nà jià fēi jī lǐ yǒu rén.

08   nà gè chuān lán yī fu de nán rén zài ná zhe shén me dōng xi.
     nà gè chuān lán yī fu de nán rén shén me dōng xi yě méi ná.
     tā men zài zhǐ zhe shéng me dōng xi.
     tā men méi zhǐ shén me dōng xi.

09   yǒu rén zài qí mǎ.
     méi yǒu rén zài qí mǎ.
     pán zi shàng yǒu dōng xi.
     pán zi shàng méi yǒu dōng xi.

10   zhuō zi shàng yǒu dōng xi.
     nà xiē zhuō zi shàng quán dōu méi yǒu dōng xi.
     yǒu rén zhèng tǎng zài zhàng péng lǐ.
     zhàng pén lǐ méi yǒu rén.

描述交通工具的动词和介词

01　一辆摩托车
　　几辆摩托车
　　一辆黄色的公共汽车
　　两辆黄色的公共汽车

02　一辆红色的小汽车
　　一辆白色的大轿车
　　一艘红色的船
　　一辆黑色的大卡车

03　那辆卡车在拖那辆轿车。
　　有人在开那辆轿车。
　　那辆红色的轿车在那辆卡车的后面。
　　那辆卡车在拖那条船。

04　那辆卡车在一座桥的上面，但在另一座桥的下面。
　　在那座桥下面有一辆卡车和一辆轿车。
　　一座桥
　　那辆轿车停在一座房子的前面。

05　那辆自行车停放着。
　　那个男人正把一辆自行车放到一辆小货车上。
　　那个女人在上那辆小货车。
　　那两艘船在河上。

06　那辆轿车在转弯。
　　那两辆轿车正在雪中行驶。
　　那些红色小汽车在游行。
　　那辆轿车在超过一辆卡车。

07　一辆黑色的大轿车
　　一辆老爷车
　　一辆敞篷轿车
　　一辆红色的跑车

08　那辆火车正在山上行驶。
　　人们在上那辆有轨电车。
　　这辆红色的轿车肇事了。
　　那辆红色的轿车没有肇事。

09　那辆红色轿车和那辆灰色的轿车肇事了。
　　那艘潜水艇正在水下。
　　那艘船有帆。
　　那辆红色轿车和那辆白色轿车停着。

10　那辆红色的轿车撞坏了。
　　那辆红色的轿车没有撞坏。
　　那艘大船在航行。
　　那辆牵引车在拖那辆轿车。

4-09

描述交通工具的動詞和介詞

01　一輛摩托車
　　幾輛摩托車
　　一輛黃色的公共汽車
　　兩輛黃色的公共汽車

02　一輛紅色的小汽車
　　一輛白色的大轎車
　　一艘紅色的船
　　一輛黑色的大卡車

03　那輛卡車在拖那輛轎車。
　　有人在開那輛轎車。
　　那輛紅色的轎車在那輛卡車的後面。
　　那輛卡車在拖那條船。

04　那輛卡車在一座橋的上面，但在另一座橋的下面。
　　在那座橋下面有一輛卡車和一輛轎車。
　　一座橋
　　那輛汽車停在一座房子的前面。

05　那輛自行車停放著。
　　那個男人正把一輛自行車放到一輛小貨車上。
　　那個女人在上那輛小貨車。
　　那兩艘船在河上。

06　那輛轎車在轉彎。
　　那兩輛轎車正在雪中行駛。
　　那些紅色小汽車在游行。
　　那輛轎車在超過一輛卡車。

07　一輛黑色的大轎車
　　一輛老爺車
　　一輛敞篷轎車
　　一輛紅色的跑車

08　那輛火車正在山上行駛。
　　人們在上那輛有軌電車。
　　這輛紅色的轎車肇事了。
　　那輛紅色的轎車沒有肇事。

09　那輛紅色轎車和那輛灰色的轎車肇事了。
　　那艘潛水艇正在水下。
　　那艘船有帆。
　　那輛紅色轎車和那輛白色轎車停著。

10　那輛紅色的轎車撞壞了。
　　那輛紅色的轎車沒有撞壞。
　　那艘大船在航行。
　　那輛牽引車在拖那輛轎車。

4-09

miáo shù jiāo tōng gōng jù de dòng cí hé jiè cí

01 yī liàng mó tuō chē
yǐ liàng mó tuō chē
yī liàng huáng sè de gōng gòng qì chē
liǎng liàng huáng sè de gōng gòng qì chē

02 yī liàng hóng sè de xiǎo qì chē
yī liàng bái sè de dà jiào chē
yī sōu hóng sè de chuán
yī liàng hēi sè de dà kǎ chē

03 nà liàng kǎ chē zài tuō nà liàng jiào chē.
yǒu rén zài kāi nà liàng jiào chē.
nà liàng hóng sè de jiào chē zài nà liàng kǎ chē de hòu miàn.
nà liàng kǎ chē zài tuō nà tiáo chuán.

04 nà liàng kǎ chē zài yī zuò qiáo de shàng miàn, dàn zài lìng yī zuò qiáo de xià miàn.
zài nà zuò qiáo xià miàn yǒu yī liàng kǎ chē hé yī liàng jiào chē.
yī zuò qiáo
nà liàng jiào chē tíng zài yī zuò fáng zi de qián miàn.

05 nà liàng zì xíng chē tíng fàng zhe.
nà gè nán rén zhèng bǎ yī liàng zì xíng chē fàng dào yī liàng xiǎo huò chē shàng.
nà gè nǚ rén zài shàng nà liàng xiǎo huò chē.
nà liǎng sōu chuán zài hé shàng.

06 nà liàng jiào chē zài zhuǎn wān.
nà liǎng liàng jiào chē zhèng zài xuě zhōng xíng shǐ.
nà xiē hóng sè xiǎo qì chē zài yóu xíng.
nà liàng jiào chē zài chāo guò yī liàng kǎ chē.

07 yī liàng hēi sè de dà jiào chē
yī liàng lǎo ye chē
yī liàng chǎng péng jiào chē
yī liàng hóng sè de pǎo chē

08 nà liàng huǒ chē zhèng zài shān shàng xíng shǐ.
rén men zài shàng nà liàng yǒu guǐ diàn chē.
zhè liàng hóng sè de jiào chē zhào shì le.
nà liàng hóng sè de jiào chē méi yǒu zhào shì.

09 nà liàng hóng sè jiào chē hé nà liàng huī sè de jiào chē zhào shì le.
nà sōu qián shuǐ tǐng zhèng zài shuǐ xià.
nà sōu chuán yǒu fān.
nà liàng hóng sè jiào chē hé nà liàng bái sè jiào chē tíng zhe.

10 nà liàng hóng sè de jiào chē zhuàng huài le.
nà liàng hóng sè de jiào chē méi yǒu zhuàng huài.
nà sōu dà chuán zài háng xíng.
nà liàng qiān yǐn chē zài tuō nà liàng jiào chē.

4-10

介词短语 "用…" 作状语

01 他在进行撑竿跳。
  她在用麦克风唱歌儿。
  那个穿红毛衣的男孩儿在玩儿。他在和朋友们一起玩儿。
  他在用双手扶把骑自行车。

02 他在跳远，没有用撑竿。
  她没有用麦克风唱歌儿。
  他没有和朋友们一起玩儿。
  他没有用双手扶把骑自行车。

03 他在进行撑竿跳。
  他在跳远，没有用撑竿。
  她在用麦克风唱歌。
  她没有用麦克风唱歌。

04 他在和朋友们一起玩儿。
  他没有和朋友们一起玩儿。
  他没有用双手扶把骑自行车。
  他在用双手扶把骑自行车。

05 那个男人在往下跳，没有用降落伞。
  那个男人在跳降落伞。
  他在顺着绳子往上爬。
  他没有顺着绳子往上爬。

06 那个男人在跑，没有穿T恤衫。
  那个穿T恤衫的男人在跑。
  那个戴着太阳镜的女人正坐着。
  那个女人正坐着，没有戴太阳镜。

07 那些打雨伞的人在走。
  那些人在走，没有打伞。
  那个戴头盔的人在骑自行车。
  那个人在骑自行车，没有戴头盔。

08 那个戴帽子的女人在走。
  那个女人在走，没有戴帽子。
  那个男人坐在箱子上，没有戴帽子。
  那个戴帽子的男人坐在箱子上。

09 那个戴帽子的男人在写字。
  那个戴帽子的男人在指着什么东西。
  那个没戴帽子的男人在指着什么东西。
  那个没戴帽子的男人在写字。

10 那个穿毛衣的男孩儿正在沙地上玩儿。
  那个没穿毛衣的男孩儿正在沙地上玩儿。
  那个穿毛衣的男孩儿正在草地上玩儿。
  那个没穿毛衣的男孩儿正在草地上玩儿。

4-10

介詞短語 "用…" 作狀語

01 他在進行撐竿跳。
  她在用麥克風唱歌兒。
  那個穿紅毛衣的男孩兒在玩兒。他在和朋友們一起玩兒。
  他在用雙手扶把騎自行車。

02 他在跳遠，沒有用撐竿。
  她沒有用麥克風唱歌兒。
  他沒有和朋友們一起玩兒。
  他沒有用雙手扶把騎自行車。

03 他在進行撐竿跳。
  他在跳遠，沒有用撐竿。
  她在用麥克風唱歌。
  她沒有用麥克風唱歌。

04 他在和朋友們一起玩兒。
  他沒有和朋友們一起玩兒。
  他沒有用雙手扶把騎自行車。
  他在用雙手扶把騎自行車。

05 那個男人在往下跳，沒有用降落傘。
  那個男人在跳降落傘。
  他在順著繩子往上爬。
  他沒有順著繩子往上爬。

06 那個男人在跑，沒有穿T恤衫。
  那個穿T恤衫的男人在跑。
  那個戴著太陽鏡的女人正坐著。
  那個女人正坐著，沒有戴太陽鏡。

07 那些打雨傘的人在走。
  那些人在走，沒有打傘。
  那個戴頭盔的人在騎自行車。
  那個人在騎自行車，沒有戴頭盔。

08 那個戴帽子的女人在走。
  那個女人在走，沒有戴帽子。
  那個男人坐在箱子上，沒有戴帽子。
  那個戴帽子的男人坐在箱子上。

09 那個戴帽子的男人在寫字。
  那個戴帽子的男人在指著甚麼東西。
  那個沒戴帽子的男人在指著甚麼東西。
  那個沒戴帽子的男人在寫字。

10 那個穿毛衣的男孩兒正在沙地上玩兒。
  那個沒穿毛衣的男孩兒正在沙地上玩兒。
  那個穿毛衣的男孩兒正在草地上玩兒。
  那個沒穿毛衣的男孩兒正在草地上玩兒。

4-10

jiè cí duǎn yǔ "yòng..." zuò zhuàng yǔ

01 tā zài jìn xín chēng gān tiào.
    tā zài yòng mài kè fēng chàng gēr.
    nà gè chuān hóng máo yī de nán háir zài wánr. tā zài hé péng yǒu men yī qǐ wánr.
    tā zài yòng shuāng shǒu fú bǎ qí zì xíng chē.

02 tā zài tiào yuǎn, méi yǒu yòng chēng gān.
    tā méi yǒu yòng mài kè fēng chàng gē.
    tā méi yǒu hé péng yǒu men yī qǐ wánr.
    tā méi yǒu yòng shuāng shǒu fú bǎ qí zì xíng chē.

03 tā zài jìn xín chēng gān tiào.
    tā zài tiào yuǎn, méi yǒu yòng chēng gān.
    tā zài yòng mài kè fēng chàng gē.
    tā méi yǒu yòng mài kè fēng chàng gē.

04 tā zài hé péng yǒu men yī qǐ wánr.
    tā méi yǒu hé péng yǒu men yī qǐ wánr.
    tā méi yǒu yòng shuāng shǒu fú bǎ qí zì xíng chē.
    tā zài yòng shuāng shǒu fú bǎ qí zì xíng chē.

05 nà gè nán rén zài wǎng xià tiào, méi yǒu yòng jiàng luò sǎn.
    nà gè nán rén zài tiào jiàng luò sǎn.
    tā zài shùn zhe shéng zi wǎng shàng pá.
    tā méi yǒu shùn zhe shéng zi wǎng shàng pá.

06 nà gè nán rén zài pǎo, méi yǒu chuān T xù shān.
    nà gè chuān T xù shān de nán rén zài pǎo.
    nà gè dài zhe tài yáng jìng de nǚ rén zhèng zuò zhe.
    nà gè nǚ rén zhèng zuò zhe, méi yǒu dài tài yáng jìng.

07 nà xiē dǎ yǔ sǎn de rén zài zǒu.
    nà xiē rén zài zǒu, méi yǒu dǎ sǎn.
    nà gè dài tóu kuī de rén zài qí zì xíng chē.
    nà gè rén zài qí zì xíng chē, méi yǒu dài tóu kuī.

08 nà gè dài mào zi de nǚ rén zài zǒu.
    nà gè nǚ rén zài zǒu, méi yǒu dài mào zi.
    nà gè nán rén zuò zài xiāng zi shàng, méi yǒu dài mào zi.
    nà gè dài mào zi de nán rén zuò zài xiāng zi shàng.

09 nà gè dài mào zi de nán rén zài xiě zì.
    nà gè dài mào zi de nán rén zài zhǐ zhe shén me dōng xi.
    nà gè méi dài mào zi de nán rén zài zhǐ zhe shén me dōng xi.
    nà gè méi dài mào zi de nán rén zài xiě zì.

10 nà gè chuān máo yī de nán háir zhèng zài shā dì shàng wánr.
    nà gè méi chuān máo yī de nán háir zhèng zài shā dì shàng wánr.
    nà gè chuān máo yī de nán háir zhèng zài cǎo dì shàng wánr.
    nà gè méi chuān máo yī de nán háir zhèng zài cǎo dì shàng wánr.

4-11

复习第四部分

01 那个男人在干什么？
   他在喝水。

   那个男人在干什么？
   他在弹吉他。

   那个男人在干什么？
   他在穿毛衣。

   那个男人在干什么？
   他正和他儿子坐在一起。

02 手分开着，脚也分开着。
   手脚并在一起。
   脚分开着，手并在一起。
   脚并在一起，手分开着。

03 七十五
   八十五
   九十五
   一百

04 那个男人现在不能讲话，因为他在喝东西。
   那个男人能讲话，因为他没有喝东西。
   那个男孩儿不能讲话，因为他在水下。
   那个男孩儿能讲话，因为他没有在水下。

05 那只猫睡着了。
   那只猫醒着。
   那个婴儿睡着了。
   那个婴儿醒着。

06 那个女人一边弹着电子琴，一边在唱歌。
   那个女人一边弹着电子琴，一边在喝东西。
   那个女人一手拿着手提包，一手在梳头。
   那个女人一边拿着手提包，一边在写字。

07 兄妹俩和他们的母亲
   一对夫妇和他们的女儿
   兄妹俩和他们的父母
   哥哥和妹妹

08 有人在骑马。
   没有人在骑马。
   盘子上有东西。
   盘子上没有东西。

09 那辆卡车在拖那辆轿车。
   有人在开那辆轿车。
   那辆红色的轿车在那辆卡车的后面。
   那辆卡车在拖那条船。

4-11

復習第四部分

01 那個男人在干什麼？
   他在喝水。

   那個男人在干什麼？
   他在彈吉他。

   那個男人在干什麼？
   他在穿毛衣。

   那個男人在干什麼？
   他正和他兒子坐在一起。

02 手分開著，腳也分開著。
   手腳並在一起。
   腳分開著，手並在一起。
   腳並在一起，手分開著。

03 七十五
   八十五
   九十五
   一百

04 那個男人現在不能講話，因為他在喝東西。
   那個男人能講話，因為他沒有喝東西。
   那個男孩兒不能講話，因為他在水下。
   那個男孩兒能講話，因為他沒有在水下。

05 那隻貓睡著了。
   那隻貓醒著。
   那個嬰兒睡著了。
   那個嬰兒醒著。

06 那個女人一邊彈著電子琴，一邊在唱歌。
   那個女人一邊彈著電子琴，一邊在喝東西。
   那個女人一手拿著手提包，一手在梳頭。
   那個女人一邊拿著手提包，一邊在寫字。

07 兄妹倆和他們的母親
   一對夫婦和他們的女兒
   兄妹倆和他們的父母
   哥哥和妹妹

08 有人在騎馬。
   沒有人在騎馬。
   盤子上有東西。
   盤子上沒有東西。

09 那輛卡車在拖那輛轎車。
   有人在開那輛轎車。
   那輛紅色的轎車在那輛卡車的後面。
   那輛卡車在拖那條船。

（继续）

4-11

fù xí dì sì bù fen

01 nà gè nán rén zài gàn shén me?
tā zài hē shuǐ.

nà gè nán rén zài gàn shén me?
tā zài tán jí tā.

nà gè nán rén zài gàn shén me?
tā zài chuān máo yī.

nà gè nán rén zài gàn shén me?
tā zhèng hé tā ér zi zuò zài yī qǐ.

02 shǒu fēn kāi zhe, jiǎo yě fēn kāi zhe.
shǒu jiǎo bìng zài yī qǐ.
jiǎo fēn kāi zhe, shǒu bìng zài yī qǐ.
jiǎo bìng zài yī qǐ, shǒu fēn kāi zhe.

03 qī shí wǔ
bā shí wǔ
jiǔ shí wǔ
yī bǎi

04 nà gè nán rén xiàn zài bù néng jiǎng huà, yīn wéi tā zài hē dōng xī.
nà gè nán rén néng jiǎng huà, yīn wéi tā méi yǒu hē dōng xī.
nà gè nán háir bù néng jiǎng huà, yīn wéi tā zài shuǐ xià.
nà gè nán háir néng jiǎng huà, yīn wéi tā méi yǒu zài shuǐ xià.

05 nà zhī māo shuì zháo le.
nà zhī māo xǐng zhe.
nà gè yīng ér shuì zháo le.
nà gè yīng ér xǐng zhe.

06 nà gè nǚ rén yī biān tán zhe diàn zi qín, yī biān zài chàng gē.
nà gè nǚ rén yī biān tán zhe diàn zi qín, yī biān zài hē dōng xi.
nà gè nǚ rén yī shǒu ná zhe shǒu tí bāo, yī shǒu zài shū tóu.
nà gè nǚ rén yī biān ná zhe shǒu tí bāo, yī biān zài xiě zì.

07 xiōng mèi liǎ hé tā men de mǔ qīn
yī duì fū fù hé tā men de nǚ ér
xiōng mèi liǎ hé tā men de fù mǔ
gē ge hé mèi mei

08 yǒu rén zài qí mǎ.
méi yǒu rén zài qí mǎ.
pán zi shàng yǒu dōng xi.
pán zi shàng méi yǒu dōng xi.

09 nà liàng kǎ chē zài tuō nà liàng jiào chē.
yǒu rén zài kāi nà liàng jiào chē.
nà liàng hóng sè de jiào chē zài nà liàng kǎ chē de hòu miàn.
nà liàng kǎ chē zài tuō nà tiáo chuán.

(jì xù)

10 那个戴帽子的男人在写字。
那个戴帽子的男人在指着什么东西。
那个没戴帽子的男人在指着什么东西。
那个没戴帽子的男人在写字。

10 那個戴帽子的男人在寫字。
那個戴帽子的男人在指著甚麼東西。
那個沒戴帽子的男人在指著甚麼東西。
那個沒戴帽子的男人在寫字。

10 nà gè dài mào zi de nán rén zài xiě zì.
    nà gè dài mào zi de nán rén zài zhǐ zhe shén me dōng xi.
    nà gè méi dài mào zi de nán rén zài zhǐ zhe shén me dōng xi.
    nà gè méi dài mào zi de nán rén zài xiě zì.

5-01

各种运算：加、减、乘、除

01　六
　　一
　　二十
　　九

02　二
　　五
　　十一
　　八

03　三
　　四
　　七
　　十

04　一加一等于二。
　　一加二等于三。
　　一加三等于四。
　　一加四等于五。

05　三加四等于七。
　　三加五等于八。
　　六减二等于四。
　　六减四等于二。

06　六加五等于十一。
　　六加六等于十二。
　　四加三等于七。
　　四加五等于九。

07　八减二等于六。
　　八减四等于四。
　　七减三等于四。
　　七减五等于二。

08　十二减五等于七。
　　十二减六等于六。
　　十二减七等于五。
　　十二减八等于四。

09　十二除以二等于六。
　　二乘六等于十二。
　　六除以三等于二。
　　二乘八等于十六。

10　十除以五等于二。
　　十五除以五等于三。
　　二十除以五等于四。
　　四乘五等于二十。

5-01

各種運算：加、減、乘、除

01　六
　　一
　　二十
　　九

02　二
　　五
　　十一
　　八

03　三
　　四
　　七
　　十

04　一加一等於二。
　　一加二等於三。
　　一加三等於四。
　　一加四等於五。

05　三加四等於七。
　　三加五等於八。
　　六減二等於四。
　　六減四等於二。

06　六加五等於十一。
　　六加六等於十二。
　　四加三等於七。
　　四加五等於九。

07　八減二等於六。
　　八減四等於四。
　　七減三等於四。
　　七減五等於二。

08　十二減五等於七。
　　十二減六等於六。
　　十二減七等於五。
　　十二減八等於四。

09　十二除以二等於六。
　　二乘六等於十二。
　　六除以三等於二。
　　二乘八等於十六。

10　十除以五等於二。
　　十五除以五等於三。
　　二十除以五等於四。
　　四乘五等於二十。

5-01

gè zhǒng yùn suàn: jiā, jiǎn, chéng, chú

01 liù
    yī
    èr shí
    jiǔ

02 èr
    wǔ
    shí yī
    bā

03 sān
    sì
    qī
    shí

04 yī jiā yī děng yú èr.
    yī jiā èr děng yú sān.
    yī jiā sān děng yú sì.
    yī jiā sì děng yú wǔ.

05 sān jiā sì děng yú qī.
    sān jiā wǔ děng yú bā.
    liù jiǎn èr děng yú sì.
    liù jiǎn sì děng yú èr.

06 liù jiā wǔ děng yú shí yī.
    liù jiā liù děng yú shí èr.
    sì jiā sān děng yú qī.
    sì jiā wǔ děng yú jiǔ.

07 bā jiǎn èr děng yú liù.
    bā jiǎn sì děng yú sì.
    qī jiǎn sān děng yú sì.
    qī jiǎn wǔ děng yú èr.

08 shí èr jiǎn wǔ děng yú qī.
    shí èr jiǎn liù děng yú liù.
    shí èr jiǎn qī děng yú wǔ.
    shí èr jiǎn bā děng yú sì.

09 shí èr chú yǐ èr děng yú liù.
    èr chéng liù děng yú shí èr.
    liù chú yǐ sān děng yú èr.
    èr chéng bā děng yú shí liù.

10 shí chú yǐ wǔ děng yú èr.
    shí wǔ chú yǐ wǔ děng yú sān.
    èr shí chú yǐ wǔ děng yú sì.
    sì chéng wǔ děng yú èr shí.

名词所有格和物主代词：他的、她的

01 一个男孩儿
  那个男孩儿和他的爸爸
  那个男孩儿和他的狗
  那个男孩儿的狗

02 一个长着金发的女人和她的狗
  一个男人和他的狗
  一个长着黑发的女人和她的狗
  一个男孩儿和他的狗

03 那个女人在遛她的狗。
  那个男孩儿在遛他的狗。
  有人在遛三只狗。
  那两个女人在遛她们的狗。

04 那个女人的帽子是黑色的。
  那个男人的安全帽是白色的。
  那个女人的马在跳。
  那个男人的马在尥蹶子。

05 那个女孩儿的袜子是白色的。
  那个女孩儿的衬衫是白色的。
  那个男人的狗很小。
  那个男人的狗在看书。

06 一个女人和她的猫
  一个女人和她的马
  一个男人和他的猫
  一个男人和他的马

07 那个男人在穿他自己的衬衫。
  这件衬衫太大了，不是那个男孩儿的。
  那个男人的衬衫在桌子上。
  这件衬衫太小了，不是那个男人的。

08 一顶女式帽子
  一顶男式帽子
  一只男人的手
  一只女人的手

09 一辆儿童游乐车
  一辆成年人开的汽车
  儿童服装
  成年人服装

10 女式手套
  男式手套
  女人们的腿
  一双女人的腿

5-02

名詞所有格和物主代詞：他的、她的

01 一個男孩兒
  那個男孩兒和他的爸爸
  那個男孩兒和他的狗
  那個男孩兒的狗

02 一個長著金髮的女人和她的狗
  一個男人和他的狗
  一個長著黑髮的女人和她的狗
  一個男孩兒和他的狗

03 那個女人在遛她的狗。
  那個男孩兒在遛他的狗。
  有人在遛三隻狗。
  那兩個女人在遛她們的狗。

04 那個女人的帽子是黑色的。
  那個男人的安全帽是白色的。
  那個女人的馬在跳。
  那個男人的馬在尥蹶子。

05 那個女孩兒的襪子是白色的。
  那個女孩兒的襯衫是白色的。
  那個男人的狗很小。
  那個男人的狗在看書。

06 一個女人和她的貓
  一個女人和她的馬
  一個男人和他的貓
  一個男人和他的馬

07 那個男人在穿他自己的襯衫。
  這件襯衫太大了，不是那個男孩兒的。
  那個男人的襯衫在桌子上。
  這件襯衫太小了，不是那個男人的。

08 一頂女式帽子
  一頂男式帽子
  一隻男人的手
  一隻女人的手

09 一輛兒童游樂車
  一輛成年人開的汽車
  兒童服裝
  成年人服裝

10 女式手套
  男式手套
  女人們的腿
  一雙女人的腿

5-02

míng cí suǒ yǒu gé hé wù zhǔ dài cí: tā de, tā de

01   yī gè nán háir
      nà gè nán háir hé tā de bà bà
      nà gè nán háir hé tā de gǒu
      nà gè nán háir de gǒu

02   yī gè zhǎng zhe jīn fà de nǚ rén hé tā de gǒu
      yī gè nán rén hé tā de gǒu
      yī gè zhǎng zhe hēi fà de nǚ rén hé tā de gǒu
      yī gè nán háir hé tā de gǒu

03   nà gè nǚ rén zài liù tā de gǒu.
      nà gè nán háir zài liù tā de gǒu.
      yǒu rén zài liù sān zhī gǒu.
      nà liǎng gè nǚ rén zài liù tā men de gǒu.

04   nà gè nǚ rén de mào zi shì hēi sè de.
      nà gè nán rén de ān quán mào shì bái sè de.
      nà gè nǚ rén de mǎ zài tiào.
      nà gè nán rén de mǎ zài liào juě zi.

05   nà gè nǚ háir de wà zi shì bái sè de.
      nà gè nǚ háir de chèn shān shì bái sè de.
      nà gè nán rén de gǒu hěn xiǎo.
      nà gè nán rén de gǒu zài kàn shū.

06   yī gè nǚ rén hé tā de māo
      yī gè nǚ rén hé tā de mǎ
      yī gè nán rén hé tā de māo
      yī gè nán rén hé tā de mǎ

07   nà gè nán rén zài chuān tā zì jǐ de chèn shān.
      zhè jiàn chèn shān tài dà le, bú shì nà gè nán háir de.
      nà gè nán rén de chèn shān zài zhuō zi shàng.
      zhè jiàn chèn shān tài xiǎo le, bú shì nà gè nán rén de.

08   yī dǐng nǚ shì mào zi
      yī dǐng nán shì mào zi
      yī zhī nán rén de shǒu
      yī zhī nǚ rén de shǒu

09   yī liàng ér tóng yóu lè chē
      yī liàng chéng nián rén kāi de qì chē
      ér tóng fú zhuāng
      chéng nián rén fú zhuāng

10   nǚ shì shǒu tào
      nán shì shǒu tào
      nǚ rén men de tuǐ
      yī shuāng nǚ rén de tuǐ

5-03

运用各种时态：现在进行时，现在完成时，用"要"、"想要"表示的将来时

01　那个女孩儿在跳绳儿。
　　那个女孩儿在走。
　　那个女孩儿在骑马。
　　那个女孩儿在笑。

02　那个男孩儿正要跳。
　　那个男孩儿要摔下来了。
　　那个男孩儿想要吃东西。
　　那个男孩儿想要骑自行车。

03　那个女人已经跳完了。
　　那个女人已经打开了抽屉。
　　那个女人已经把球扔了过去。
　　那个女人已经睡着了。

04　那个男人和那个女人想要拥抱。
　　那个男人和那个女人在拥抱。
　　这幅作品是毕加索所画。
　　这幅作品不是毕加索所画。

05　那只天鹅在游。
　　那只鸟在飞。
　　那只鸟在走。
　　那只天鹅在拍打翅膀，但没有飞。

06　那条狗正要接飞盘。
　　那条狗已经接住了飞盘。
　　那条狗正要拣帽子。
　　那条狗已经把帽子拣了起来。

07　那匹马已经跳过去了。
　　那匹马已经把那个牛仔从背上甩了下来。
　　那匹马已经上去了。
　　那匹马已经下去了。

08　那些孩子想要从桌子上跳下来。
　　那些孩子正从桌子上跳下来。
　　那些孩子已经从桌子上跳了下来。
　　那些孩子正绕着桌子走。

09　那个穿白衬衫的男人想要爬墙。
　　那个穿白衬衫的男人在爬墙。
　　那头骆驼正要张嘴。
　　那头骆驼已经张开了嘴。

10　那个男人想打手提电话。他正把它从兜里拿出来。
　　那个男人在打手提电话。
　　那个男人正拿着手提电话，但没有打。
　　那个男人在用一部红色的电话。

5-03

運用個種時態：現在進行時，現在完成時，用"要"、"想要"表示的將來時

01　那個女孩兒在跳繩兒。
　　那個女孩兒在走。
　　那個女孩兒在騎馬。
　　那個女孩兒在笑。

02　那個男孩兒正要跳。
　　那個男孩兒要摔下來了。
　　那個男孩兒想要吃東西。
　　那個男孩兒想要騎自行車。

03　那個女人已經跳完了。
　　那個女人已經打開了抽屜。
　　那個女人已經把球扔了過去。
　　那個女人已經睡著了。

04　那個男人和那個女人想要擁抱。
　　那個男人和那個女人在擁抱。
　　這幅作品是畢加索所畫。
　　這幅作品不是畢加索所畫。

05　那隻天鵝在游。
　　那隻鳥在飛。
　　那隻鳥在走。
　　那隻天鵝在拍打翅膀，但沒有飛。

06　那條狗正要接飛盤。
　　那條狗已經接住了飛盤。
　　那條狗正要撿帽子。
　　那條狗已經把帽子撿了起來。

07　那匹馬已經跳過去了。
　　那匹馬已經把那個牛仔從背上甩了下來。
　　那匹馬已經上去了。
　　那匹馬已經下去了。

08　那些孩子想要從桌子上跳下來。
　　那些孩子正從桌子上跳下來。
　　那些孩子已經從桌子上跳了下來。
　　那些孩子正繞著桌子走。

09　那個穿白襯衫的男人想要爬牆。
　　那個穿白襯衫的男人在爬牆。
　　那頭駱駝正要張嘴。
　　那頭駱駝已經張開了嘴。

10　那個男人想打手提電話。他正把它從兜裡拿出來。
　　那個男人在打手提電話。
　　那個男人正拿著手提電話，但沒有打。
　　那個男人在用一部紅色的電話。

5-03

yùn yòng gè zhǒng shí tài: xiàn zài jìn xíng shí, xiàn zài wán chéng shí, yòng "yào", "xiǎng yào" biǎo shì de jiāng lái shí

01 nà gè nǚ háir zài tiào shéngr.
    nà gè nǚ háir zài zǒu.
    nà gè nǚ háir zài qí mǎ.
    nà gè nǚ háir zài xiào.

02 nà gè nán háir zhèng yào tiào.
    nà gè nán háir yào shuāi xià lái le.
    nà gè nán háir xiǎng yào chī dōng xi.
    nà gè nán háir xiǎng yào qí zì xíng chē.

03 nà gè nǚ rén yǐ jīng tiào wán le.
    nà gè nǚ rén yǐ jīng dǎ kāi le chōu tì.
    nà gè nǚ rén yǐ jīng bǎ qiú rēng le guò qù.
    nà gè nǚ rén yǐ jīng shuì zháo le.

04 nà gè nán rén hé nà gè nǚ rén xiǎng yào yōng bào.
    nà gè nán rén hé nà gè nǚ rén zài yōng bào.
    zhè fú zuò pǐn shì bì jiā suǒ suǒ huà.
    zhè fú zuò pǐn bú shì bì jiā suǒ suǒ huà.

05 nà zhī tiān é zài yóu.
    nà zhī niǎo zài fēi.
    nà zhī niǎo zài zǒu.
    nà zhī tiān é zài pāi dǎ chì bǎng, dàn méi yǒu fēi.

06 nà tiáo gǒu zhèng yào jiē fēi pán.
    nà tiáo gǒu yǐ jīng jiē zhù le fēi pán.
    nà tiáo gǒu zhèng yào jiǎn mào zi.
    nà tiáo gǒu yǐ jīng bǎ mào zi jiǎn le qǐ lái.

07 nà pǐ mǎ yǐ jīng tiào guò qù le.
    nà pǐ mǎ yǐ jīng bǎ nà gè niú zǎi cóng bèi shàng shuǎi le xià lái.
    nà pǐ mǎ yǐ jīng shàng qù le.
    nà pǐ mǎ yǐ jīng xià qù le.

08 nà xiē hái zi xiǎng yào cóng zhuō zi shàng tiào xià lái.
    nà xiē hái zi zhèng cóng zhuō zi shàng tiào xià lái.
    nà xiē hái zi yǐ jīng cóng zhuō zi shàng tiào le xià lái.
    nà xiē hái zi zhèng rào zhe zhuō zi zǒu.

09 nà gè chuān bái chèn shān de nán rén xiǎng yào pá qiáng.
    nà gè chuān bái chèn shān de nán rén zài pá qiáng.
    nà tóu luò tuó zhèng yào zhāng zuǐ.
    nà tóu luò tuó yǐ jīng zhāng kāi le zuǐ.

10 nà gè nán rén xiǎng dǎ shǒu tí diàn huà. tā zhèng bǎ tā cóng dōu lǐ ná chū lái.
    nà gè nán rén zài dǎ shǒu tí diàn huà.
    nà gè nán rén zhèng ná zhe shǒu tí diàn huà, dàn méi yǒu dǎ.
    nà gè nán rén zài yòng yī bù hóng sè de diàn huà.

十以上的数字表示法

01 十七
    二十七
    三十七
    三十八

02 四十三
    三十四
    六十三
    三十六

03 七十八
    八十七
    九十五
    五十九

04 一百四十五
    一百五十四
    二百七十八
    二百八十七

05 三百二十五
    三百五十二
    四百二十五
    四百五十二

06 五百四十九
    五百五十九
    六百六十九
    六百九十六

07 七百三十四
    七百四十三
    八百三十四
    八百四十三

08 九百二十六
    九百六十二
    一千零八十七
    一千零七十八

09 一千八百五十七
    二千八百五十七
    一千八百七十五
    二千八百七十五

10 三千一百二十五
    七千一百二十五
    九千一百二十五
    一万零一百二十五

5-04

十以上的數字表示法

01 十七
    二十七
    三十七
    三十八

02 四十三
    三十四
    六十三
    三十六

03 七十八
    八十七
    九十五
    五十九

04 一百四十五
    一百五十四
    二百七十八
    二百八十七

05 三百二十五
    三百五十二
    四百二十五
    四百五十二

06 五百四十九
    五百五十九
    六百六十九
    六百九十六

07 七百三十四
    七百四十三
    八百三十四
    八百四十三

08 九百二十六
    九百六十二
    一千零八十七
    一千零七十八

09 一千八百五十七
    二千八百五十七
    一千八百七十五
    二千八百七十五

10 三千一百二十五
    七千一百二十五
    九千一百二十五
    一萬零一百二十五

5-04

shí yǐ shàng de shù zì biǎo shì fǎ

01 shí qī
   èr shí qī
   sān shí qī
   sān shí bā

02 sì shí sān
   sān shí sì
   liù shí sān
   sān shí liù

03 qī shí bā
   bā shí qī
   jiǔ shí wǔ
   wǔ shí jiǔ

04 yī bǎi sì shí wǔ
   yī bǎi wǔ shí sì
   èr bǎi qī shí bā
   èr bǎi bā shí qī

05 sān bǎi èr shí wǔ
   sān bǎi wǔ shí èr
   sì bǎi èr shí wǔ
   sì bǎi wǔ shí èr

06 wǔ bǎi sì shí jiǔ
   wǔ bǎi wǔ shí jiǔ
   liù bǎi liù shí jiǔ
   liù bǎi jiǔ shí liù

07 qī bǎi sān shí sì
   qī bǎi sì shí sān
   bā bǎi sān shí sì
   bā bǎi sì shí sān

08 jiǔ bǎi èr shí liù
   jiǔ bǎi liù shí èr
   yī qiān líng bā shí qī
   yī qiān líng qī shí bā

09 yī qiān bā bǎi wǔ shí qī
   èr qiān bā bǎi wǔ shí qī
   yī qiān bā bǎi qī shí wǔ
   èr qiān bā bǎi qī shí wǔ

10 sān qiān yī bǎi èr shí wǔ
   qī qiān yī bǎi èr shí wǔ
   jiǔ qiān yī bǎi èr shí wǔ
   yī wàn líng yī bǎi èr shí wǔ

直接宾语和间接宾语

01　那个男人在推自行车。
　　那个男人在推四轮车。
　　那个女人在推那些箱子。
　　那些男人在推那个垫子。

02　那个男人在拉四轮车。
　　那匹小马在拉车。
　　他们在拉那个垫子。
　　他们在推那个垫子。

03　他在拉四轮车。
　　他在推四轮车。
　　他们在推那个垫子。
　　他们在拉那个垫子。

04　那个男人在修理自行车。
　　那个男人在骑自行车。
　　那个女人在遛狗。
　　那个女人在逗狗玩儿。

05　那个女孩儿戴着帽子。
　　那个女孩儿拿着帽子。
　　那个男人正拿着那杯水。他没有喝。
　　那个男人在喝那杯水。

06　那个女人在上台阶。
　　那个女人在推那些箱子。
　　那个男人扛着那个小孩儿。
　　那个男人在推四轮车。

07　那个女人在给那个男孩儿钱。
　　那个男人在给那个女人药。
　　那个女人正把吉他递给那个男孩儿。
　　那个男人正把吉他递给那个女孩儿。

08　那个男孩儿正从那个女人手里接过钱。
　　那个男孩儿正从那个女人手里接过吉他。
　　那个女孩儿正从那个男人手里接过吉他。
　　那个女人正从那个男人手里接过药。

09　那个女孩儿在拿盘子。
　　有人在给那个男人一盘食物。
　　有人在给那个女人一盘食物。
　　那个男人正把吉他递给那个女孩儿。

10　那个女人在给那个男孩儿钱。
　　有人在给那个女人什么东西。
　　那个男人在拿一杯牛奶。
　　那个男人给了那个女人一杯牛奶。

5-05

直接賓語和間接賓語

01　那個男人在推自行車。
　　那個男人在推四輪車。
　　那個女人在推那些箱子。
　　那些男人在推那個墊子。

02　那個男人在拉四輪車。
　　那匹小馬在拉車。
　　他們在拉那個墊子。
　　他們在推那個墊子。

03　他在拉四輪車。
　　他在推四輪車。
　　他們在推那個墊子。
　　他們在拉那個墊子。

04　那個男人在修理自行車。
　　那個男人在騎自行車。
　　那個女人在遛狗。
　　那個女人在逗狗玩兒。

05　那個女孩兒戴著帽子。
　　那個女孩兒拿著帽子。
　　那個男人正拿著那杯水。他沒有喝。
　　那個男人在喝那杯水。

06　那個女人在上臺階。
　　那個女人在推那些箱子。
　　那個男人扛著那個小孩兒。
　　那個男人在推四輪車。

07　那個女人在給那個男孩兒錢。
　　那個男人在給那個女人藥。
　　那個女人正把吉他遞給那個男孩兒。
　　那個男人正把吉他遞給那個女孩兒。

08　那個男孩兒正從那個女人手裡接過錢。
　　那個男孩兒正從那個女人手裡接過吉他。
　　那個女孩兒正從那個男人手裡接過吉他。
　　那個女人正從那個男人手裡接過藥。

09　那個女孩兒在拿盤子。
　　有人在給那個男人一盤食物。
　　有人在給那個女人一盤食物。
　　那個男人正把吉他遞給那個女孩兒。

10　那個女人在給那個男孩兒錢。
　　有人在給那個女人甚麼東西。
　　那個男人在拿一杯牛奶。
　　那個男人給了那個女人一杯牛奶。

5-05

zhí jiē bīn yǔ hé jiàn jiē bīn yǔ

01   nà gè nán rén zài tuī zì xíng chē.
      nà gè nán rén zài tuī sì lún chē.
      nà gè nǚ rén zài tuī nà xiē xiāng zi.
      nà xiē nán rén zài tuī nà gè diàn zi.

02   nà gè nán rén zài lā sì lún chē.
      nà pǐ xiǎo mǎ zài lā chē.
      tā men zài lā nà gè diàn zi.
      tā men zài tuī nà gè diàn zi.

03   tā zài lā sì lún chē.
      tā zài tuī sì lún chē.
      tā men zài tuī nà gè diàn zi.
      tā men zài lā nà gè diàn zi.

04   nà gè nán rén zài xiū lǐ zì xíng chē.
      nà gè nán rén zài qí zì xíng chē.
      nà gè nǚ rén zài liù gǒu.
      nà gè nǚ rén zài dòu gǒu wánr.

05   nà gè nǚ háir dài zhe mào zi.
      nà gè nǚ háir ná zhe mào zi.
      nà gè nán rén zhèng ná zhe nà bēi shuǐ. tā méi yǒu hē.
      nà gè nán rén zài hē nà bēi shuǐ.

06   nà gè nǚ rén zài shàng tái jiē.
      nà gè nǚ rén zài tuī nà xiē xiāng zi.
      nà gè nán rén káng zhe nà gè xiǎo háir.
      nà gè nán rén zài tuī sì lún chē.

07   nà gè nǚ rén zài gěi nà gè nán háir qián.
      nà gè nán rén zài gěi nà gè nǚ rén yào.
      nà gè nǚ rén zhèng bǎ jí tā dì gěi nà gè nán háir.
      nà gè nán rén zhèng bǎ jí tā dì gěi nà gè nǚ háir.

08   nà gè nán háir zhèng cóng nà gè nǚ rén shǒu lǐ jiē guò qián.
      nà gè nán háir zhèng cóng nà gè nǚ rén shǒu lǐ jiē guò jí tā.
      nà gè nǚ háir zhèng cóng nà gè nán rén shǒu lǐ jiē guò jí tā.
      nà gè nǚ rén zhèng cóng nà gè nán rén shǒu lǐ jiē guò yào.

09   nà gè nǚ háir zài ná pán zi.
      yǒu rén zài gěi nà gè nán rén yī pán shí wù.
      yǒu rén zài gěi nà gè nǚ rén yī pán shí wù.
      nà gè nán rén zhèng bǎ jí tā dì gěi nà gè nǚ háir.

10   nà gè nǚ rén zài gěi nà gè nán háir qián.
      yǒu rén zài gěi nà gè nǚ rén shén me dōng xi.
      nà gè nán rén zài ná yī bēi niú nǎi.
      nà gè nán rén gěi le nà gè nǚ rén yī bēi niú nǎi.

热、冷

01　火
　　太阳
　　雪
　　冰

02　火是热的。
　　太阳是热的。
　　雪是冷的。
　　冰是冷的。

03　一棵树、紫色的花儿
　　一支蜡烛
　　雪快把树盖上了。
　　雪快把山盖上了。

04　那些树着火了。
　　那支蜡烛在燃烧。
　　太阳在树后面。
　　太阳在云彩后面。

05　火冒着黑烟。
　　火冒着白烟。
　　那只小炉子冒着蓝火。
　　那支火柴冒着黄火。

06　夏天热。
　　冬天冷。
　　那些面包是热的。
　　那些面包不是热的。

07　天很冷，这两个人都戴着帽子和围巾。
　　天很热，这两个人都在晒太阳。
　　天热的时候，人们去水里玩儿。
　　天冷的时候，人们去雪里玩儿。

08　热天
　　冷天
　　冷食
　　热食

09　天很热。
　　天很冷。
　　冷饮
　　热饮

10　他很热。
　　他很冷。
　　太阳照在那个女人身上。
　　太阳照在草地上。

5-06

熱、冷

01　火
　　太陽
　　雪
　　冰

02　火是熱的。
　　太陽是熱的。
　　雪是冷的。
　　冰是冷的。

03　一棵樹、紫色的花兒
　　一支蠟燭
　　雪快把樹蓋上了。
　　雪快把山蓋上了。

04　那些樹著火了。
　　那支蠟燭在燃燒。
　　太陽在樹後面。
　　太陽在雲彩後面。

05　火冒著黑煙。
　　火冒著白煙。
　　那隻小爐子冒著藍火。
　　那支火柴冒著黃火。

06　夏天熱。
　　冬天冷。
　　那些面包是熱的。
　　那些面包不是熱的。

07　天很冷，這兩個人都戴著帽子和圍巾。
　　天很熱，這兩個人都在晒太陽。
　　天熱的時候，人們去水裡玩兒。
　　天冷的時候，人們去雪裡玩兒。

08　熱天
　　冷天
　　冷食
　　熱食

09　天很熱。
　　天很冷。
　　冷飲
　　熱飲

10　他很熱。
　　他很冷。
　　太陽照在那個女人身上。
　　太陽照在草地上。

5-06

rè, lěng

01 huǒ
   tài yáng
   xuě
   bīng

02 huǒ shì rè de.
   tài yáng shì rè de.
   xuě shì lěng de.
   bīng shì lěng de.

03 yī kē shù, zǐ sè de huār
   yī zhī là zhú
   xuě kuài bǎ shù gài shàng le.
   xuě kuài bǎ shān gài shàng le.

04 nà xiē shù zháo huǒ le.
   nà zhī là zhú zài rán shāo.
   tài yáng zài shù hòu miàn.
   tài yáng zài yún cǎi hòu miàn.

05 huǒ mào zhe hēi yān.
   huǒ mào zhe bái yān.
   nà zhī xiǎo lú zi mào zhe lán huǒ.
   nà zhī huǒ chái mào zhe huáng huǒ.

06 xià tiān rè.
   dōng tiān lěng.
   nà xiē miàn bāo shì rè de.
   nà xiē miàn bāo bú shì rè de.

07 tiān hěn lěng, zhè liǎng gè rén dōu dài zhe mào zi hé wéi jīn.
   tiān hěn rè, zhè liǎng gè rén dōu zài shài tài yáng.
   tiān rè de shí hòu, rén men qù shuǐ lǐ wánr.
   tiān lěng de shí hòu, rén men qù xuě lǐ wánr.

08 rè tiān
   lěng tiān
   lěng shí
   rè shí

09 tiān hěn rè.
   tiān hěn lěng.
   lěng yǐn
   rè yǐn

10 tā hěn rè.
   tā hěn lěng.
   tài yáng zhào zài nà gè nǚ rén shēn shàng.
   tài yáng zhào zài cǎo dì shàng.

111

植物、动物和食物

01 花儿是一种植物。
草是一种植物。
树是一种植物。
灌木和花儿是两种植物。

02 两种花儿
一种花儿
几种水果
一种水果

03 葡萄是一种水果。
香蕉是一种水果。
苹果是一种水果。
梨是一种水果。

04 狗是一种动物。
猫是一种动物。
羊是一种动物。
鸭子是一种动物。

05 两种鸭子
一种鸭子
两种狗
一种狗

06 肉是一种食物。
水果是一种食物。
面包是一种食物。
冰淇淋是一种食物。

07 葡萄是食物。
香蕉是食物。
苹果是食物。
梨是食物。

08 两种动物
一种动物
一种植物
几种植物

09 狗是动物。
花儿是植物。
马和牛都是动物。
鸭子是动物。

10 很多种食物
很多种植物
一种植物和一种动物
两种动物

5-07

植物、動物和食物

01 花兒是一種植物。
草是一種植物。
樹是一種植物。
灌木和花兒是兩種植物。

02 兩種花兒
一種花兒
幾種水果
一種水果

03 葡萄是一種水果。
香蕉是一種水果。
苹果是一種水果。
梨是一種水果。

04 狗是一種動物。
貓是一種動物。
羊是一種動物。
鴨子是一種動物。

05 兩種鴨子
一種鴨子
兩種狗
一種狗

06 肉是一種食物。
水果是一種食物。
面包是一種食物。
冰淇淋是一種食物。

07 葡萄是食物。
香蕉是食物。
苹果是食物。
梨是食物。

08 兩種動物
一種動物
一種植物
幾種植物

09 狗是動物。
花兒是植物。
馬和牛都是動物。
鴨子是動物。

10 很多種食物
很多種植物
一種植物和一種動物
兩種動物

5-07

zhí wù, dòng wù hé shí wù

01 huār shì yī zhǒng zhí wù.
cǎo shì yī zhǒng zhí wù.
shù shì yī zhǒng zhí wù.
guàn mù hé huār shì liǎng zhǒng zhí wù.

02 liǎng zhǒng huār
yī zhǒng huār
jǐ zhǒng shuǐ guǒ
yī zhǒng shuǐ guǒ

03 pú táo shì yī zhǒng shuǐ guǒ.
xiāng jiāo shì yī zhǒng shuǐ guǒ.
píng guǒ shì yī zhǒng shuǐ guǒ.
lí shì yī zhǒng shuǐ guǒ.

04 gǒu shì yī zhǒng dòng wù.
māo shì yī zhǒng dòng wù.
yáng shì yī zhǒng dòng wù.
yā zi shì yī zhǒng dòng wù.

05 liǎng zhǒng yā zi
yī zhǒng yā zi
liǎng zhǒng gǒu
yī zhǒng gǒu

06 ròu shì yī zhǒng shí wù.
shuǐ guǒ shì yī zhǒng shí wù.
miàn bāo shì yī zhǒng shí wù.
bīng qí lín shì yī zhǒng shí wù.

07 pú táo shì shí wù.
xiāng jiāo shì shí wù.
píng guǒ shì shí wù.
lí shì shí wù.

08 liǎng zhǒng dòng wù
yī zhǒng dòng wù
yī zhǒng zhí wù
jǐ zhǒng zhí wù

09 gǒu shì dòng wù.
huār shì zhí wù.
mǎ hé niú dōu shì dòng wù.
yā zi shì dòng wù.

10 hěn duō zhǒng shí wù
hěn duō zhǒng zhí wù
yī zhǒng zhí wù hé yī zhǒng dòng wù
liǎng zhǒng dòng wù

5-08

家具、服装及乐器

01 桌子是家具。
椅子是家具。
床是家具。
沙发是家具。

02 餐桌和椅子都是家具。
书桌和椅子都是家具。
床是用来在上面睡觉的家具。
沙发是用来在上面坐着的家具。

03 桌子是家具。
椅子是家具。
长椅是用来在上面坐着的家具。
衣橱是用来装衣服的家具。

04 连衣裙是服装。
夹克是服装。
衬衫和领带都是服装。
儿童服装

05 那个小丑儿在穿衣服。
那个小丑儿已经打扮好了。
那个女人在穿衣服。
那个女人已经穿戴好了。

06 这些人穿戴得很正式。
这些人打扮得象牛仔似的。
这两个人穿着游泳衣。
这些人打扮得象小丑儿似的。

07 那个男人一边抱着萨克斯风，一边在弹钢琴。
吉他是乐器。
小提琴是乐器。
笛子是乐器。

08 有人在弹电贝丝。
有人在吹笛子。
有人在弹电子琴。
有人在打鼓。

09 那个鼓手在听那个吹笛子的人演奏。
那个男人拿着两把吉他。
有人在弹吉他。
那两个孩子在弹钢琴。

10 几件家具
服装
乐器
一件家具

5-08

家具、服裝及樂器

01 桌子是家具。
椅子是家具。
床是家具。
沙發是家具。

02 餐桌和椅子都是家具。
書桌和椅子都是家具。
床是用來在上面睡覺的家具。
沙發是用來在上面坐著的家具。

03 桌子是家具。
椅子是家具。
長椅是用來在上面坐著的家具。
衣櫥是用來裝衣服的家具。

04 連衣裙是服裝。
茄克是服裝。
襯衫和領帶都是服裝。
兒童服裝

05 那個小醜兒在穿衣服。
那個小醜兒已經打扮好了。
那個女人在穿衣服。
那個女人已經穿戴好了。

06 這些人穿戴得很正式。
這些人打扮得象牛仔似的。
這兩個人穿著游泳衣。
這些人打扮得象小醜兒似的。

07 那個男人一邊抱著薩克斯風，一邊在彈鋼琴。
吉他是樂器。
小提琴是樂器。
笛子是樂器。

08 有人在彈電貝絲。
有人在吹笛子。
有人在彈電子琴。
有人在打鼓。

09 那個鼓手在聽那個吹笛子的人演奏。
那個男人拿著兩把吉他。
有人在彈吉他。
那兩個孩子在彈鋼琴。

10 幾件家具
服裝
樂器
一件家具

5-08

jiā jù, fú zhuāng jí yuè qì

01 zhuō zi shì jiā jù.
    yǐ zi shì jiā jù.
    chuáng shì jiā jù.
    shā fā shì jiā jù.

02 cān zhuō hé yǐ zi dōu shì jiā jù.
    shū zhuō hé yǐ zi dōu shì jiā jù.
    chuáng shì yòng lái zài shàng miàn shuì jiào de jiā jù.
    shā fā shì yòng lái zài shàng miàn zuò zhe de jiā jù.

03 zhuō zi shì jiā jù.
    yǐ zi shì jiā jù.
    cháng yǐ shì yòng lái zài shàng miàn zuò zhe de jiā jù.
    yī chú shì yòng lái zhuāng yī fu de jiā jù.

04 lián yī qún shì fú zhuāng.
    jiá kè shì fú zhuāng.
    chèn shān hé lǐng dài dōu shì fú zhuāng.
    ér tóng fú zhuāng

05 nà gè xiǎo chǒur zài chuān yī fu.
    nà gè xiǎo chǒur yǐ jīng dǎ bàn hǎo le.
    nà gè nǚ rén zài chuān yī fu.
    nà gè nǚ rén yǐ jīng chuān dài hǎo le.

06 zhè xiē rén chuān dài de hěn zhèng shì.
    zhè xiē rén dǎ bàn de xiàng niú zǎi shì de.
    zhè liǎng gè rén chuān zhe yóu yǒng yī.
    zhè xiē rén dǎ bàn de xiàng xiǎo chǒur shì de.

07 nà gè nán rén yī biān bào zhe sà kè sī fēng, yī biān zài tán gāng qín.
    jí tā shì yuè qì.
    xiǎo tí qín shì yuè qì.
    dí zi shì yuè qì.

08 yǒu rén zài tán diàn bèi sī.
    yǒu rén zài chuī dí zi.
    yǒu rén zài tán diàn zǐ qín.
    yǒu rén zài dǎ gǔ.

09 nà gè gǔ shǒu zài tīng nà gè chuī dí zi de rén yǎn zòu.
    nà gè nán rén ná zhe liǎng bǎ jí tā.
    yǒu rén zài tán jí tā.
    nà liǎng gè hái zi zài tán gāng qín.

10 jǐ jiàn jiā jù
    fú zhuāng
    yuè qì
    yī jiàn jiā jù

比较多少；可数及不可数名词

01 两个人骑着一辆自行车。
一个人站在两个骑自行车的人中间。
一个人在骑自行车，两个人在走。
许多人在骑自行车。

02 椅子比桌子多。
绿苹果比红苹果多。
那个女人杯子里的牛奶和那个女孩儿杯子里的一样
多。
那个男人左手里的糖比右手里的多。

03 桌子比椅子少。
红苹果比绿苹果少。
两个杯子里的牛奶一样多。
那个男人右手里的糖比左手里的少。

04 这个托盘上有一点儿食物。
这个托盘上有很多食物。
这幅画里水比陆地少。
这幅画里水比陆地多。

05 这幅画里沙子比草多。
这幅画里沙子比草少。
那个女孩儿杯子里的牛奶比那个女人杯子里的多。
那个女孩儿杯子里的牛奶比那个女人杯子里的少。

06 我们能数出有多少个男孩儿：一个、两个、三个。
我们能数出有多少个男孩儿：一个、两个、三个、四
个。
我们能数出有多少个男孩儿：一个、两个、三个、四
个、五个、六个。
我们能数出有多少根蜡烛：一根、两根、三根、四
根、五根。

07 硬币多得数不清。
鸟多得数不清。
花儿多得数不清。
气球多得数不清。

08 几个气球
数不清的气球
几个人
数不清的人

09 人多得数不清。
只有几个人。
帽子多得数不清。
只有几顶帽子。

10 有很多，很多的花儿。
只有几朵花儿。
动物多得数不清。
只有两只动物。

5-09

比較多少；可數及不可數名詞

01 兩個人騎著一輛自行車。
一個人站在兩個騎自行車的人中間。
一個人在騎自行車，兩個人在走。
許多人在騎自行車。

02 椅子比桌子多。
綠苹果比紅苹果多。
那個女人杯子裡的牛奶和那個女孩兒杯子裡的一樣
多。
那個男人左手裡的糖比右手裡的多。

03 桌子比椅子少。
紅苹果比綠苹果少。
兩個杯子裡的牛奶一樣多。
那個男人右手裡的糖比左手裡的少。

04 這個托盤上有一點兒食物。
這個托盤上有很多食物。
這幅畫裡水比陸地少。
這幅畫裡水比陸地多。

05 這幅畫裡沙子比草多。
這幅畫裡沙子比草少。
那個女孩兒杯子裡的牛奶比那個女人杯子裡的多。
那個女孩兒杯子裡的牛奶比那個女人杯子裡的少。

06 我們能數出有多少個男孩兒：一個、二個、三個。
我們能數出有多少個男孩兒：一個、二個、三個、四
個。
我們能數出有多少個男孩兒：一個、二個、三個、四
個、五個、六個。
我們能數出有多少根蠟燭：一根、二根、三根、四
根、五根。

07 硬幣多得數不清。
鳥多得數不清。
花兒多得數不清。
氣球多得數不清。

08 幾個氣球
數不清的氣球
幾個人
數不清的人

09 人多得數不清。
祇有幾個人。
帽子多得數不清。
祇有幾頂帽子。

10 有很多，很多的花兒。
祇有幾朵花兒。
動物多得數不清。
祇有兩隻動物。

5-09

bǐ jiào duō shǎo; kě shǔ jí bù kě shǔ míng cí

01 liǎng gè rén qí zhe yī liàng zì xíng chē.
    yī gè rén zhàn zài liǎng gè qí zì xíng chē de rén zhōng jiān.
    yī gè rén zài qí zì xíng chē, liǎng gè rén zài zǒu.
    xǔ duō rén zài qí zì xíng chē.

02 yǐ zi bǐ zhuō zi duō.
    lǜ píng guǒ bǐ hóng píng guǒ duō.
    nà gè nǚ rén bēi zi lǐ de niú nǎi hé nà gè nǚ háir bēi zi lǐ de yī yàng duō.
    nà gè nán rén zuǒ shǒu lǐ de táng bǐ yòu shǒu lǐ de duō.

03 zhuō zi bǐ yǐ zi shǎo.
    hóng píng guǒ bǐ lǜ píng guǒ shǎo.
    liǎng gè bēi zi lǐ de niú nǎi yī yàng duō.
    nà gè nán rén yòu shǒu lǐ de táng bǐ zuǒ shǒu lǐ de shǎo.

04 zhè gè tuō pán shàng yǒu yī diǎnr shí wù.
    zhè gè tuō pán shàng yǒu hěn duō shí wù.
    zhè fú huà lǐ shuǐ bǐ lù dì shǎo.
    zhè fú huà lǐ shuǐ bǐ lù dì duō.

05 zhè fú huà lǐ shā zi bǐ cǎo duō.
    zhè fú huà lǐ shā zi bǐ cǎo shǎo.
    nà gè nǚ háir bēi zi lǐ de niú nǎi bǐ nà gè nǚ rén bēi zi lǐ de duō.
    nà gè nǚ háir bēi zi lǐ de niú nǎi bǐ nà gè nǚ rén bēi zi lǐ de shǎo.

06 wǒ men néng shǔ chū yǒu duō shǎo gè nán háir: yī gè, liǎng gè, sān gè.
    wǒ men néng shǔ chū yǒu duō shǎo gè nán háir: yī gè, liǎng gè, sān gè, sì gè.
    wǒ men néng shǔ chū yǒu duō shǎo gè nán háir: yī gè, liǎng gè, sān gè, sì gè, wǔ gè, liù gè.
    wǒ men néng shǔ chū yǒu duō shǎo gēn là zhú: yī gēn, liǎng gēn, sān gēn, sì gēn, wǔ gēn.

07 yìng bì duō de shǔ bù qīng.
    niǎo duō de shǔ bù qīng.
    huār duō de shǔ bù qīng.
    qì qiú duō de shǔ bù qīng.

08 jǐ gè qì qiú
    shǔ bù qīng de qì qiú
    jǐ gè rén
    shǔ bù qīng de rén.

09 rén duō de shǔ bù qīng.
    zhǐ yǒu jǐ gè rén.
    mào zi duō de shǔ bù qīng.
    zhǐ yǒu jǐ dǐng mào zi.

10 yǒu hěn duō, hěn duō de huār.
    zhǐ yǒu jǐ duǒ huār.
    dòng wù duō de shǔ bù qīng.
    zhǐ yǒu liǎng zhī dòng wù.

人的动作和手势

01　那些孩子在挥手。
　　那个女孩儿在挥手。
　　那个男人在挥手。
　　那个女人在挥手。

02　那些小丑中有一个在挥手。
　　那些小丑中有一个双手放在兜里。
　　那两个小丑在挥手。
　　那个坐着的小丑在挥手。

03　那个女人在咳嗽。
　　那个男人在打喷嚏。
　　那个男孩儿正把风筝线叼在嘴里。
　　那个男孩儿在伸舌头。

04　那个小伙子两臂抱在一起。
　　那个小伙子在打哈欠。
　　那个男人在打喷嚏。
　　那个男人在擤鼻子。

05　这个男人在系鞋带。
　　这个男人在挠脖子。
　　那个小丑在指着自己的鼻子。
　　那个小丑在挠头。

06　坐在长椅上的那个女人累了。
　　那个男人很累。
　　那个小伙子累了，所以他在打哈欠。
　　那个男孩儿在哭。

07　那个女人很伤心。
　　那个男人在思考。
　　这些男人不累。
　　这两个男人很累。

08　那个女人很伤心。她在参加葬礼。
　　那个男人很高兴。
　　这两个男人刚赛跑完。他们很累。
　　这个男人要赛跑。他在活动身体。

09　两个赛跑的人快跑到终点了。那个穿红背心的人要赢
　　了。
　　那个男人很高兴。他已经得了两块金牌。
　　这个女人唱得很高兴。
　　那个男孩儿很伤心，所以他在哭。

10　这个男人在挠额头。
　　这个男人在思考。
　　那个孩子正把东西从地上拣起来。
　　那个女人正把东西从地上拣起来。

5-10

人的動作和手勢

01　那些孩子在揮手。
　　那個女孩兒在揮手。
　　那個男人在揮手。
　　那個女人在揮手。

02　那些小醜中有一個在揮手。
　　那些小醜中有一個雙手放在兜裡。
　　那兩個小醜在揮手。
　　那個坐著的小醜在揮手。

03　那個女人在咳嗽。
　　那個男人在打噴嚏。
　　那個男孩兒正把風箏線叼在嘴裡。
　　那個男孩兒在伸舌頭。

04　那個小夥子兩臂抱在一起。
　　那個小夥子在打呵欠。
　　那個男人在打噴嚏。
　　那個男人在擤鼻子。

05　這個男人在系鞋帶。
　　這個男人在撓脖子。
　　那個小醜在指著自己的鼻子。
　　那個小醜在撓頭。

06　坐在長椅上的那個女人累了。
　　那個男人很累。
　　那個小夥子累了，所以他在打呵欠。
　　那個男孩兒在哭。

07　那個女人很傷心。
　　那個男人在思考。
　　這些男人不累。
　　這兩個男人很累。

08　那個女人很傷心。她在參加葬禮。
　　那個男人很高興。
　　這兩個男人剛賽跑完。他們很累。
　　這個男人要賽跑。他在活動身體。

09　兩個賽跑的人快跑到終點了。那個穿紅背心的人要贏
　　了。
　　那個男人很高興。他已經得了兩塊金牌。
　　這個女人唱得很高興。
　　那個男孩兒很傷心，所以他在哭。

10　這個男人在撓額頭。
　　這個男人在思考。
　　那個孩子正把東西從地上撿起來。
　　那個女人正把東西從地上撿起來。

5-10

rén de dòng zuò hé shǒu shì

01 nà xiē hái zi zài huī shǒu.
   nà gè nǚ háir zài huī shǒu.
   nà gè nán rén zài huī shǒu.
   nà gè nǚ rén zài huī shǒu.

02 nà xiē xiǎo chǒu zhōng yǒu yī gè zài huī shǒu.
   nà xiē xiǎo chǒu zhōng yǒu yī gè shuāng shǒu fàng zài dōu lǐ.
   nà liǎng gè xiǎo chǒu zài huī shǒu.
   nà gè zuò zhe de xiǎo chǒu zài huī shǒu.

03 nà gè nǚ rén zài ké sòu.
   nà gè nán rén zài dǎ pēn tì.
   nà gè nán háir zhèng bǎ fēng zhēng xiàn diāo zài zuǐ lǐ.
   nà gè nán háir zài shēn shé tóu.

04 nà gè xiǎo huǒ zi liǎng bì bào zài yī qǐ.
   nà gè xiǎo huǒ zi zài dǎ hā qiàn.
   nà gè nán rén zài dǎ pēn tì.
   nà gè nán rén zài xǐng bí zi.

05 zhè gè nán rén zài jì xié dài.
   zhè gè nán rén zài náo bó zi.
   nà gè xiǎo chǒu zài zhǐ zhe zì jǐ de bí zi.
   nà gè xiǎo chǒu zài náo tóu.

06 zuò zài cháng yǐ shàng de nà gè nǚ rén lèi le.
   nà gè nán rén hěn lèi.
   nà gè xiǎo huǒ zi lèi le, suǒ yǐ tā zài dǎ hā qiàn.
   nà gè nán háir zài kū.

07 nà gè nǚ rén hěn shāng xīn.
   nà gè nán rén zài sī kǎo.
   zhè xiē nán rén bú lèi.
   zhè liǎng gè nán rén hěn lèi.

08 nà gè nǚ rén hěn shāng xīn, tā zài cān jiā zàng lǐ.
   nà gè nán rén hěn gāo xìng.
   zhè liǎng gè nán rén gāng sài pǎo wán, tā men hěn lèi.
   zhè gè nán rén yào sài pǎo, tā zài huó dòng shēn tǐ.

09 liǎng gè sài pǎo de rén kuài pǎo dào zhōng diǎn le, nà gè chuān hóng bèi xīn de rén yào yíng le.
   nà gè nán rén hěn gāo xìng, tā yǐ jīng dé le liǎng kuài jīn pái.
   zhè gè nǚ rén chàng de hěn gāo xìng.
   nà gè nán háir hěn shāng xīn, suǒ yǐ tā zài kū.

10 zhè gè nán rén zài náo é tóu.
   zhè gè nán rén zài sī kǎo.
   nà gè hái zi zhèng bǎ dōng xi cóng dì shàng jiǎn qǐ lái.
   nà gè nǚ rén zhèng bǎ dōng xi cóng dì shàng jiǎn qǐ lái.

感觉和心情

01 我的头发是红色的。
我戴着帽子。
我的头发是黑色的。
我秃顶。

02 我们很冷。
我们很热。
我很冷。
我很热。

03 我很累。
我不累。我在跳。
我们很累。
我们不累。

04 我很壮。
我很弱。
我们在跑，我们不累。
我们在跑，我们很累。

05 我病了。
我很健康。
我是一只蓝色的鸟。
我是一只长着红头的鸟。

06 那个男人说: "我饿了。"
那个男人说: "我吃饱了。"
那个女人说: "我饿了。"
那个女人说: "我吃饱了。"

07 我们很高兴。
我们不高兴。
我很高兴。
我不高兴。

08 我们很累。
我很累，那个男孩儿不累。
我们不累，他很累。
我很累，那个女人不累。

09 我病了。
我渴了。
我冷了。
我有钱。

10 我没喝东西，你在喝东西。
我饿了。
我们冷了。
我们又热又累。

5-11

感覺和心情

01 我的頭髮是紅色的。
我戴著帽子。
我的頭髮是黑色的。
我秃頂。

02 我們很冷。
我們很熱。
我很冷。
我很熱。

03 我很累。
我不累，我在跳。
我們很累。
我們不累。

04 我很壯。
我很弱。
我們在跑，我們不累。
我們在跑，我們很累。

05 我病了。
我很健康。
我是一隻藍色的鳥。
我是一隻長著紅頭的鳥。

06 那個男人説："我餓了。"
那個男人説："我吃飽了。"
那個女人説："我餓了。"
那個女人説："我吃飽了。"

07 我們很高興。
我們不高興。
我很高興。
我不高興。

08 我們很累。
我很累，那個男孩兒不累。
我們不累，他很累。
我很累，那個女人不累。

09 我病了。
我渴了。
我冷了。
我有錢。

10 我沒喝東西，你在喝東西。
我餓了。
我們冷了。
我們又熱又累。

5-11

gǎn jué hé xīn qíng

01 wǒ de tóu fà shì hóng sè de.
    wǒ dài zhe mào zi.
    wǒ de tóu fà shì hēi sè de.
    wǒ tū dǐng.

02 wǒ men hěn lěng.
    wǒ men hěn rè.
    wǒ hěn lěng.
    wǒ hěn rè.

03 wǒ hěn lèi.
    wǒ bú lèi, wǒ zài tiào.
    wǒ men hěn lèi.
    wǒ men bú lèi.

04 wǒ hěn zhuàng.
    wǒ hěn ruò.
    wǒ men zài pǎo, wǒ men bú lèi.
    wǒ men zài pǎo, wǒ men hěn lèi.

05 wǒ bìng le.
    wǒ hěn jiàn kāng.
    wǒ shì yī zhī lán sè de niǎo.
    wǒ shì yī zhī zhǎng zhe hóng tóu de niǎo.

06 nà gè nán rén shuō: "wǒ è le."
    nà gè nán rén shuō: "wǒ chī bǎo le."
    nà gè nǚ rén shuō: "wǒ è le."
    nà gè nǚ rén shuō: "wǒ chī bǎo le."

07 wǒ men hěn gāo xìng.
    wǒ men bù gāo xìng.
    wǒ hěn gāo xìng.
    wǒ bù gāo xìng.

08 wǒ men hěn lèi.
    wǒ hěn lèi. nà gè nán háir bú lèi.
    wǒ men bú lèi. tā hěn lèi.
    wǒ hěn lèi. nà gè nǚ rén bú lèi.

09 wǒ bìng le.
    wǒ kě le.
    wǒ lěng le.
    wǒ yǒu qián.

10 wǒ méi hē dōng xi, nǐ zài hē dōng xi.
    wǒ è le.
    wǒ men lěng le.
    wǒ men yòu rè yòu lèi.

5-12

复习第五部分

01 六加五等于十一。
六加六等于十二。
四加三等于七。
四加五等于九。

02 女式手套
男式手套
女人们的腿
一双女人的腿

03 那个男人想打手提电话。他正把它从兜里拿出来。
那个男人在打手提电话。
那个男人正拿着手提电话，但没有打。
那个男人在用一部红色的电话。

04 七百三十四
七百四十三
八百三十四
八百四十三

05 那个女人在给那个男孩儿钱。
那个男人在给那个女人药。
那个女人正把吉他递给那个男孩儿。
那个男人正把吉他递给那个女孩儿。

06 很多种食物
很多种植物
一种植物和一种动物
两种动物

07 那个小丑儿在穿衣服。
那个小丑儿已经打扮好了。
那个女人在穿衣服。
那个女人已经穿戴好了。

08 这幅画里沙子比草多。
这幅画里沙子比草少。
那个女孩儿杯子里的牛奶比那个女人杯子里的多。
那个女孩儿杯子里的牛奶比那个女人杯子里的少。

09 这个男人在系鞋带。
这个男人在挠脖子。
那个小丑在指着自己的鼻子。
那个小丑在挠头。

10 我们很累。
我很累，那个男孩儿不累。
我们不累，他很累。
我很累，那个女人不累。

5-12

復習第五部分

01 六加五等於十一。
六加六等於十二。
四加三等於七。
四加五等於九。

02 女式手套
男式手套
女人們的腿
一雙女人的腿

03 那個男人想打手提電話。他正把它從兜裡拿出來。
那個男人在打手提電話。
那個男人正拿著手提電話，但沒有打。
那個男人在用一部紅色的電話。

04 七百三十四
七百四十三
八百三十四
八百四十三

05 那個女人在給那個男孩兒錢。
那個男人在給那個女人藥。
那個女人正把吉他遞給那個男孩兒。
那個男人正把吉他遞給那個女孩兒。

06 很多種食物
很多種植物
一種植物和一種動物
兩種動物

07 那個小醜兒在穿衣服。
那個小醜兒已經打扮好了。
那個女人在穿衣服。
那個女人已經穿戴好了。

08 這幅畫裡沙子比草多。
這幅畫裡沙子比草少。
那個女孩兒杯子裡的牛奶比那個女人杯子裡的多。
那個女孩兒杯子裡的牛奶比那個女人杯子裡的少。

09 這個男人在系鞋帶。
這個男人在撓脖子。
那個小醜在指著自己的鼻子。
那個小醜在撓頭。

10 我們很累。
我很累，那個男孩兒不累。
我們不累，他很累。
我很累，那個女人不累。

5-12

fù xí dì wǔ bù fen

01 liù jiā wǔ děng yú shí yī.
    liù jiā liù děng yú shí èr.
    sì jiā sān děng yú qī.
    sì jiā wǔ děng yú jiǔ.

02 nǚ shì shǒu tào
    nán shì shǒu tào
    nǚ rén men de tuǐ
    yī shuāng nǚ rén de tuǐ

03 nà gè nán rén xiǎng dǎ shǒu tí diàn huà. tā zhèng bǎ tā cóng dōu lǐ ná chū lái.
    nà gè nán rén zài dǎ shǒu tí diàn huà.
    nà gè nán rén zhèng ná zhe shǒu tí diàn huà, dàn méi yǒu dǎ.
    nà gè nán rén zài yòng yī bù hóng sè de diàn huà.

04 qī bǎi sān shí sì
    qī bǎi sì shí sān
    bā bǎi sān shí sì
    bā bǎi sì shí sān

05 nà gè nǚ rén zài gěi nà gè nán háir qián.
    nà gè nán rén zài gěi nà gè nǚ rén yào.
    nà gè nǚ rén zhèng bǎ jí tā dì gěi nà gè nán háir.
    nà gè nán rén zhèng bǎ jí tā dì gěi nà gè nǚ háir.

06 hěn duō zhǒng shí wù
    hěn duō zhǒng zhí wù
    yī zhǒng zhí wù hé yī zhǒng dòng wù
    liǎng zhǒng dòng wù

07 nà gè xiǎo chǒur zài chuān yī fu.
    nà gè xiǎo chǒur yǐ jīng dǎ bàn hǎo le.
    nà gè nǚ rén zài chuān yī fu.
    nà gè nǚ rén yǐ jīng chuān dài hǎo le.

08 zhè fú huà lǐ shā zi bǐ cǎo duō.
    zhè fú huà lǐ shā zi bǐ cǎo shǎo.
    nà gè nǚ háir bēi zi lǐ de niú nǎi bǐ nà gè nǚ rén bēi zi lǐ de duō.
    nà gè nǚ háir bēi zi lǐ de niú nǎi bǐ nà gè nǚ rén bēi zi lǐ de shǎo.

09 zhè gè nán rén zài jì xié dài.
    zhè gè nán rén zài náo bó zi.
    nà gè xiǎo chǒu zài zhǐ zhe zì jǐ de bí zi.
    nà gè xiǎo chǒu zài náo tóu.

10 wǒ men hěn lèi.
    wǒ hěn lèi. nà gè nán háir bú lèi.
    wǒ men bú lèi. tā hěn lèi.
    wǒ hěn lèi. nà gè nǚ rén bú lèi.

6-01

用"刚才…"、"在…"表示过去和现在发生的事

01 那些孩子在公园里。
    那个男孩儿在飞机里。
    那只狗叼着一个飞盘。
    那只杯子是满的。

02 这就是刚才在公园里的那些孩子。
    那个男孩儿刚才在飞机里。
    那只狗刚才叼着一个飞盘。
    那只杯子刚才是满的。

03 那个男孩儿张着嘴。
    那些孩子站在桌子上。
    那个男孩儿刚才张着嘴。
    那些孩子刚才站在桌子上。

04 那个女人拿着一个箱子。
    这就是刚才拿着箱子的那个女人。
    那两个女孩儿拿着一条绳子。
    这就是刚才拿着绳子的那两个女孩儿。

05 那个男人头上戴着帽子。
    这就是刚才头上戴着帽子的那个男人。
    那个穿蓝衣服的男孩儿手里拿着一把耙子。
    那个穿蓝衣服的男孩儿刚才手里拿了一把耙子。

06 这些人在参加自行车比赛。
    这些人刚才参加了一场自行车比赛。
    这个男人在参加自行车比赛。
    这个男人刚才参加了一场自行车比赛。

07 那个男孩儿站在桌子上。
    那个男孩儿刚才站在桌子上。
    那个女人拿着一个笔记本。
    那个女人刚才拿着一个笔记本。

08 这个人正在水里。
    这个人刚才在水里。
    那个男孩儿在墙上。他在爬墙。
    那个男孩儿刚才在墙上。他已经从墙上摔下来了。

09 这些人在游行。
    这些人刚才在游行。
    那个男人在卡车里。
    那个男人刚才在卡车里。

10 那个男孩儿在屋里。
    那个男孩儿刚才在屋里。现在他在屋外。
    那个小丑戴着帽子。
    那个小丑刚才戴着帽子。

6-01

用"剛才…"、"在…"表示過去和現在發生的事

01 那些孩子在公園裡。
    那個男孩兒在飛機裡。
    那隻狗叼著一個飛盤。
    那隻杯子是滿的。

02 這就是剛才在公園裡的那些孩子。
    那個男孩兒剛才在飛機裡。
    那隻狗剛才叼著一個飛盤。
    那隻杯子剛才是滿的。

03 那個男孩兒張著嘴。
    那些孩子站在桌子上。
    那個男孩兒剛才張著嘴。
    那些孩子剛才站在桌子上。

04 那個女人拿著一個箱子。
    這就是剛才拿著箱子的那個女人。
    那兩個女孩兒拿著一條繩子。
    這就是剛才拿著繩子的那兩個女孩兒。

05 那個男人頭上戴著帽子。
    這就是剛才頭上戴著帽子的那個男人。
    那個穿藍衣服的男孩兒手裡拿著一把耙子。
    那個穿藍衣服的男孩兒剛才手裡拿了一把耙子。

06 這些人在參加自行車比賽。
    這些人剛才參加了一場自行車比賽。
    這個男人在參加自行車比賽。
    這個男人剛才參加了一場自行車比賽。

07 那個男孩兒站在桌子上。
    那個男孩兒剛才站在桌子上。
    那個女人拿著一個筆記本。
    那個女人剛才拿著一個筆記本。

08 這個人正在水裡。
    這個人剛才在水裡。
    那個男孩兒在牆上。他在爬牆。
    那個男孩兒剛才在牆上。他已經從牆上摔下來了。

09 這些人在游行。
    這些人剛才在游行。
    那個男人在卡車裡。
    那個男人剛才在卡車裡。

10 那個男孩兒在屋裡。
    那個男孩兒剛才在屋裡。現在他在屋外。
    那個小醜戴著帽子。
    那個小醜剛才戴著帽子。

6-01

yòng "gāng cái...", "zài...", biǎo shì guò qù hé xiàn zài fā shēng de shì

01 nà xiē hái zi zài gōng yuán lǐ.
nà gè nán háir zài fēi jī lǐ.
nà zhī gǒu diāo zhe yī gè fēi pán.
nà zhī bēi zi shì mǎn de.

02 zhè jiù shì gāng cái zài gōng yuán lǐ de nà xiē hái zi.
nà gè nán háir gāng cái zài fēi jī lǐ.
nà zhī gǒu gāng cái diāo zhe yī gè fēi pán.
nà zhī bēi zi gāng cái shì mǎn de.

03 nà gè nán háir zhāng zhe zuǐ.
nà xiē hái zi zhàn zài zhuō zi shàng.
nà gè nán háir gāng cái zhāng zhe zuǐ.
nà xiē hái zi gāng cái zhàn zài zhuō zi shàng.

04 nà gè nǚ rén ná zhe yī gè xiāng zi.
zhè jiù shì gāng cái ná zhe xiāng zi de nà gè nǚ rén.
nà liǎng gè nǚ háir ná zhe yī tiáo shéng zi.
zhè jiù shì gāng cái ná zhe shéng zi de nà liǎng gè nǚ háir.

05 nà gè nán rén tóu shàng dài zhe mào zi.
zhè jiù shì gāng cái tóu shàng dài zhe mào zi de nà gè nán rén.
nà gè chuān lán yī fu de nán háir shǒu lǐ ná zhe yī bǎ pá zi.
nà gè chuān lán yī fu de nán háir gāng cái shǒu lǐ ná le yī bǎ pá zi.

06 zhè xiē rén zài cān jiā zì xíng chē bǐ sài.
zhè xiē rén gāng cái cān jiā le yī chǎng zì xíng chē bǐ sài.
zhè gè nán rén zài cān jiā zì xíng chē bǐ sài.
zhè gè nán rén gāng cái cān jiā le yī chǎng zì xíng chē bǐ sài.

07 nà gè nán háir zhàn zài zhuō zi shàng.
nà gè nán háir gāng cái zhàn zài zhuō zi shàng.
nà gè nǚ rén ná zhe yī gè bǐ jì běn.
nà gè nǚ rén gāng cái ná zhe yī gè bǐ jì běn.

08 zhè gè rén zhèng zài shuǐ lǐ.
zhè gè rén gāng cái zài shuǐ lǐ.
nà gè nán háir zài qiáng shàng. tā zài pá qiáng.
nà gè nán háir gāng cái zài qiáng shàng. tā yǐ jīng cóng qiáng shàng shuāi xià lái le.

09 zhè xiē rén zài yóu xíng.
zhè xiē rén gāng cái zài yóu xíng.
nà gè nán rén zài kǎ chē lǐ.
nà gè nán rén gāng cái zài kǎ chē lǐ.

10 nà gè nán háir zài wū lǐ.
nà gè nán háir gāng cái zài wū lǐ, xiàn zài tā zài wū wài.
nà gè xiǎo chǒu dài zhe mào zi.
nà gè xiǎo chǒu gāng cái dài zhe mào zi.

6-02

现在进行时，现在完成时及用"要"、"正要"、"快要"表示的一般将来时

01 那个男人正要上轿车。
    那个男人在上轿车。
    那个男人正要上马车。
    那个男人在上马车。

02 那个男孩儿正要跳。
    那个男孩儿在跳。
    那个男孩儿已经跳了。
    那个男孩儿要扔球。

03 那个女人正要写字。
    那个女人在写字。
    那个男孩儿正在往下掉。
    那个男孩儿已经掉下来了。

04 那个男孩儿快要从水里出来了。
    那个男孩儿正要滑水。
    那个男孩儿在滑水。
    那个男孩儿已经滑进水里了。

05 那个男孩儿快要跳了。
    那个男孩儿在跳。
    那些人快要过街了。
    那些人在过街。

06 那个男孩儿在看着那个球。
    那个男孩儿正要扔那个球。
    那个男人正要把那个男孩儿抛起来。
    那个男人已经把那个男孩儿抛了起来。

07 那个女人正要把什么东西放进袋子里。
    那个女人已经把什么东西放进了袋子里。
    那个女人正要亲那个男人。
    那个女人在亲那个男人。

08 那个女人正要走进那家商店。
    那个女人正走进那家商店。
    那个男人正要关轿车的行李箱。
    那个男人已经把轿车的行李箱关上了。

09 那些人要上台阶。
    那些人在上台阶。
    那些人已经上完了台阶。
    那些人在下台阶。

10 那两个人要下台阶。
    那两个人在下台阶。
    那两个人已经走下了台阶。
    那两个人在上台阶。

6-02

現在進行時，現在完成時及用"要"、"正要"、"快要"表示的一般將來時

01 那個男人正要上轎車。
    那個男人在上轎車。
    那個男人正要上馬車。
    那個男人在上馬車。

02 那個男孩兒正要跳。
    那個男孩兒在跳。
    那個男孩兒已經跳了。
    那個男孩兒要扔球。

03 那個女人正要寫字。
    那個女人在寫字。
    那個男孩兒正在往下掉。
    那個男孩兒已經掉下來了。

04 那個男孩兒快要從水裡出來了。
    那個男孩兒正要滑水。
    那個男孩兒在滑水。
    那個男孩兒已經滑進水裡了。

05 那個男孩兒快要跳了。
    那個男孩兒在跳。
    那些人快要過街了。
    那些人在過街。

06 那個男孩兒在看著那個球。
    那個男孩兒正要扔那個球。
    那個男人正要把那個男孩兒抛起來。
    那個男人已經把那個男孩兒抛了起來。

07 那個女人正要把甚麼東西放進袋子裡。
    那個女人已經把甚麼東西放進了袋子裡。
    那個女人正要親那個男人。
    那個女人在親那個男人。

08 那個女人正要走進那家商店。
    那個女人正走進那家商店。
    那個男人正要關轎車的行李箱。
    那個男人已經把轎車的行李箱關上了。

09 那些人要上臺階。
    那些人在上臺階。
    那些人已經上完了臺階。
    那些人在下臺階。

10 那兩個人要下臺階。
    那兩個人在下臺階。
    那兩個人已經走下了臺階。
    那兩個人在上臺階。

6-02

xiàn zài jìn xíng shí, xiàn zài wán chéng shí jí yòng "yào", "zhèng yào", "kuài yào" biǎo shì de yī bān jiāng lái shí

01 nà gè nán rén zhèng yào shàng jiào chē.
nà gè nán rén zài shàng jiào chē.
nà gè nán rén zhèng yào shàng mǎ chē.
nà gè nán rén zài shàng mǎ chē.

02 nà gè nán háir zhèng yào tiào.
nà gè nán háir zài tiào.
nà gè nán háir yǐ jīng tiào le.
nà gè nán háir yào rēng qiú.

03 nà gè nǚ rén zhèng yào xiě zì.
nà gè nǚ rén zài xiě zì.
nà gè nán háir zhèng zài wǎng xià diào.
nà gè nán háir yǐ jīng diào xià lái le.

04 nà gè nán háir kuài yào cóng shuǐ lǐ chū lái le.
nà gè nán háir zhèng yào huá shuǐ.
nà gè nán háir zài huá shuǐ.
nà gè nán háir yǐ jīng huá jìn shuǐ lǐ le.

05 nà gè nán háir kuài yào tiào le.
nà gè nán háir zài tiào.
nà xiē rén kuài yào guò jiē le.
nà xiē rén zài guò jiē.

06 nà gè nán háir zài kàn zhe nà gè qiú.
nà gè nán háir zhèng yào rēng nà gè qiú.
nà gè nán rén zhèng yào bǎ nà gè nán háir pāo qǐ lái.
nà gè nán rén yǐ jīng bǎ nà gè nán háir pāo le qǐ lái.

07 nà gè nǚ rén zhèng yào bǎ shén me dōng xi fàng jìn dài zi lǐ.
nà gè nǚ rén yǐ jīng bǎ shén me dōng xi fàng jìn le dài zi lǐ.
nà gè nǚ rén zhèng yào qīn nà gè nán rén.
nà gè nǚ rén zài qīn nà gè nán rén.

08 nà gè nǚ rén zhèng yào zǒu jìn nà jiā shāng diàn.
nà gè nǚ rén zhèng zǒu jìn nà jiā shāng diàn.
nà gè nán rén zhèng yào guān jiào chē de xíng lǐ xiāng.
nà gè nán rén yǐ jīng bǎ jiào chē de xíng lǐ xiāng guān shàng le.

09 nà xiē rén yào shàng tái jiē.
nà xiē rén zài shàng tái jiē.
nà xiē rén yǐ jīng shàng wán le tái jiē.
nà xiē rén zài xià tái jiē.

10 nà liǎng gè rén yào xià tái jiē.
nà liǎng gè rén zài xià tái jiē.
nà liǎng gè rén yǐ jīng zǒu xià le tái jiē.
nà liǎng gè rén zài shàng tái jiē.

6-03

描述人物特征

01 那位老人长着白胡子。
那个秃顶的人正看着一块地毯。
那个秃顶的人留着胡子。
戴红领结的那个男人留着胡子。

02 那个男人留着胡子。
那个男人秃顶。
那个男人没有留胡子。
那个女人没有长胡子。

03 这两个人穿着制服。
这两个人没有穿制服。
这个男人穿着制服。
这个男人没有穿制服。

04 这个人唇上留着胡子，可是没有留络腮胡子。
这个人留着络腮胡子，可是唇上没有留胡子。
这个人唇上和下巴上都留着胡子。
这个人唇上和下巴上都没有长胡子。

05 这座塑像唇上留着胡子。
这座塑像留着络腮胡子。
那个留长头发的女人戴着一只耳环。
那个留短头发的女人戴着一只耳环。

06 这对夫妇穿戴得很正式。
这对夫妇穿戴得很随便。
这些个男人穿戴得很正式。
这些男人穿戴得很随便。

07 这个女孩儿长着黑头发，黑皮肤。
那个穿红毛衣的男孩儿长着黑皮肤。
长着红头发的那个女孩儿长着白皮肤。
那个穿黑衬衫的男孩儿长着白皮肤。

08 哪个年轻女人长着黑皮肤？
哪个年轻女人长着白皮肤？
哪个小伙子长着黑皮肤？
哪个小伙子长着白皮肤？

09 那个女人长着白皮肤，留着短发。
那个女人长着白皮肤，留着长长的金发。
这个人长着黑皮肤，留着短发。
这个人长着黑皮肤，留着长发。

10 这个男人长着黑皮肤，唇上留着胡子。
这个男人长着白皮肤，留着络腮胡子。
这个男人长着白皮肤，唇上和下巴上都没留胡子。
这个男人长着黑皮肤，唇上和下巴上都没留胡子。

6-03

描述人物特征

01 那位老人長著白胡子。
那個禿頂的人正看著一塊地毯。
那個禿頂的人留著胡子。
戴紅領結的那個男人留著胡子。

02 那個男人留著胡子。
那個男人禿頂。
那個男人沒有留胡子。
那個女人沒有長胡子。

03 這兩個人穿著制服。
這兩個人沒有穿制服。
這個男人穿著制服。
這個男人沒有穿制服。

04 這個人唇上留著胡子，可是沒有留絡鰓胡子。
這個人留著絡鰓胡子，可是唇上沒有留胡子。
這個人唇上和下巴上都留著胡子。
這個人唇上和下巴上都沒有長胡子。

05 這座塑像唇上留著胡子。
這座塑像留著絡鰓胡子。
那個留長頭髮的女人戴著一隻耳環。
那個留短頭髮的女人戴著一隻耳環。

06 這對夫婦穿戴得很正式。
這對夫婦穿戴得很隨便。
這些個男人穿戴得很正式。
這些男人穿戴得很隨便。

07 這個女孩兒長著黑頭髮，黑皮膚。
那個穿紅毛衣的男孩兒長著黑皮膚。
長著紅頭髮的那個女孩兒長著白皮膚。
那個穿黑襯衫的男孩兒長著白皮膚。

08 哪個年輕女人長著黑皮膚？
哪個年輕女人長著白皮膚？
哪個小夥子長著黑皮膚？
哪個小夥子長著白皮膚？

09 那個女人長著白皮膚，留著短髮。
那個女人長著白皮膚，留著長長的金髮。
這個人長著黑皮膚，留著短髮。
這個人長著黑皮膚，留著長髮。

10 這個男人長著黑皮膚，唇上留著胡子。
這個男人長著白皮膚，留著絡腮胡子。
這個男人長著白皮膚，唇上和下巴上都沒留胡子。
這個男人長著黑皮膚，唇上和下巴上都沒留胡子。

6-03

miáo shù rén wù tè zhēng

01 nà wèi lǎo rén zhǎng zhe bái hú zi.
    nà gè tū dǐng de rén zhèng kàn zhe yī kuài dì tǎn.
    nà gè tū dǐng de rén liú zhe hú zi.
    dài hóng lǐng jié de nà gè nán rén liú zhe hú zi.

02 nà gè nán rén liú zhe hú zi.
    nà gè nán rén tū dǐng.
    nà gè nán rén méi yǒu liú hú zi.
    nà gè nǚ rén méi yǒu zhǎng hú zi.

03 zhè liǎng gè rén chuān zhe zhì fú.
    zhè liǎng gè rén méi yǒu chuān zhì fú.
    zhè gè nán rén chuān zhe zhì fú.
    zhè gè nán rén méi yǒu chuān zhì fú.

04 zhè gè rén chún shàng liú zhe hú zi, kě shì méi yǒu liú luò sāi hú zi.
    zhè gè rén liú zhe luò sāi hú zi, kě shì chún shàng méi yǒu liú hú zi.
    zhè gè rén chún shàng hé xià ba shàng dōu liú zhe hú zi.
    zhè gè rén chún shàng hé xià ba shàng dōu méi yǒu zhǎng hú zi.

05 zhè zuò sù xiàng chún shàng liú zhe hú zi.
    zhè zuò sù xiàng liú zhe luò sāi hú zi.
    nà gè liú cháng tóu fà de nǚ rén dài zhe yī zhī ěr huán.
    nà gè liú duǎn tóu fà de nǚ rén dài zhe yī zhī ěr huán.

06 zhè duì fū fù chuān dài de hěn zhèng shì.
    zhè duì fū fù chuān dài de hěn suí biàn.
    zhè xiē gè nán rén chuān dài de hěn zhèng shì.
    zhè xiē nán rén chuān dài de hěn suí biàn.

07 zhè gè nǚ háir zhǎng zhe hēi tóu fà, hēi pí fū.
    nà gè chuān hóng máo yī de nán háir zhǎng zhe hēi pí fū.
    zhǎng zhe hóng tóu fà de nà gè nǚ háir zhǎng zhe bái pí fū.
    nà gè chuān hēi chèn shān de nán háir zhǎng zhe bái pí fū.

08 nǎ gè nián qīng nǚ rén zhǎng zhe hēi pí fū?
    nǎ gè nián qīng nǚ rén zhǎng zhe bái pí fū?
    nǎ gè xiǎo huǒ zi zhǎng zhe hēi pí fū?
    nǎ gè xiǎo huǒ zi zhǎng zhe bái pí fū?

09 nà gè nǚ rén zhǎng zhe bái pí fū, liú zhe duǎn fà.
    nà gè nǚ rén zhǎng zhe bái pí fū, liú zhe cháng cháng de jīn fà.
    zhè gè rén zhǎng zhe hēi pí fū, liú zhe duǎn fà.
    zhè gè rén zhǎng zhe hēi pí fū, liú zhe cháng fà.

10 zhè gè nán rén zhǎng zhe hēi pí fū, chún shàng liú zhe hú zi.
    zhè gè nán rén zhǎng zhe bái pí fū, liú zhe luò sāi hú zi.
    zhè gè nán rén zhǎng zhe bái pí fū, chún shàng hé xià ba shàng dōu méi liú hú zi.
    zhè gè nán rén zhǎng zhe hēi pí fū, chún shàng hé xià ba shàng dōu méi liú hú zi.

使用量词: 副、双、卷、袋等

01　一袋鱼
　　一袋葡萄
　　许多袋面包
　　一个空纸袋

02　一卷纸巾
　　一张纸巾
　　一袋炸薯片
　　一塑料袋葡萄

03　满满一瓶子果汁
　　半瓶子果汁
　　一个空玻璃瓶
　　一卷手纸

04　两卷纸巾
　　满满一纸袋
　　一个空塑料袋
　　一个空纸袋

05　一个空玻璃瓶
　　满满一瓶子
　　许多面包
　　六块面包

06　一卷纸巾
　　一卷手纸
　　满满一纸袋
　　一个空纸袋

07　一个西红柿
　　许多西红柿
　　许多箱苹果
　　几块西瓜

08　一双靴子
　　一副太阳镜
　　几篮苹果
　　几箱苹果

09　一副太阳镜
　　一副手套和一双鞋
　　一双靴子
　　一副色子

10　一束花儿
　　三束花儿
　　一个香蕉
　　几串香蕉

6-04

使用量詞：副、雙、卷、袋等

01　一袋魚
　　一袋葡萄
　　許多袋麵包
　　一個空紙袋

02　一卷紙巾
　　一張紙巾
　　一袋炸薯片
　　一塑料袋葡萄

03　滿滿一瓶子果汁
　　半瓶子果汁
　　一個空玻璃瓶
　　一卷手紙

04　兩卷紙巾
　　滿滿一紙袋
　　一個空塑料袋
　　一個空紙袋

05　一個空玻璃瓶
　　滿滿一瓶子
　　許多麵包
　　六塊麵包

06　一卷紙巾
　　一卷手紙
　　滿滿一紙袋
　　一個空紙袋

07　一個西紅柿
　　許多西紅柿
　　許多箱苹果
　　幾塊西瓜

08　一雙靴子
　　一副太陽鏡
　　幾籃苹果
　　幾箱苹果

09　一副太陽鏡
　　一副手套和一雙鞋
　　一雙靴子
　　一副色子

10　一束花兒
　　三束花兒
　　一個香蕉
　　幾串香蕉

6-04

shǐ yòng liàng cí: fù, shuāng, juǎn, dài děng

01 yī dài yú
    yī dài pú táo
    xǔ duō dài miàn bāo
    yī gè kōng zhǐ dài

02 yī juǎn zhǐ jīn
    yī zhāng zhǐ jīn
    yī dài zhá shǔ piàn
    yī sù liào dài pú táo

03 mǎn mǎn yī píng zi guǒ zhī
    bàn píng zi guǒ zhī
    yī gè kōng bō li píng
    yī juǎn shǒu zhǐ

04 liǎng juǎn zhǐ jīn
    mǎn mǎn yī zhǐ dài
    yī gè kōng sù liào dài
    yī gè kōng zhǐ dài

05 yī gè kōng bō li píng
    mǎn mǎn yī píng zi
    xǔ duō miàn bāo
    liù kuài miàn bāo

06 yī juǎn zhǐ jīn
    yī juǎn shǒu zhǐ
    mǎn mǎn yī zhǐ dài
    yī gè kōng zhǐ dài

07 yī gè xī hóng shì
    xǔ duō xī hóng shì
    xǔ duō xiāng píng guǒ
    jǐ kuài xī guā

08 yī shuāng xuē zi
    yī fù tài yáng jìng
    jǐ lán píng guǒ
    jǐ xiāng píng guǒ

09 yī fù tài yáng jìng
    yī fù shǒu tào hé yī shuāng xié
    yī shuāng xuē zi
    yī fù shǎi zi

10 yī shù huār
    sān shù huār
    yī gè xiāng jiāo
    jǐ chuàn xiāng jiāo

6-05

運用"既不 ... 也不"、"兩个 ... 都不"、
"兩个 ... 都"

01 那个女人在骑马。
　　那个女人现在不骑马了。
　　那些男人在骑自行车。
　　那些男人现在不骑自行车了。

02 那些男人在跑。
　　那两个男人现在不跑了。
　　那两个小伙子在唱歌。
　　那两个小伙子现在不唱歌了。

03 那个男人和那个女人在唱歌。
　　那个男人和那个女人现在不唱歌了。
　　那个小丑在打扮。
　　那个小丑已经打扮完了。

04 这个女人在吃东西。
　　这个女人在打电话。
　　这个女人既不在打电话，也不在吃东西。
　　这个男人既不在打电话，也不在吃东西。

05 这个女人一边唱歌，一边弹琴。
　　这个女人既不在唱歌，也不在弹琴。
　　这两个女人一边敲着鼓，一边笑着。
　　这两个女人既不在敲鼓，也不在笑。

06 两个人都在唱歌。
　　两个人都不在唱歌。
　　这些人中只有一个在唱歌。
　　六个人都在唱歌。

07 穿白衣服的那个男人正站在人行道上。
　　穿白衣服的那个男人现在不在人行道上站着了。
　　那辆公共汽车正停在人行道上。
　　那辆公共汽车现在不在人行道上停着了。

08 这四个人都在走。
　　这四个人都不在走。
　　这三个人都在走。
　　这三个人都不在走。

09 那两个小伙子都在唱歌。他们俩谁都不在和女人亲
　　吻。
　　那个男人和那个女人都不在讲话。
　　那个男人和那个女人都不在亲吻。
　　那个穿黑 T 恤衫的男人在站着，他的朋友们都没站
　　着。

10 那个男人和那个女人都打着伞。
　　那个男人和那个女人都没打着伞。
　　那个男人和那个男孩儿都戴着帽子。
　　那个男人和那个男孩儿都没戴帽子。

6-05

運用"既不…也不"、"兩個…都不"、
"兩個…都"

01 那個女人在騎馬。
　　那個女人現在不騎馬了。
　　那些男人在騎自行車。
　　那些男人現在不騎自行車了。

02 那些男人在跑。
　　那兩個男人現在不跑了。
　　那兩個小夥子在唱歌。
　　那兩個小夥子現在不唱歌了。

03 那個男人和那個女人在唱歌。
　　那個男人和那個女人現在不唱歌了。
　　那個小醜在打扮。
　　那個小醜已經打扮完了。

04 這個女人在吃東西。
　　這個女人在打電話。
　　這個女人既不在打電話，也不在吃東西。
　　這個男人既不在打電話，也不在吃東西。

05 這個女人一邊唱歌，一邊彈琴。
　　這個女人既不在唱歌，也不在彈琴。
　　這兩個女人一邊敲著鼓，一邊笑著。
　　這兩個女人既不在敲鼓，也不在笑。

06 兩個人都在唱歌。
　　兩個人都不在唱歌。
　　這些人中只有一個在唱歌。
　　六個人都在唱歌。

07 穿白衣服的那個男人正站在人行道上。
　　穿白衣服的那個男人現在不在人行道上站著了。
　　那輛公共汽車正停在人行道上。
　　那輛公共汽車現在不在人行道上停著了。

08 這四個人都在走。
　　這四個人都不在走。
　　這三個人都在走。
　　這三個人都不在走。

09 那兩個小夥子都在唱歌，他們倆誰都不在和女人親
　　吻。
　　那個男人和那個女人都不在講話。
　　那個男人和那個女人都不在親吻。
　　那個穿黑 T 恤衫的男人在站著，他的朋友們都沒站
　　著。

10 那個男人和那個女人都打著傘。
　　那個男人和那個女人都沒打著傘。
　　那個男人和那個男孩兒都戴著帽子。
　　那個男人和那個男孩兒都沒戴帽子。

6-05

yùn yòng "jì bù...yě bù" , "liǎng gè...dōu bù", "liǎng gè...dōu"

01 nà gè nǔ rén zài qí mǎ.
    nà gè nǔ rén xiàn zài bù qí mǎ le.
    nà xiē nán rén zài qí zì xíng chē.
    nà xiē nán rén xiàn zài bù qí zì xíng chē le.

02 nà xiē nán rén zài pǎo.
    nà liǎng gè nán rén xiàn zài bù pǎo le.
    nà liǎng gè xiǎo huǒ zi zài chàng gē.
    nà liǎng gè xiǎo huǒ zi xiàn zài bú chàng gē le.

03 nà gè nán rén hé nà gè nǔ rén zài chàng gē.
    nà gè nán rén hé nà gè nǔ rén xiàn zài bú chàng gē le.
    nà gè xiǎo chǒu zài dǎ bàn.
    nà gè xiǎo chǒu yǐ jīng dǎ bàn wán le.

04 zhè gè nǔ rén zài chī dōng xi.
    zhè gè nǔ rén zài dǎ diàn huà.
    zhè gè nǔ rén jì bú zài dǎ diàn huà, yě bú zài chī dōng xi.
    zhè gè nán rén jì bú zài dǎ diàn huà, yě bú zài chī dōng xi.

05 zhè gè nǔ rén yī biān chàng gē, yī biān tán qín.
    zhè gè nǔ rén jì bú zài chàng gē, yě bú zài tán qín.
    zhè liǎng gè nǔ rén yī biān qiāo zhe gǔ, yī biān xiào zhe.
    zhè liǎng gè nǔ rén jì bú zài qiāo gǔ, yě bú zài xiào.

06 liǎng gè rén dōu zài chàng gē.
    liǎng gè rén dōu bú zài chàng gē.
    zhè xiē rén zhōng zhǐ yǒu yī gè zài chàng gē.
    liù gè rén dōu zài chàng gē.

07 chuān bái yī fu de nà gè nán rén zhèng zhàn zài rén xíng dào shàng.
    chuān bái yī fu de nà gè nán rén xiàn zài bú zài rén xíng dào shàng zhàn zhe le.
    nà liàng gōng gòng qì chē zhèng tíng zài rén xíng dào shàng.
    nà liàng gōng gòng qì chē xiàn zài bú zài rén xíng dào shàng tíng zhe le.

08 zhè sì gè rén dōu zài zǒu.
    zhè sì gè rén dōu bú zài zǒu.
    zhè sān gè rén dōu zài zǒu.
    zhè sān gè rén dōu bú zài zǒu.

09 nà liǎng gè xiǎo huǒ zi dōu zài chàng gē, tā mén liǎ shéi dōu bú zài hé nǔ rén qīn wěn.
    nà gè nán rén hé nà gè nǔ rén dōu bú zài jiǎng huà.
    nà gè nán rén hé nà gè nǔ rén dōu bú zài qīn wěn.
    nà gè chuān hēi T xù shān de nán rén zài zhàn zhe, tā de péng yǒu men dōu méi zhàn zhe.

10 nà gè nán rén hé nà gè nǔ rén dōu dǎ zhe sǎn.
    nà gè nán rén hé nà gè nǔ rén dōu méi dǎ zhe sǎn.
    nà gè nán rén hé nà gè nán háir dōu dài zhe mào zi.
    nà gè nán rén hé nà gè nán háir dōu méi dài mào zi.

动词的现在时和过去时："在…"、"刚才…"

01 这些人在参加自行车比赛。
 这些人刚才在参加自行车比赛。
 那个小丑戴着帽子。
 那个小丑刚才戴着帽子。

02 那个年轻妇女在看书。
 那个年轻妇女刚才在看书。
 那个男孩儿在钓鱼。
 那个男孩儿刚才在钓鱼。

03 那个女孩儿在跳绳。
 那个女孩儿刚才在跳绳。
 那个女人在喝东西。
 那个女人刚才在喝东西。

04 爸爸和两个儿子在挖地。
 爸爸和两个儿子刚才在挖地。
 那只狗在望着那本书。
 那只狗刚才望着那本书。

05 那个男人穿着一件衬衫，可是衬衫太小了。
 那个男人刚才穿着一件衬衫，可是衬衫太小了。
 那个男人穿着自己的衬衫。
 那个男人刚才穿着这件衬衫，可是现在这件衬衫穿在
　 那个男孩儿身上。

06 那个男人在弹吉他。
 那个男人刚才在弹吉他。
 那个女人拿着吉他。
 那个女人刚才拿着吉他，可是现在吉他拿在那个男孩
　 儿手里。

07 交通灯是红色的。
 交通灯刚才是红色的。
 那个男人在爬梯子。
 那个男人已经爬着梯子上去了。

08 有两个人在开车。
 有人刚才在开车，可是现在不开了。
 有人要开车。
 汽车钥匙

09 这只狗在打哈欠。
 这只狗叼着一个飞盘。
 这个小伙子在打哈欠。
 这个小伙子在吃东西。

10 这就是刚才打哈欠的那只狗。
 这就是刚才叼着飞盘的那只狗。
 这就是刚才打哈欠的那个小伙子。
 这就是刚才吃东西的那个小伙子。

6-06

動詞的現在時和過去時："在…"、"剛才…"

01 這些人在參加自行車比賽。
 這些人剛才在參加自行車比賽。
 那個小醜戴著帽子。
 那個小醜剛才戴著帽子。

02 那個年輕婦女在看書。
 那個年輕婦女剛才在看書。
 那個男孩兒在釣魚。
 那個男孩兒剛才在釣魚。

03 那個女孩兒在跳繩。
 那個女孩兒剛才在跳繩。
 那個女人在喝東西。
 那個女人剛才在喝東西。

04 爸爸和兩個兒子在挖地。
 爸爸和兩個兒子剛才在挖地。
 那隻狗在望著那本書。
 那隻狗剛才望著那本書。

05 那個男人穿著一件襯衫，可是襯衫太小了。
 那個男人剛才穿著一件襯衫，可是襯衫太小了。
 那個男人穿著自己的襯衫。
 那個男人剛才穿著這件襯衫，可是現在這件襯衫穿在
　 那個男孩兒身上。

06 那個男人在彈吉他。
 那個男人剛才在彈吉他。
 那個女人拿著吉他。
 那個女人剛才拿著吉他，可是現在吉他拿在那個男孩
　 兒手里。

07 交通燈是紅色的。
 交通燈剛才是紅色的。
 那個男人在爬梯子。
 那個男人已經爬著梯子上去了。

08 有兩個人在開車。
 有人剛才在開車，可是現在不開了。
 有人要開車。
 汽車鑰匙

09 這隻狗在打呵欠。
 這隻狗叼著一個飛盤。
 這個小夥子在打呵欠。
 這個小夥子在吃東西。

10 這就是剛才打呵欠的那隻狗。
 這就是剛才叼著飛盤的那隻狗。
 這就是剛才打呵欠的那個小夥子。
 這就是剛才吃東西的那個小夥子。

6-06

dòng cí de xiàn zài shí hé guò qù shí: "zài...", "gāng cái..."

01 zhè xiē rén zài cān jiā zì xíng chē bǐ sài.
zhè xiē rén gāng cái zài cān jiā zì xíng chē bǐ sài.
nà gè xiǎo chǒu dài zhe mào zi.
nà gè xiǎo chǒu gāng cái dài zhe mào zi.

02 nà gè nián qīng fù nǚ zài kàn shū.
nà gè nián qīng fù nǚ gāng cái zài kàn shū.
nà gè nán háir zài diào yú.
nà gè nán háir gāng cái zài diào yú.

03 nà gè nǚ háir zài tiào shéng.
nà gè nǚ háir gāng cái zài tiào shéng.
nà gè nǚ rén zài hē dōng xi.
nà gè nǚ rén gāng cái zài hē dōng xi.

04 bà bà hé liǎng gè ér zi zài wā dì.
bà bà hé liǎng gè ér zi gāng cái zài wā dì.
nà zhī gǒu zài wàng zhe nà běn shū.
nà zhī gǒu gāng cái wàng zhe nà běn shū.

05 nà gè nán rén chuān zhe yī jiàn chèn shān, kě shì chèn shān tài xiǎo le.
nà gè nán rén gāng cái chuān zhe yī jiàn chèn shān, kě shì chèn shān tài xiǎo le.
nà gè nán rén chuān zhe zì jǐ de chèn shān.
nà gè nán rén gāng cái chuān zhe zhè jiàn chèn shān, kě shì xiàn zài zhè jiàn chèn shān chuān zài nà gè
    nán háir shēn shàng.

06 nà gè nán rén zài tán jí tā.
nà gè nán rén gāng cái zài tán jí tā.
nà gè nǚ rén ná zhe jí tā.
nà gè nǚ rén gāng cái ná zhe jí ta, kě shì xiàn zài jí ta ná zài nà gè nán háir shǒu lǐ.

07 jiāo tōng dēng shì hóng sè de.
jiāo tōng dēng gāng cái shì hóng sè de.
nà gè nán rén zài pá tī zi.
nà gè nán rén yǐ jīng pá zhe tī zi shàng qù le.

08 yǒu liǎng gè rén zài kāi chē.
yǒu rén gāng cái zài kāi chē, kě shì xiàn zài bù kāi le.
yǒu rén yào kāi chē.
qì chē yào shi

09 zhè zhī gǒu zài dǎ hā qiàn.
zhè zhī gǒu diāo zhe yī gè fēi pán.
zhè gè xiǎo huǒ zi zài dǎ hā qiàn.
zhè gè xiǎo huǒ zi zài chī dōng xi.

10 zhè jiù shì gāng cái dǎ hā qiàn de nà zhī gǒu.
zhè jiù shì gāng cái diāo zhe fēi pán de nà zhī gǒu.
zhè jiù shì gāng cái dǎ hā qiàn de nà gè xiǎo huǒ zi.
zhè jiù shì gāng cái chī dōng xi de nà gè xiǎo huǒ zi.

姓名

01 两个男人，一个女人
   四个男人
   一个男人
   三个男人，一个女人

02 左边的那个男人是查尔斯王子。
   左边的那个男人是罗纳德．里根。
   那个讲话的男人是米哈依尔．戈尔巴乔夫。
   同歌手们在一起的那个女人是南西．里根。

03 左边那个男人的名字叫查尔斯。
   左边那个男人的名字叫罗纳德。
   那个男人的名字叫米哈依尔。
   站在歌手们前面的那个女人的名字叫南西。

04 查尔斯王子正同罗纳德．里根握手。
   罗纳德．里根正同三个男人站在一起。
   米哈依尔．戈尔巴乔夫在讲话。
   南西．里根正朝歌手们微笑。

05 这是桑德拉，她是一个小姑娘。
   这是霍克，他是一个男孩儿。
   这是莫丽萨，她是一个女人。
   这是普拉诺夫，他是一个男人。

06 那个小姑娘儿说："我叫桑德拉，四岁了。"
   那个男孩儿说："我叫霍克，十岁了。"
   那个女人说："我叫莫丽萨，二十二岁。"
   那个男人说："我叫普拉诺夫，二十三岁。"

07 莫丽萨想要上台阶。
   莫丽萨正在上台阶。
   莫丽萨正在下台阶。
   莫丽萨已经下了台阶。

08 桑德拉拿着一个气球。
   霍克拿着一个气球。
   普拉诺夫站在树上。
   莫丽萨站在树上。

09 桑德拉说："看看我的气球！"
   霍克说："看看我的气球！"
   普拉诺夫说："瞧，我站在树上！"
   莫丽萨说："瞧，我站在树上！"

10 莫丽萨和普拉诺夫在上墙。
   莫丽萨和普拉诺夫站在墙上。
   莫丽萨和普拉诺夫刚刚从墙上跳下来，脚还没落地。
   莫丽萨和普拉诺夫已经从墙上跳到了地上。

6-07

姓名

01 兩個男人，一個女人
   四個男人
   一個男人
   三個男人，一個女人

02 左邊的那個男人是查爾斯王子。
   左邊的那個男人是羅納德．里根。
   那個講話的男人是米哈依爾．戈爾巴喬夫。
   同歌手們在一起的那個女人是南西．里根。

03 左邊那個男人的名字叫查爾斯。
   左邊那個男人的名字叫羅納德。
   那個男人的名字叫米哈依爾。
   站在歌手們前面的那個女人的名字叫南西。

04 查爾斯王子正同羅納德．里根握手。
   羅納德．里根正同三個男人站在一起。
   米哈依爾．戈爾巴喬夫在講話。
   南西．里根正朝歌手們微笑。

05 這是桑德拉，她是一個小姑娘。
   這是霍克，他是一個男孩兒。
   這是莫麗薩，她是一個女人。
   這是普拉諾夫，他是一個男人。

06 那個小姑娘兒說："我叫桑德拉，四歲了。"
   那個男孩說："我叫霍克，十歲了。"
   那個女人說："我叫莫麗薩，二十二歲。"
   那個男人說："我叫普拉諾夫，二十三歲。"

07 莫麗薩想要上臺階。
   莫麗薩正在上臺階。
   莫麗薩正在下臺階。
   莫麗薩已經下了臺階。

08 桑德拉拿著一個氣球。
   霍克拿著一個氣球。
   普拉諾夫站在樹上。
   莫麗薩站在樹上。

09 桑德拉說："看看我的氣球！"
   霍克說："看看我的氣球！"
   普拉諾夫說："瞧，我站在樹上！"
   莫麗薩說："瞧，我站在樹上！"

10 莫麗薩和普拉諾夫在上牆。
   莫麗薩和普拉諾夫站在牆上。
   莫麗薩和普拉諾夫剛剛從牆上跳下來，腳還沒落地。
   莫麗薩和普拉諾夫已經從牆上跳到了地上。

6-07

xìng míng

01 liǎng gè nán rén, yī gè nǚ rén
   sì gè nán rén
   yī gè nán rén
   sān gè nán rén, yī gè nǚ rén

02 zuǒ biān de nà gè nán rén shì chá ěr sī wáng zǐ.
   zuǒ biān de nà gè nán rén shì luó nà dé . lǐ gēn.
   nà gè jiǎng huà de nán rén shì mǐ hā yī ěr . gē ěr bā qiáo fū.
   tóng gē shǒu men zài yī qǐ de nà gè nǚ rén shì nán xī . lǐ gēn.

03 zuǒ biān nà gè nán rén de míng zi jiào chá ěr sī.
   zuǒ biān nà gè nán rén de míng zi jiào luó nà dé.
   nà gè nán rén de míng zi jiào mǐ hā yī ěr.
   zhàn zài gē shǒu men qián miàn de nà gè nǚ rén de míng zi jiào nán xī.

04 chá ěr sī wáng zǐ zhèng tóng luó nà dé . lǐ gēn wò shǒu.
   luó nà dé . lǐ gēn zhèng tóng sān gè nán rén zhàn zài yī qǐ.
   mǐ hā yī ěr . gē ěr bā qiáo fū zài jiǎng huà.
   nán xī . lǐ gēn zhèng cháo gē shǒu men wēi xiào.

05 zhè shì sāng dé lā, tā shì yī gè xiǎo gū niang.
   zhè shì huò kè, tā shì yī gè nán háir.
   zhè shì mò lì sà, tā shì yī gè nǚ rén.
   zhè shì pǔ lā nuò fū, tā shì yī gè nán rén.

06 nà gè xiǎo gū niáng shuō: "wǒ jiào sāng dé lā, sì suì le."
   nà gè nán háir shuō: "wǒ jiào huò kè, shí suì le."
   nà gè nǚ rén shuō: "wǒ jiào mò lì sà, èr shí èr suì."
   nà gè nán rén shuō: "wǒ jiào pǔ lā nuò fū, èr shí sān suì."

07 mò lì sà xiǎng yào shàng tái jiē.
   mò lì sà zhèng zài shàng tái jiē.
   mò lì sà zhèng zài xià tái jiē.
   mò lì sà yǐ jīng xià le tái jiē.

08 sāng dé lā ná zhe yī gè qì qiú.
   huò kè ná zhe yī gè qì qiú.
   pǔ lā nuò fū zhàn zài shù shàng.
   mò lì sà zhàn zài shù shàng.

09 sāng dé lā shuō: "kàn kàn wǒ de qì qiú!"
   huò kè shuō: "kàn kàn wǒ de qì qiú!"
   pǔ lā nuò fū shuō: "qiáo, wǒ zhàn zài shù shàng!"
   mò lì sà shuō: "qiáo, wǒ zhàn zài shù shàng!"

10 mò lì sà hé pǔ lā nuò fū zài shàng qiáng.
   mò lì sà hé pǔ lā nuò fū zhàn zài qiáng shàng.
   mò lì sà hé pǔ lā nuò fū gāng gāng cóng qiáng shàng tiào xià lái, jiǎo hái méi luò dì.
   mò lì sà hé pǔ lā nuò fū yǐ jīng cóng qiáng shàng tiào dào le dì shàng.

6-08

运用现在进行时，现在完成时及用 "要"、"正要"、"快要" 表示的一般将来时

01 那个男人正要亲他的妻子。
那个男人在亲他的妻子。
那个女人要扔球。
那个女人在扔球。

02 那个小姑娘在同那个男人说话。
那个女人没有和谁说话，她在做饭。
那个女人正坐在那个男人身上。
那个女人正坐在摇椅上。

03 那个女人在骑马。
没人骑马。
没人骑车。
有人在骑车。

04 那匹马在亲那个女人。
那匹马谁也没亲。
那个男孩儿在踢球。
没人踢球。

05 那匹马在亲那个女人。
没人在亲那个女人。
那个男孩儿在踢球。
那个男孩儿什么都没踢。

06 那个男孩儿要摔倒了。
那个男孩儿已经摔倒了。
那个男人在爬梯子。
那个男人已经爬着梯子上去了。

07 那些男人快要赛跑了。
那些男人在赛跑。
那两个男人已经赛跑完了。
那些女人快要赛跑了。

08 那个女人正要把那只猫抱起来。
那个女人正把那只猫抱起来。
那个女人已经把那只猫抱了起来，现在正把猫抱在怀里。
那个女人在看报纸。

09 那个女人正要穿连衣裙。
那个女人在穿连衣裙。
那个女人已经穿上了连衣裙。
那个男人在穿 T 恤衫。

10 那个小姑娘要把水浇到头上。
那个小姑娘正把水浇到头上。
那个女人正要看书。
那个女人在看书。

6-08

運用現在進行時，現在完成時及用 "要"、"正要"、"快要" 表示的一般將來時

01 那個男人正要親他的妻子。
那個男人在親他的妻子。
那個女人要扔球。
那個女人在扔球。

02 那個小姑娘在同那個男人說話。
那個女人沒有和誰說話，她在做飯。
那個女人正坐在那個男人身上。
那個女人正坐在搖椅上。

03 那個女人在騎馬。
沒人騎馬。
沒人騎車。
有人在騎車。

04 那匹馬在親那個女人。
那匹馬誰也沒親。
那個男孩兒在踢球。
沒人踢球。

05 那匹馬在親那個女人。
沒人在親那個女人。
那個男孩兒在踢球。
那個男孩兒甚麼都沒踢。

06 那個男孩兒要摔倒了。
那個男孩兒已經摔倒了。
那個男人在爬梯子。
那個男人已經爬著梯子上去了。

07 那些男人快要賽跑了。
那些男人在賽跑。
那兩個男人已經賽跑完了。
那些女人快要賽跑了。

08 那個女人正要把那隻貓抱起來。
那個女人正把那隻貓抱起來。
那個女人已經把那隻貓抱了起來，現在正把貓抱在懷裡。
那個女人在看報紙。

09 那個女人正要穿連衣裙。
那個女人在穿連衣裙。
那個女人已經穿上了連衣裙。
那個男人在穿 T 恤衫。

10 那個小姑娘要把水澆到頭上。
那個小姑娘正把水澆到頭上。
那個女人正要看書。
那個女人在看書。

6-08

yùn yòng xiàn zài jìn xíng shí, xiàn zài wán chéng shí jí yòng "yào", "zhèng yào", "kuài yào" biǎo shì de yī bān jiāng lái shí

01 nà gè nán rén zhèng yào qīn tā de qī zi.
    nà gè nán rén zài qīn tā de qī zi.
    nà gè nǚ rén yào rēng qiú.
    nà gè nǚ rén zài rēng qiú.

02 nà gè xiǎo gū niang zài tóng nà gè nán rén shuō huà.
    nà gè nǚ rén méi yǒu hé shéi shuō huà, tā zài zuò fàn.
    nà gè nǚ rén zhèng zuò zài nà gè nán rén shēn shàng.
    nà gè nǚ rén zhèng zuò zài yáo yǐ shàng.

03 nà gè nǚ rén zài qí mǎ.
    méi rén qí mǎ.
    méi rén qí chē.
    yǒu rén zài qí chē.

04 nà pǐ mǎ zài qīn nà gè nǚ rén.
    nà pǐ mǎ shéi yě méi qīn.
    nà gè nán háir zài tī qiú.
    méi rén tī qiú.

05 nà pǐ mǎ zài qīn nà gè nǚ rén.
    méi rén zài qīn nà gè nǚ rén.
    nà gè nán háir zài tī qiú.
    nà gè nán háir shén me dōu méi tī.

06 nà gè nán háir yào shuāi dǎo le.
    nà gè nán háir yǐ jīng shuāi dǎo le.
    nà gè nán rén zài pá tī zi.
    nà gè nán rén yǐ jīng pá zhe tī zi shàng qù le.

07 nà xiē nán rén kuài yào sài pǎo le.
    nà xie nán rén zài sài pǎo.
    nà liǎng gè nán rén yǐ jīng sài pǎo wán le.
    nà xiē nǚ rén kuài yào sài pǎo le.

08 nà gè nǚ rén zhèng yào bǎ nà zhī māo bào qǐ lái.
    nà gè nǚ rén zhèng bǎ nà zhī māo bào qǐ lái.
    nà gè nǚ rén yǐ jīng bǎ nà zhī māo bào le qǐ lái, xiàn zài zhèng bǎ māo bào zài huái lǐ.
    nà gè nǚ rén zài kàn bào zhǐ.

09 nà gè nǚ rén zhèng yào chuān lián yī qún.
    nà gè nǚ rén zài chuān lián yī qún.
    nà gè nǚ rén yǐ jīng chuān shàng le lián yī qún.
    nà gè nán rén zài chuān T xù shān.

10 nà gè xiǎo gū niang yào bǎ shuǐ jiāo dào tóu shàng.
    nà gè xiǎo gū niang zhèng bǎ shuǐ jiāo dào tóu shàng.
    nà gè nǚ rén zhèng yào kàn shū.
    nà gè nǚ rén zài kàn shū.

使用更多的量词：串、朵、个、套、对等

01　很多串香蕉
　　一串香蕉
　　很多串葡萄
　　一串葡萄

02　一串香蕉
　　一个香蕉
　　一串葡萄
　　一颗葡萄

03　一对娃娃
　　许多洋娃娃
　　几朵花儿
　　很多束花儿

04　一对蜡烛
　　很多成对的蜡烛
　　一副手套
　　很多副手套

05　一束花儿
　　一朵花儿
　　两面旗
　　很多旗

06　很多气球
　　几个气球
　　一个骑自行车的人
　　一群骑自行车的人

07　一副色子
　　两副色子
　　一个赛跑的人
　　一组赛跑的人

08　一套工具
　　一套餐厅家具
　　一套行李
　　一套餐刀

09　一套银餐具
　　一对双胞胎
　　一副棋具
　　一套盘子

10　一对乘自动扶梯下楼的夫妇
　　两对夫妇
　　一对娃娃
　　一套俄罗斯娃娃

6-09

使用更多的量詞：串、朵、個、套、對等

01　很多串香蕉
　　一串香蕉
　　很多串葡萄
　　一串葡萄

02　一串香蕉
　　一個香蕉
　　一串葡萄
　　一顆葡萄

03　一對娃娃
　　許多洋娃娃
　　幾朵花兒
　　很多束花兒

04　一對蠟燭
　　很多成對的蠟燭
　　一副手套
　　很多副手套

05　一束花兒
　　一朵花兒
　　兩面旗
　　很多旗

06　很多氣球
　　幾個氣球
　　一個騎自行車的人
　　一群騎自行車的人

07　一副色子
　　兩副色子
　　一個賽跑的人
　　一組賽跑的人

08　一套工具
　　一套餐廳家具
　　一套行李
　　一套餐刀

09　一套銀餐具
　　一對雙胞胎
　　一副棋具
　　一套盤子

10　一對乘自動扶梯下樓的夫婦
　　兩對夫婦
　　一對娃娃
　　一套俄羅斯娃娃

6-09

shǐ yòng gèng duō de liàng cí: chuàn, duǒ, gè, tào, duì děng

01 hěn duō chuàn xiāng jiāo
    yī chuàn xiāng jiāo
    hěn duō chuàn pú táo
    yī chuàn pú táo

02 yī chuàn xiāng jiāo
    yī gè xiāng jiāo
    yī chuàn pú táo
    yī kē pú táo

03 yī duì wá wá
    xǔ duō yáng wá wá
    jǐ duǒ huār
    hěn duō shù huār

04 yī duì là zhú
    hěn duō chéng duì de là zhú
    yī fù shǒu tào
    hěn duō fù shǒu tào

05 yī shù huār
    yī duǒ huār
    liǎng miàn qí
    hěn duō qí

06 hěn duō qì qiú
    jǐ gè qì qiú
    yī gè qí zì xíng chē de rén
    yī qún qí zì xíng chē de rén

07 yī fù shǎi zi
    liǎng fù shǎi zi
    yī gè sài pǎo de rén
    yī zǔ sài pǎo de rén

08 yī tào gōng jù
    yī tào cān tīng jiā jù
    yī tào xíng lǐ
    yī tào cān dāo

09 yī tào yín cān jù
    yī duì shuāng bāo tāi
    yī fù qí jù
    yī tào pán zi

10 yī duì chèng zì dòng fú tī xià lóu de fū fù.
    liǎng duì fū fù
    yī duì wá wá
    yī tào é luó sī wá wá

6-10

单独的（地）、人群和朋友

01 那个小姑娘没有和其他人在一起。
那个小姑娘和朋友们在一起。
那个小姑娘和父母在一起。
那个小姑娘和小狗在一起。

02 那个拿红色麦克风的歌手在独唱。
那个歌手在和一个朋友唱歌。
那个女人在同合唱团一起唱歌。
那个女人一边弹钢琴，一边独唱。

03 那个女人周围都是花儿。
那个女人周围都是灌木丛。
那个女人周围都是书。
那个女人周围都是人。

04 那个女人周围都是花儿。
那个女人周围都是灌木丛。
那个女人周围都是书。
那个女人周围都是人。

05 那座城堡耸立在山顶上，四周没有其它建筑物。
那座堡垒耸立在沙漠上，四周没有其它建筑物。
那座城堡四周都是建筑物。
那座教堂四周都是建筑物。

06 那个女人没有和其他人在一起。
那个女人和另一个人在一起。
那个女人周围都是人。
那张桌子四周放着椅子。

07 独自一人
一对夫妇
几个人
一群人

08 那个女孩儿在自己看书。
那个女孩儿在和一个朋友玩儿。
那个女孩儿在和老师玩儿。
那个女孩儿在同老师和朋友散步。

09 有个人在下台阶。
几个人在下台阶。
有一大群人站在台阶上。
有一群人正在人行道上走。

10 一大群人在赛跑。
几个人在赛跑。
这两个人在赛跑，但她们不是对手。
这个人自己在跑，不是在比赛。

6-10

單獨的（地）、人群和朋友

01 那個小姑娘沒有和其他人在一起。
那個小姑娘和朋友們在一起。
那個小姑娘和父母在一起。
那個小姑娘和小狗在一起。

02 那個拿紅色麥克風的歌手在獨唱。
那個歌手在和一個朋友唱歌。
那個女人在同合唱團一起唱歌。
那個女人一邊彈鋼琴，一邊獨唱。

03 那個女人週圍都是花兒。
那個女人週圍都是灌木叢。
那個女人週圍都是書。
那個女人週圍都是人。

04 那個女人週圍都是花兒。
那個女人週圍都是灌木叢。
那個女人週圍都是書。
那個女人週圍都是人。

05 那座城堡聳立在山頂上，四週沒有其它建築物。
那座堡壘聳立在沙漠上，四週沒有其它建築物。
那座城堡四週都是建築物。
那座教堂四週都是建築物。

06 那個女人沒有和其他人在一起。
那個女人和另一個人在一起。
那個女人週圍都是人。
那張桌子四週放著椅子。

07 獨自一人
一對夫婦
幾個人
一群人

08 那個女孩兒在自己看書。
那個女孩兒在和一個朋友玩兒。
那個女孩兒在和老師玩兒。
那個女孩兒在同老師和朋友散步。

09 有個人在下臺階。
幾個人在下臺階。
有一大群人站在臺階上。
有一群人正在人行道上走。

10 一大群人在賽跑。
幾個人在賽跑。
這兩個人在賽跑，但她們不是對手。
這個人自己在跑，不是在比賽。

6-10

dān dú de(de), rén qún hé péng yǒu

01 nà gè xiǎo gū niáng méi yǒu hé qí tā rén zài yī qǐ.
    nà gè xiǎo gū niáng hé péng yǒu men zài yī qǐ.
    nà gè xiǎo gū niáng hé fù mǔ zài yī qǐ.
    nà gè xiǎo gū niáng hé xiǎo gǒu zài yī qǐ.

02 nà gè ná hóng sè mài kè fēng de gē shǒu zài dú chàng.
    nà gè gē shǒu zài hé yī gè péng yǒu chàng gē.
    nà gè nǚ rén zài tóng hé chàng tuán yī qǐ chàng gē.
    nà gè nǚ rén yī biān tán gāng qín, yī biān dú chàng.

03 nà gè nǚ rén zhōu wéi dōu shì huār.
    nà gè nǚ rén zhōu wéi dōu shì guàn mù cóng.
    nà gè nǚ rén zhōu wéi dōu shì shū.
    nà gè nǚ rén zhōu wéi dōu shì rén.

04 nà gè nǚ rén zhōu wéi dōu shì huār.
    nà gè nǚ rén zhōu wéi dōu shì guàn mù cóng.
    nà gè nǚ rén zhōu wéi dōu shì shū.
    nà gè nǚ rén zhōu wéi dōu shì rén.

05 nà zuò chéng bǎo sǒng lì zài shān dǐng shàng, sì zhōu méi yǒu qí tā jiàn zhù wù.
    nà zuò bǎo lěi sǒng lì zài shā mò shàng, sì zhōu méi yǒu qí tā jiàn zhù wù.
    nà zuò chéng bǎo sì zhōu dōu shì jiàn zhù wù.
    nà zuò jiào táng sì zhōu dōu shì jiàn zhù wù.

06 nà gè nǚ rén méi yǒu hé qí tā rén zài yī qǐ.
    nà gè nǚ rén hé lìng yī gè rén zài yī qǐ.
    nà gè nǚ rén zhōu wéi dōu shì rén.
    nà zhāng zhuō zi sì zhōu fàng zhe yǐ zi.

07 dú zì yī rén
    yī duì fū fù
    jǐ gè rén
    yī qún rén

08 nà gè nǚ háir zài zì jǐ kàn shū.
    nà gè nǚ háir zài hé yī gè péng yǒu wánr.
    nà gè nǚ háir zài hé lǎo shī wánr.
    nà gè nǚ háir zài tóng lǎo shī hé péng yǒu sàn bù.

09 yǒu gè rén zài xià tái jiē.
    jǐ gè rén zài xià tái jiē.
    yǒu yī dà qún rén zhàn zài tái jiē shàng.
    yǒu yī qún rén zhèng zài rén xíng dào shàng zǒu.

10 yī dà qún rén zài sài pǎo.
    jǐ gè rén zài sài pǎo.
    zhè liǎng gè rén zài sài pǎo, dàn tā mén bú shì duì shǒu.
    zhè gè rén zì jǐ zài pǎo, bú shì zài bǐ sài.

6-11

各种职业；感觉及各种活动

01　我是医生。
　　我是护士。
　　我是机械工。
　　我是学生。

02　我是警察。
　　我是牙医。
　　我是木匠。
　　我是科学家。

03　我是秘书。
　　我是厨师。
　　我是老师。
　　我是服务员。

04　我很尴尬。
　　我脚疼。
　　我不害怕，他很害怕。
　　我病了。

05　我冷了。
　　我又热又渴。
　　我很害怕。
　　我是医生，我在给病人看病。

06　我为我的儿子感到骄傲。
　　我很喜欢我的轿车。
　　我很瘦。
　　我很胖。

07　我在银行外面。
　　我在警察局。
　　我很有钱。
　　我在银行里。

08　哎哟！我的脚呀！
　　我戴着帽子。
　　我穿着蓝裙子。
　　我很尴尬。

09　我病了，你没病，你是护士。
　　我是医生，我没有病，你病了。
　　我在修车。
　　我在给人治牙。

10　我在烤面包。
　　我在用打字机打字。
　　我在教学生。
　　我们在读书。

6-11

各種職業；感覺及各種活動

01　我是醫生。
　　我是護士。
　　我是機械工。
　　我是學生。

02　我是警察。
　　我是牙醫。
　　我是木匠。
　　我是科學家。

03　我是秘書。
　　我是廚師。
　　我是老師。
　　我是服務員。

04　我很尷尬。
　　我腳疼。
　　我不害怕，他很害怕。
　　我病了。

05　我冷了。
　　我又熱又渴。
　　我很害怕。
　　我是醫生，我在給病人看病。

06　我為我的兒子感到驕傲。
　　我很喜歡我的轎車。
　　我很瘦。
　　我很胖。

07　我在銀行外面。
　　我在警察局。
　　我很有錢。
　　我在銀行裡。

08　哎喲！我的腳呀！
　　我戴著帽子。
　　我穿著藍裙子。
　　我很尷尬。

09　我病了，你沒病，你是護士。
　　我是醫生，我沒有病，你病了。
　　我在修車。
　　我在給人治牙。

10　我在烤麵包。
　　我在用打字機打字。
　　我在教學生。
　　我們在讀書。

6-11

gè zhǒng zhí yè; gǎn jué jí gè zhǒng huó dòng

01 wǒ shì yī shēng.
    wǒ shì hù shì.
    wǒ shì jī xiè gōng.
    wǒ shì xué shēng.

02 wǒ shì jǐng chá.
    wǒ shì yá yī.
    wǒ shì mù jiàng.
    wǒ shì kē xué jiā.

03 wǒ shì mì shū.
    wǒ shì chú shī.
    wǒ shì lǎo shī.
    wǒ shì fú wù yuán.

04 wǒ hěn gān gà.
    wǒ jiǎo téng.
    wǒ bú hài pà, tā hěn hài pà.
    wǒ bìng le.

05 wǒ lěng le.
    wǒ yòu rè yòu kě.
    wǒ hěn hài pà.
    wǒ shì yī shēng, wǒ zài gěi bìng rén kàn bìng.

06 wǒ wèi wǒ de ér zi gǎn dào jiāo ào.
    wǒ hěn xǐ huān wǒ de jiào chē.
    wǒ hěn shòu.
    wǒ hěn pàng.

07 wǒ zài yín háng wài miàn.
    wǒ zài jǐng chá jú.
    wǒ hěn yǒu qián.
    wǒ zài yín háng lǐ.

08 āi yō! wǒ de jiǎo ya!
    wǒ dài zhe mào zi.
    wǒ chuān zhe lán qún zi.
    wǒ hěn gān gà.

09 wǒ bìng le, nǐ méi bìng, nǐ shì hù shì.
    wǒ shì yī shēng, wǒ méi yǒu bìng, nǐ bìng le.
    wǒ zài xiū chē.
    wǒ zài géi rén zhì yá.

10 wǒ zài kǎo miàn bāo.
    wǒ zài yòng dǎ zì jī dǎ zì.
    wǒ zài jiāo xué shēng.
    wǒ men zài dú shū.

6-12

复习第六部分

01 这些人在游行。
这些人刚才在游行。
那个男人在卡车里。
那个男人刚才在卡车里。

02 那个女人正要走进那家商店。
那个女人正走进那家商店。
那个男人正要关轿车的行李箱。
那个男人已经把轿车的行李箱关上了。

03 这对夫妇穿戴得很正式。
这对夫妇穿戴得很随便。
这两个男人穿戴得很正式。
这些男人穿戴得很随便。

04 两卷纸巾
满满一纸袋
一个空塑料袋
一个空纸袋

05 两个人都在唱歌。
两个人都不在唱歌。
这些人中只有一个在唱歌。
六个人都在唱歌。

06 爸爸和两个儿子在挖地。
爸爸和两个儿子刚才在挖地。
那只狗在望着那本书。
那只狗刚才望着那本书。

07 那个女人正要把那只猫抱起来。
那个女人正把那只猫抱起来。
那个女人已经把那只猫抱了起来，现在正把猫抱在怀里。
那个女人在看报纸。

08 一套银餐具
一对双胞胎
一副棋具
一套盘子

09 那个拿红色麦克风的歌手在独唱。
那个歌手在和一个朋友唱歌。
那个女人在同合唱团一起唱歌。
那个女人一边弹钢琴，一边独唱。

10 我是警察。
我是牙医。
我是木匠。
我是科学家。

6-12

復習第六部分

01 這些人在游行。
這些人剛才在游行。
那個男人在卡車裡。
那個男人剛才在卡車裡。

02 那個女人正要走進那家商店。
那個女人正走進那家商店。
那個男人正要關轎車的行李箱。
那個男人已經把轎車的行李箱關上了。

03 這對夫婦穿戴得很正式。
這對夫婦穿戴得很隨便。
這兩個男人穿戴得很正式。
這些男人穿戴得很隨便。

04 兩卷紙巾
滿滿一紙袋
一個空塑料袋
一個空紙袋

05 兩個人都在唱歌。
兩個人都不在唱歌。
這些人中只有一個在唱歌。
六個人都在唱歌。

06 爸爸和兩個兒子在挖地。
爸爸和兩個兒子剛才在挖地。
那隻狗在望著那本書。
那隻狗剛才望著那本書。

07 那個女人正要把那隻貓抱起來。
那個女人正把那隻貓抱起來。
那個女人已經把那隻貓抱了起來，現在正把貓抱在懷裡。
那個女人在看報紙。

08 一套銀餐具
一對雙胞胎
一副棋具
一套盤子

09 那個拿紅色麥克風的歌手在獨唱。
那個歌手在和一個朋友唱歌。
那個女人在同合唱團一起唱歌。
那個女人一邊彈鋼琴，一邊獨唱。

10 我是警察。
我是牙醫。
我是木匠。
我是科學家。

6-12

fù xí dì liù bù fen

01 zhè xiē rén zài yóu xíng.
    zhè xiē rén gāng cái zài yóu xíng.
    nà gè nán rén zài kǎ chē lǐ.
    nà gè nán rén gāng cái zài kǎ chē lǐ.

02 nà gè nǚ rén zhèng yào zǒu jìn nà jiā shāng diàn.
    nà gè nǚ rén zhèng zǒu jìn nà jiā shāng diàn.
    nà gè nán rén zhèng yào guān jiào chē de xíng lǐ xiāng.
    nà gè nán rén yǐ jīng bǎ jiào chē de xíng lǐ xiāng guān shàng le.

03 zhè duì fū fù chuān dài de hěn zhèng shì.
    zhè duì fū fù chuān dài de hěn suí biàn.
    zhè liǎng gè nán rén chuān dài de hěn zhèng shì.
    zhè xiē nán rén chuān dài de hěn suí biàn.

04 liǎng juǎn zhǐ jīn
    mǎn mǎn yī zhǐ dài
    yī gè kōng sù liào dài
    yī gè kōng zhǐ dài

05 liǎng gè rén dōu zài chàng gē.
    liǎng gè rén dōu bú zài chàng gē.
    zhè xiē rén zhōng zhǐ yǒu yī gè zài chàng gē.
    liù gè rén dōu zài chàng gē.

06 bà bà hé liǎng gè ér zi zài wā dì.
    bà bà hé liǎng gè ér zi gāng cái zài wā dì.
    nà zhī gǒu zài wàng zhe nà běn shū.
    nà zhī gǒu gāng cái wàng zhe nà běn shū.

07 nà gè nǚ rén zhèng yào bǎ nà zhī māo bào qǐ lái.
    nà gè nǚ rén zhèng bǎ nà zhī māo bào qǐ lái.
    nà gè nǚ rén yǐ jīng bǎ nà zhī māo bào le qǐ lái, xiàn zài zhèng bǎ māo bào zài huái lǐ.
    nà gè nǚ rén zài kàn bào zhǐ.

08 yī tào yín cān jù
    yī duì shuāng bāo tāi
    yī fù qí jù
    yī tào pán zi

09 nà gè ná hóng sè mài kè fēng de gē shǒu zài dú chàng.
    nà gè gē shǒu zài hé yī gè péng yǒu chàng gē.
    nà gè nǚ rén zài tóng hé chàng tuán yī qǐ chàng gē.
    nà gè nǚ rén yī biān tán gāng qín, yī biān dú chàng.

10 wǒ shì jǐng chá.
    wǒ shì yá yī.
    wǒ shì mù jiàng.
    wǒ shì kē xué jiā.

使用更多的动词：指点、拉、挖、接等

01 那个女孩儿在上船。
    那个男孩儿正从水里出来。
    那个男孩儿已经从水里出来了。
    那个男孩儿要从水里出来了。

02 那个男人和那个女人在指着什么东西。
    两个女人在指着什么东西。
    左边的那个男孩儿在指着什么东西。
    有个女人在指着什么东西，还有个女人什么东西也没
    指。

03 那个男人在放风筝。
    那个男人在试着放风筝。
    地上有三个风筝。
    那个男孩儿在放风筝。

04 那个男孩儿在往下看。
    那个男孩儿在往上看。
    那个小丑在往下看。
    那个小丑在往上看。

05 那个穿红衬衫的男孩儿在放风筝。
    那个男孩儿一边拿着杯子喝水，一边在放风筝。
    那个男人在试着让牛张嘴。
    有个男人在试着放风筝。

06 那个穿蓝衣服的男孩儿快要被土块儿打着了。
    那个男孩儿被土块儿打着了。
    那个男人在干活儿。
    那个男人不在干活儿。

07 爸爸在给两个儿子念书。
    爸爸在和两个儿子干活儿。
    爸爸一手拿着铁锹，一手拿着书。
    爸爸在给狗念书。

08 那些马在干活儿。
    那些马不在干活儿。
    爸爸在指着什么东西。
    爸爸在和两个男孩儿干活儿。

09 那两个男孩儿在抢耙子。
    那个男孩儿在挖地。
    那个穿白衣服的男孩儿在接耙子。
    那个穿蓝衣服的男孩儿在接耙子。

10 那个女孩儿要给马喂草。
    那个女孩儿在给马喂草。
    那个女孩儿已经给马喂了草。
    那个牛仔要给牛喂草。

使用更多的動詞：指點、拉、挖、接等

01 那個女孩兒在上船。
    那個男孩兒正從水裡出來。
    那個男孩兒已經從水裡出來了。
    那個男孩兒要從水裡出來了。

02 那個男人和那個女人在指著甚麼東西。
    兩個女人在指著甚麼東西。
    左邊的那個男孩兒在指著甚麼東西。
    有個女人在指著甚麼東西，還有個女人甚麼東西也沒
    指。

03 那個男人在放風箏。
    那個男人在試著放風箏。
    地上有三個風箏。
    那個男孩兒在放風箏。

04 那個男孩兒在往下看。
    那個男孩兒在往上看。
    那個小醜在往下看。
    那個小醜在往上看。

05 那個穿紅襯衫的男孩兒在放風箏。
    那個男孩兒一邊拿著杯子喝水，一邊在放風箏。
    那個男人在試著讓牛張嘴。
    有個男人在試著放風箏。

06 那個穿藍衣服的男孩兒快要被土塊兒打著了。
    那個男孩兒被土塊兒打著了。
    那個男人在幹活兒。
    那個男人不在幹活兒。

07 爸爸在給兩個兒子唸書。
    爸爸在和兩個兒子幹活兒。
    爸爸一手拿著鐵鍬，一手拿著書。
    爸爸在給狗唸書。

08 那些馬在幹活兒。
    那些馬不在幹活兒。
    爸爸在指著甚麼東西。
    爸爸在和兩個男孩兒幹活兒。

09 那兩個男孩兒在搶耙子。
    那個男孩兒在挖地。
    那個穿白衣服的男孩兒在接耙子。
    那個穿藍衣服的男孩兒在接耙子。

10 那個女孩兒要給馬喂草。
    那個女孩兒在給馬喂草。
    那個女孩兒已經給馬喂了草。
    那個牛仔要給牛喂草。

7-01

shǐ yòng gèng duō de dòng cí: zhǐ diǎn, lā, wā, jiē děng

01   nà gè nǚ háir zài shàng chuán.
     nà gè nán háir zhèng cóng shuǐ lǐ chū lái.
     nà gè nán háir yǐ jīng cóng shuǐ lǐ chū lái le.
     nà gè nán háir yào cóng shuǐ lǐ chū lái le.

02   nà gè nán rén hé nà gè nǚ rén zài zhǐ zhe shén me dōng xi.
     liǎng gè nǚ rén zài zhǐ zhe shén me dōng xi.
     zuǒ biān de nà gè nán háir zài zhǐ zhe shén me dōng xi.
     yǒu gè nǚ rén zài zhǐ zhe shén me dōng xi, hái yǒu gè nǚ rén shén me dōng xi yě méi zhǐ.

03   nà gè nán rén zài fàng fēng zhēng.
     nà gè nán rén zài shì zhe fàng fēng zhēng.
     dì shàng yǒu sān gè fēng zhēng.
     nà gè nán háir zài fàng fēng zhēng.

04   nà gè nán háir zài wǎng xià kàn.
     nà gè nán háir zài wǎng shàng kàn.
     nà gè xiǎo chǒu zài wǎng xià kàn.
     nà gè xiǎo chǒu zài wǎng shàng kàn.

05   nà gè chuān hóng chèn shān de nán háir zài fàng fēng zhēng.
     nà gè nán háir yī biān ná zhe bēi zi hē shuǐ, yī biān zài fàng fēng zhēng.
     nà gè nán rén zài shì zhe ràng niú zhāng zuǐ.
     yǒu gè nán rén zài shì zhe fàng fēng zhēng.

06   nà gè chuān lán yī fu de nán háir kuài yào bèi tǔ kuàir dǎ zhe le.
     nà gè nán háir bèi tǔ kuàir dǎ zhe le.
     nà gè nán rén zài gàn huór.
     nà gè nán rén bú zài gàn huór.

07   bà bà zài gěi liǎng gè ér zi niàn shū.
     bà bà zài hé liǎng gè ér zi gàn huór.
     bà bà yī shǒu ná zhe tiě qiāo, yī shǒu ná zhe shū.
     bà bà zài gěi gǒu niàn shū.

08   nà xiē mǎ zài gàn huór.
     nà xiē mǎ bú zài gàn huór.
     bà bà zài zhǐ zhe shén me dōng xi.
     bà bà zài hé liǎng gè nán háir gàn huór.

09   nà liǎng gè nán háir zài qiǎng pá zi.
     nà gè nán háir zài wā dì.
     nà gè chuān bái yī fu de nán háir zài jiē pá zi.
     nà gè chuān lán yī fu de nán háir zài jiē pá zi.

10   nà gè nǚ háir yào gěi mǎ wèi cǎo.
     nà gè nǚ háir zài gěi mǎ wèi cǎo.
     nà gè nǚ háir yǐ jīng gěi mǎ wèi le cǎo.
     nà gè niú zǎi yào gěi niú wèi cǎo.

更多的动词；疑问代词：谁、哪；副词：平时

01 这只天鹅在拍打翅膀。
这两只鸟都张着翅膀。
这个男人手上的那只鸟张着翅膀。
这只鸟没有张着翅膀。

02 骆驼有四条腿。
人有两条腿。
鸭子有两条腿。
象有四条腿。

03 宇航员穿宇航服。
有时候，姑娘们穿连衣裙。
飞机有机翼。
鸟有翅膀。

04 钟有针。
自行车有轮子。
水手住在船上。
士兵拿枪。

05 谁穿宇航服？
谁穿连衣裙？
谁拿枪？
谁住在船上？

06 哪只动物只有两条腿？
哪只动物四条腿着地？
哪只动物两条腿着地，还有两条腿没着地？
哪只动物四条腿都没着地？

07 这个人是卖面包的。
这个人是卖太阳镜的。
这个人是卖西红柿的。
这个人是卖花草的。

08 马平时是驮人的，可这匹马现在没人骑。
这匹马驮着人。
飞机平时是飞行的，可这架飞机现在没有飞行。
飞机平时是飞行的，这架飞机正在飞行。

09 这个工人戴着安全帽。
这个工人平时戴着安全帽，可现在没有戴安全帽。
士兵平时带着枪。可这些士兵现在没有带着枪。
士兵平时带着枪。这些士兵现在拿着枪。

10 这两个穿蓝西装的小伙子在唱歌。
这两个穿蓝西装的小伙子是唱歌的，可现在没有唱
　　歌。
狗一般不穿衣服，这只狗没有穿衣服。
狗一般不穿衣服，可这只狗穿着衣服。

7-02

更多的動詞；疑問代詞：誰、哪；副詞：平時

01 這隻天鵝在拍打翅膀。
這兩隻鳥都張著翅膀。
這個男人手上的那隻鳥張著翅膀。
這隻鳥沒有張著翅膀。

02 駱駝有四條腿。
人有兩條腿。
鴨子有兩條腿。
象有四條腿。

03 宇航員穿宇航服。
有時候，姑娘們穿連衣裙。
飛機有機翼。
鳥有翅膀。

04 鍾有針。
自行車有輪子。
水手住在船上。
士兵拿槍。

05 誰穿宇航服？
誰穿連衣裙？
誰拿槍？
誰住在船上？

06 哪隻動物只有兩條腿？
哪隻動物四條腿著地？
哪隻動物兩條腿著地，還有兩條腿沒著地？
哪隻動物四條腿都沒著地？

07 這個人是賣面包的。
這個人是賣太陽鏡的。
這個人是賣西紅柿的。
這個人是賣花草的。

08 馬平時是馱人的，可這匹馬沒人騎。
這匹馬馱著人。
飛機平時是飛行的，可這架飛機現在沒有飛行。
飛機平時是飛行的，這架飛機正在飛行。

09 這個工人戴著安全帽。
這個工人平時戴著安全帽，可現在沒有戴安全帽。
士兵平時帶著槍，可這些士兵現在沒有帶著槍。
士兵平時帶著槍，這些士兵現在拿著槍。

10 這兩個穿藍西裝的小夥子在唱歌。
這兩個穿藍西裝的小夥子是唱歌的，可現在沒有唱
　　歌。
狗一般不穿衣服，這隻狗沒有穿衣服。
狗一般不穿衣服，可這隻狗穿著衣服。

7-02

gèng duō de dòng cí; yí wèn dài cí: shéi, nǎ; fù cí: píng shí

01   zhè zhī tiān é zài pāi dǎ chì bǎng.
      zhè liǎng zhī niǎo dōu zhāng zhe chì bǎng.
      zhè gè nán rén shǒu shàng de nà zhī niǎo zhāng zhe chì bǎng.
      zhè zhī niǎo méi yǒu zhāng zhe chì bǎng.

02   luò tuó yǒu sì tiáo tuǐ.
      rén yǒu liǎng tiáo tuǐ.
      yā zi yǒu liǎng tiáo tuǐ.
      xiàng yǒu sì tiáo tuǐ.

03   yǔ háng yuán chuān yǔ háng fú.
      yǒu shí hòu, gū niáng men chuān lián yī qún.
      fēi jī yǒu jī yì.
      niǎo yǒu chì bǎng.

04   zhōng yǒu zhēn.
      zì xíng chē yǒu lún zi.
      shuǐ shǒu zhù zài chuán shàng.
      shì bīng ná qiāng.

05   shéi chuān yǔ háng fú?
      shéi chuān lián yī qún?
      shéi ná qiāng?
      shéi zhù zài chuán shàng?

06   nǎ zhī dòng wù zhǐ yǒu liǎng tiáo tuǐ?
      nǎ zhī dòng wù sì tiáo tuǐ zhuó dì?
      nǎ zhī dòng wù liǎng tiáo tuǐ zhuó dì, hái yǒu liǎng tiáo tuǐ méi zhuó dì?
      nǎ zhī dòng wù sì tiáo tuǐ dōu méi zhuó dì?

07   zhè gè rén shì mài miàn bāo de.
      zhè gè rén shì mài tài yáng jìng de.
      zhè gè rén shì mài xī hóng shì de.
      zhè gè rén shì mài huā cǎo de.

08   mǎ píng shí shì tuó rén de, kě zhè pǐ mǎ xiàn zài méi rén qí.
      zhè pǐ mǎ tuó zhe rén.
      fēi jī píng shí shì fēi xíng de, kě zhè jià fēi jī xiàn zài méi yǒu fēi xíng.
      fēi jī píng shí shì fēi xíng de, zhè jià fēi jī zhèng zài fēi xíng.

09   zhè gè gōng rén dài zhe ān quán mào.
      zhè gè gōng rén píng shí dài zhe ān quán mào, kě xiàn zài méi yǒu dài ān quán mào.
      shì bīng píng shí dài zhe qiāng. kě zhè xiē shì bīng xiàn zài méi yǒu dài zhe qiāng.
      shì bīng píng shí dài zhe qiāng. zhè xiē shì bīng xiàn zài ná zhe qiāng.

10   zhè liǎng gè chuān lán xī zhuāng de xiǎo huǒ zi zài chàng gē.
      zhè liǎng gè chuān lán xī zhuāng de xiǎo huǒ zi shì chàng gē de, kě xiàn zài méi yǒu chàng gē.
      gǒu yī bān bù chuān yī fu, zhè zhī gǒu méi yǒu chuān yī fu.
      gǒu yī bān bù chuān yī fu, kě zhè zhī gǒu chuān zhe yī fu.

7-03

快、慢

01 这个女人跑得很快。
这些男人骑车骑得很快。
这个男孩儿滑雪滑得很快。
这匹马跑得很快。

02 这匹马没有快跑，它在慢慢地走。
这辆轿车开得很慢。
这辆轿车开得很慢。
这个女人骑马骑得很快。

03 这匹马跑得很快。
这匹马在慢慢地走。
这匹马呆在原地。
这头公牛跑得很快。

04 这个女人游得很快。
这个游泳的人在水里，但是这会儿没有游泳。
这个滑雪的人滑得很快。
这个滑雪的人滑得很慢。

05 这个小姑娘在穿旱冰鞋。
这个小姑娘在溜旱冰。
这个滑雪的人在往山下滑。
这个滑雪的人已经跳了起来。

06 一个滑冰的人
一个滑雪的人
一个游泳的人
一个赛跑的人

07 这个骑自行车的人骑得很慢。
这个人正在水中向前游泳。
这座塑像一动不动。
有个人正急匆匆地过街。

08 这两个身穿红色军装的士兵一动不动地站着。
这些身穿黑色军装的士兵一动不动地保持着那个姿势。
这些宇航员在一动不动地站着。
这个溜冰的人一动不动地保持着那个姿势。

09 这些骑自行车的人骑得很快。
这些骑自行车的人骑得很慢。
这架飞机飞得很快。
这架飞机在慢慢地移动。

10 这不是一只动物，它行驶得很慢。
这不是一只动物，它飞得很快。
这是一只动物，爬得很慢。
这是一只动物，跑得很快。

7-03

快、慢

01 這個女人跑得很快。
這些男人騎車騎得很快。
這個男孩兒滑雪滑得很快。
這匹馬跑得很快。

02 這匹馬沒有快跑，它在慢慢地走。
這輛轎車開得很慢。
這輛轎車開得很慢。
這個女人騎馬騎得很快。

03 這匹馬跑得很快。
這匹馬在慢慢地走。
這匹馬呆在原地。
這頭公牛跑得很快。

04 這個女人游得很快。
這個游泳的人在水裡，但是這會兒沒有游泳。
這個滑雪的人滑得很快。
這個滑雪的人滑得很慢。

05 這個小姑娘在穿旱冰鞋。
這個小姑娘在溜旱冰。
這個滑雪的人在往山下滑。
這個滑雪的人已經跳了起來。

06 一個滑冰的人
一個滑雪的人
一個游泳的人
一個賽跑的人

07 這個騎自行車的人騎得很慢。
這個人正在水中向前游泳。
這座塑像一動不動。
有個人正急匆匆地過街。

08 這兩個身穿紅色軍裝的士兵一動不動地站著。
這些身穿黑色軍裝的士兵一動不動地保持著那個姿勢。
這些宇航員在一動不動地站著。
這個溜冰的人一動不動地保持著那個姿勢。

09 這些騎自行車的人騎得很快。
這些騎自行車的人騎得很慢。
這架飛機飛得很快。
這架飛機在慢慢地移動。

10 這不是一隻動物，它行駛得很慢。
這不是一隻動物，它飛得很快。
這是一隻動物，爬得很慢。
這是一隻動物，跑得很快。

7-03

kuài, màn

01 zhè gè nǚ rén pǎo de hěn kuài.
 zhè xiē nán rén qí chē qí de hěn kuài.
 zhè gè nán háir huá xuě huá de hěn kuài.
 zhè pǐ mǎ pǎo de hěn kuài.

02 zhè pǐ mǎ méi yǒu kuài pǎo, tā zài màn màn de zǒu.
 zhè liàng jiào chē kāi de hěn màn.
 zhè liàng jiào chē kāi de hěn kuài.
 zhè gè nǚ rén qí mǎ qí de hěn kuài.

03 zhè pǐ mǎ pǎo de hěn kuài.
 zhè pǐ mǎ zài màn màn de zǒu.
 zhè pǐ mǎ dāi zài yuán dì.
 zhè tóu gōng niú pǎo de hěn kuài.

04 zhè gè nǚ rén yóu de hěn kuài.
 zhè gè yóu yǒng de rén zài shuǐ lǐ, dàn shì zhè huìr méi yǒu yóu yǒng.
 zhè gè huá xuě de rén huá de hěn kuài.
 zhè gè huá xuě de rén huá de hěn màn.

05 zhè gè xiǎo gū niang zài chuān hàn bīng xié.
 zhè gè xiǎo gū niang zài liū hàn bīng.
 zhè gè huá xuě de rén zài wǎng shān xià huá.
 zhè gè huá xuě de rén yǐ jīng tiào le qǐ lái.

06 yī gè huá bīng de rén
 yī gè huá xuě de rén
 yī gè yóu yǒng de rén
 yī gè sài pǎo de rén

07 zhè gè qí zì xíng chē de rén qí de hěn màn.
 zhè gè rén zhèng zài shuǐ zhōng xiàng qián yóu yǒng.
 zhè zuò sù xiàng yī dòng bú dòng.
 yǒu gè rén zhèng jí cōng cōng de guò jiē.

08 zhè liǎng gè shēn chuān hóng sè jūn zhuāng de shì bīng yī dòng bú dòng de zhàn zhe.
 zhè xiē shēn chuān hēi sè jūn zhuāng de shì bīng yī dòng bú dòng de bǎo chí zhe nà gè zī shì.
 zhè xiē yǔ háng yuán zài yī dòng bú dòng de zhàn zhe.
 zhè gè liū bīng de rén yī dòng bú dòng de bǎo chí zhe nà gè zī shì.

09 zhè xiē qí zì xíng chē de rén qí de hěn kuài.
 zhè xiē qí zì xíng chē de rén qí de hěn màn.
 zhè jià fēi jī fēi de hěn kuài.
 zhè jià fēi jī zài màn màn de yí dòng.

10 zhè bú shì yī zhī dòng wù, tā xíng shǐ de hěn màn.
 zhè bú shì yī zhī dòng wù, tā fēi de hěn kuài.
 zhè shì yī zhī dòng wù, pá de hěn màn.
 zhè shì yī zhī dòng wù, pǎo de hěn kuài.

四季

01　这座房子在很多绿树前面。
　　这辆轿车在两旁都是绿树的马路上。
　　这些轿车在两旁都是树的停车场上。这些树开着白色
　　　和粉色的花儿。
　　那座白色建筑物前面有一棵绿树。

02　天不冷，这些树还都绿着。
　　天冷了，这些树盖满了雪。
　　天不冷，那座白色楼房前面有一棵开着粉红花儿的
　　　树。
　　天很暖和，有一棵树开着白花儿，还有一棵树开着粉
　　　红花儿。

03　那架红色飞机后面的山上有雪。
　　穿红 T 恤衫的男人站着的那座山上没有雪。
　　穿红 T 恤衫的男人站着的那座山上有雪。
　　那座山上没有雪，也没有人。

04　现在是冬天，山上有雪。
　　现在是冬天，树上有雪。
　　现在是秋天，树都黄了。
　　现在是春天，树上开满了粉红花儿和白花儿。

05　现在是冬天，树上有雪。
　　现在是夏天，树是绿色的。
　　现在是夏天，这两个人在游泳池里。
　　现在是秋天，树都黄了，地上全是树叶。

06　冬天
　　夏天
　　春天
　　秋天

07　夏天
　　秋天
　　冬天
　　春天

08　太阳在落下去，我们把这叫日落。
　　夜晚时的大桥
　　白天
　　夜晚时的城市

09　太阳在升起来，我们把这叫日出。
　　晚上，我们能看见月亮。
　　夜晚时的建筑物
　　白天时的建筑物

10　现在是冬天，这是白天。现在是冬季的白天。
　　现在是冬天，这是晚上。现在是冬季的夜晚。
　　现在是夏天，这是白天。现在是夏季的白天。
　　现在是夏天，这是晚上。现在是夏季的夜晚。

7-04

四季

01　這座房子在很多綠樹前面。
　　這輛轎車在兩旁都是綠樹的馬路上。
　　這些轎車在兩旁都是樹的停車場上。這些樹開著白色
　　　和粉色的花兒。
　　那座白色建筑物前面有一棵綠樹。

02　天不冷，這些樹還都綠著。
　　天冷了，這些樹蓋滿了雪。
　　天不冷，那座白色樓房前面有一棵開著粉紅花兒的
　　　樹。
　　天很暖和，有一棵樹開著白花兒，還有一棵樹開著粉
　　　紅花兒。

03　那架紅色飛機後面的山上有雪。
　　穿紅 T 恤衫的男人站著的那座山上沒有雪。
　　穿紅 T 恤衫的男人站著的那座山上有雪。
　　那座山上沒有雪，也沒有人。

04　現在是冬天，山上有雪。
　　現在是冬天，樹上有雪。
　　現在是秋天，樹都黃了。
　　現在是春天，樹上開滿了粉紅花兒和白花兒。

05　現在是冬天，樹上有雪。
　　現在是夏天，樹是綠色的。
　　現在是夏天，這兩個人在游泳池裡。
　　現在是秋天，樹都黃了，地上全是樹葉。

06　冬天
　　夏天
　　春天
　　秋天

07　夏天
　　秋天
　　冬天
　　春天

08　太陽在落下去，我們把這叫日落。
　　夜晚時的大橋
　　白天
　　夜晚時的城市

09　太陽在升起來，我們把這叫日出。
　　晚上，我們能看見月亮。
　　夜晚時的建筑物
　　白天時的建筑物

10　現在是冬天，這是白天。現在是冬季的白天。
　　現在是冬天，這是晚上。現在是冬季的夜晚。
　　現在是夏天，這是白天。現在是夏季的白天。
　　現在是夏天，這是晚上。現在是夏季的夜晚。

sì jì

01 zhè zuò fáng zi zài hěn duō lǜ shù qián miàn.
    zhè liàng jiào chē zài liǎng páng dōu shì lǜ shù de mǎ lù shàng.
    zhè xiē jiào chē zài liǎng páng dōu shì shù de tíng chē chǎng shàng. zhè xiē shù kāi zhe bái sè hé fěn sè
        de huār.
    nà zuò bái sè jiàn zhù wù qián miàn yǒu yī kē lǜ shù.

02 tiān bù lěng, zhè xiē shù hái dōu lǜ zhe.
    tiān lěng le, zhè xiē shù gài mǎn le xuě.
    tiān bù lěng, nà zuò bái sè lóu fáng qián miàn yǒu yī kē kāi zhe fěn hóng huār de shù.
    tiān hěn nuǎn he, yǒu yī kē shù kāi zhe bái huār, hái yǒu yī kē shù kāi zhe fěn hóng huār.

03 nà jià hóng sè fēi jī hòu miàn de shān shàng yǒu xuě.
    chuān hóng T xù shān de nán rén zhàn zhe de nà zuò shān shàng méi yǒu xuě.
    chuān hóng T xù shān de nán rén zhàn zhe de nà zuò shān shàng yǒu xuě.
    nà zuò shān shàng méi yǒu xuě, yě méi yǒu rén.

04 xiàn zài shì dōng tiān, shān shàng yǒu xuě.
    xiàn zài shì dōng tiān, shù shàng yǒu xuě.
    xiàn zài shì qiū tiān, shù dōu huáng le.
    xiàn zài shì chūn tiān, shù shàng kāi mǎn le fěn hóng huār hé bái huār.

05 xiàn zài shì dōng tiān, shù shàng yǒu xuě.
    xiàn zài shì xià tiān, shù shì lǜ sè de.
    xiàn zài shì xià tiān, zhè liǎng gè rén zài yóu yǒng chí lǐ.
    xiàn zài shì qiū tiān, shù dōu huáng le, dì shàng quán shì shù yè.

06 dōng tiān
    xià tiān
    chūn tiān
    qiū tiān

07 xià tiān
    qiū tiān
    dōng tiān
    chūn tiān

08 tài yáng zài luò xià qù, wǒ men bǎ zhè jiào rì luò.
    yè wǎn shí de dà qiáo
    bái tiān
    yè wǎn shí de chéng shì

09 tài yáng zài shēng qǐ lái, wǒ men bǎ zhè jiào rì chū.
    wǎn shàng, wǒ men néng kàn jiàn yuè liàng.
    yè wǎn shí de jiàn zhù wù
    bái tiān shí de jiàn zhù wù

10 xiàn zài shì dōng tiān, zhè shì bái tiān. xiàn zài shì dōng jì de bái tiān.
    xiàn zài shì dōng tiān, zhè shì wǎn shàng. xiàn zài shì dōng jì de yè wǎn.
    xiàn zài shì xià tiān, zhè shì bái tiān. xiàn zài shì xià jì de bái tiān.
    xiàn zài shì xià tiān, zhè shì wǎn shàng. xiàn zài shì xia jì de yè wǎn.

7-05

全都、全都不、一些、大多数、两个、另外等

01 这些花儿是白色的。
    这些花儿是红色的。
    这些花儿是黄色的。
    这些花儿是蓝色的。

02 这些花儿全都是白色的。
    这些花儿全都是红色的。
    这些花儿全都是黄色的。
    这些花儿全都是蓝色的。

03 这些花儿中有些是白色的。
    这些花儿中有些是蓝色的。
    这些盘子中有两个是黄色的。
    这些人中有些戴着帽子。

04 这些花儿中有些是黄色的，有些是白色的。
    这些花儿中有些是黄色的，有些是蓝色的。
    这些苹果中有些是红色的，有些是绿色的。
    这些人中有两个是男的，有两个是女的。

05 这些人大多数戴着黄帽子，但有一个人没戴。
    这些花儿大多数是白色的，但也有些是黄色的。
    这朵花儿大部分是红色的，但还带一点儿黑色。
    这朵花儿大部分是红色的，但还带一点儿黄色。

06 两只动物都是马。
    两朵花儿的花瓣儿都是白色的，但花蕊是黄色的。
    两个孩子都是女孩儿。
    两只水禽都是鸭子。

07 两只动物都是马。
    两只动物都不是马。
    两个孩子都是女孩儿。
    两个孩子都不是女孩儿。

08 这些花儿中有些是红色的。
    这些花儿全都不是红色的。
    这两只鸭子中有一只是白色的。
    这些鸭子全都不是白色的。

09 这些花儿中有些是黄色的，另外一些是蓝色的。
    这些花儿全都是黄色的。
    这两只鸭子中有一只的头是白色的，另一只的头是绿
      色的。
    这些鸭子的头全都是黑色的。

10 两个人都在指着什么东西。
    两个人什么东西也没指。
    一个人在指着什么东西，另一个人什么东西也没指。
    这两只动物中有一只是鸟，另一只不是。

7-05

全都、全都不、一些、大多數、兩個、另外等

01 這些花兒是白色的。
    這些花兒是紅色的。
    這些花兒是黃色的。
    這些花兒是藍色的。

02 這些花兒全都是白色的。
    這些花兒全都是紅色的。
    這些花兒全都是黃色的。
    這些花兒全都是藍色的。

03 這些花兒中有些是白色的。
    這些花兒中有些是藍色的。
    這些盤子中有兩個是黃色的。
    這些人中有些戴著帽子。

04 這些花兒中有些是黃色的，有些是白色的。
    這些花兒中有些是黃色的，有些是藍色的。
    這些苹果中有些是紅色的，有些是綠色的。
    這些人中有兩個是男的，有兩個是女的。

05 這些人大多數戴著黃帽子，但有一個人沒戴。
    這些花兒大多數是白色的，但也有些是黃色的。
    這朵花兒大部分是紅色的，但還帶一點兒黑色。
    這朵花兒大部分是紅色的，但還帶一點兒黃色。

06 兩隻動物都是馬。
    兩朵花兒的花瓣兒都是白色的，但花蕊是黃色的。
    兩個孩子都是女孩兒。
    兩隻水禽都是鴨子。

07 兩隻動物都是馬。
    兩隻動物都不是馬。
    兩個孩子都是女孩兒。
    兩個孩子都不是女孩兒。

08 這些花兒中有些是紅色的。
    這些花兒全都不是紅色的。
    這兩隻鴨子中有一隻是白色的。
    這些鴨子全都不是白色的。

09 這些花兒中有些是黃色的，另外一些是藍色的。
    這些花兒全都是黃色的。
    這兩隻鴨子中有一隻的頭是白色的，另一隻的頭是綠
      色的。
    這些鴨子的頭全都是黑色的。

10 兩個人都在指著甚麼東西。
    兩個人甚麼東西也沒指。
    一個人在指著甚麼東西，另一個人甚麼東西也沒指。
    這兩隻動物中有一隻是鳥，另一隻不是。

7-05

quán dōu, quán dōu bù, yī xiē, dà duō shù, liǎng gè, lìng wài dĕng

01 zhè xiē huār shì bái sè de.
    zhè xiē huār shì hóng sè de.
    zhè xiē huār shì huáng sè de.
    zhè xiē huār shì lán sè de.

02 zhè xiē huār quán dōu shì bái sè de.
    zhè xiē huār quán dōu shì hóng sè de.
    zhè xiē huār quán dōu shì huáng sè de.
    zhè xiē huār quán dōu shì lán sè de.

03 zhè xiē huār zhōng yǒu xiē shì bái sè de.
    zhè xiē huā zhōng yǒu xiē shì lán sè de.
    zhè xiē pán zi zhōng yǒu liǎng gè shì huáng sè de.
    zhè xiē rén zhōng yǒu xiē dài zhe mào zi.

04 zhè xiē huār zhōng yǒu xiē shì huáng sè de, yǒu xiē shì bái sè de.
    zhè xiē huār zhōng yǒu xiē shì huáng sè de, yǒu xiē shì lán sè de.
    zhè xiē píng guǒ zhōng yǒu xiē shì hóng sè de, yǒu xiē shì lǜ sè de.
    zhè xiē rén zhōng yǒu liǎng gè shì nán de, yǒu liǎng gè shì nǚ de.

05 zhè xiē rén dà duō shù dài zhe huáng mào zi, dàn yǒu yī gè rén méi dài.
    zhè xiē huār dà duō shù shì bái sè de, dàn yě yǒu xiē shì huáng sè de.
    zhè duǒ huār dà bù fen shì hóng sè de, dàn hái dài yī diǎnr hēi sè.
    zhè duǒ huār dà bù fen shì hóng sè de, dàn hái dài yī diànr huáng sè.

06 liǎng zhī dòng wù dōu shì mǎ.
    liǎng duǒ huār de huā bànr dōu shì bái sè de, dàn huā ruǐ shì huáng sè de.
    liǎng gè hái zi dōu shì nǚ háir.
    liǎng zhī shuǐ qín dōu shì yā zi.

07 liǎng zhī dòng wù dōu shì mǎ.
    liǎng zhī dòng wù dōu bú shì mǎ.
    liǎng gè hái zi dōu shì nǚ háir.
    liǎng gè hái zi dōu bú shì nǚ háir.

08 zhè xiē huār zhōng yǒu xiē shì hóng sè de.
    zhè xiē huār quán dōu bú shì hóng sè de.
    zhè liǎng zhī yā zi zhōng yǒu yī zhī shì bái sè de.
    zhè xiē yā zi quán dōu bú shì bái sè de.

09 zhè xiē huār zhōng yǒu xiē shì huáng sè de, lìng wài yī xiē shì lán sè de.
    zhè xiē huār quán dōu shì huáng sè de.
    zhè liǎng zhī yā zi zhōng yǒu yī zhī de tóu shì bái sè de, lìng yī zhī de tóu shì lǜ sè de.
    zhè xiē yā zi de tóu quán dōu shì hēi sè de.

10 liǎng gè rén dōu zài zhǐ zhe shén me dōng xi.
    liǎng gè rén shén me dōng xi yě méi zhǐ.
    yī gè rén zài zhǐ zhe shén me dōng xi, lìng yī gè rén shén me dōng xi yě méi zhǐ.
    zhè liǎng zhī dòng wù zhōng yǒu yī zhī shì niǎo, lìng yī zhī bú shì.

全都不、都、两个

01 这个人是女的。
   这只动物是狗。
   这个人是女孩儿。
   这只动物是马。

02 这个人不是孩子。
   这只动物不是马。
   这个孩子不是男孩儿。
   这只动物不是狗。

03 这些人是男的。
   这些人是女的。
   这些动物是鱼。
   这些动物是马。

04 这些人全都不是女的。
   这些人全都不是男的。
   这些动物全都不是马。
   这些动物全都不是鱼。

05 这些孩子全都是男孩儿。
   这些孩子全都不是男孩儿。
   这些动物全都是牛。
   这些动物全都不是牛。

06 这些孩子全都不是女孩儿。
   这些孩子全都是女孩儿。
   这些动物全都不是鱼。
   这些动物全都是鱼。

07 这两个人在喝牛奶。
   这两个人在指着杯里的牛奶。
   这两个人中的一个人在指着另一个人。
   这两个人在骑马。

08 这两个人都在喝牛奶。
   这两个人都在指着杯里的牛奶。
   这两个人中只有一个人在指着什么东西。
   这两个人都在骑马。

09 这两个人都不在喝牛奶。
   这两个人中的一个人在喝牛奶。
   两个人都在喝牛奶。
   有个人在喝桔汁。

10 这个女人在喝牛奶，但是那个女孩儿没有。
   这个女孩儿在喝牛奶，但是那个女人没有。
   这个女人和这个女孩儿都在喝牛奶。
   有个人在喝什么东西，但是他喝的不是牛奶。

7-06

全都不、都、兩個

01 這個人是女的。
   這隻動物是狗。
   這個人是女孩兒。
   這隻動物是馬。

02 這個人不是孩子。
   這隻動物不是馬。
   這個孩子不是男孩兒。
   這隻動物不是狗。

03 這些人是男的。
   這些人是女的。
   這些動物是魚。
   這些動物是馬。

04 這些人全都不是女的。
   這些人全都不是男的。
   這些動物全都不是馬。
   這些動物全都不是魚。

05 這些孩子全都是男孩兒。
   這些孩子全都不是男孩兒。
   這些動物全都是牛。
   這些動物全都不是牛。

06 這些孩子全都不是女孩兒。
   這些孩子全都是女孩兒。
   這些動物全都不是魚。
   這些動物全都是魚。

07 這兩個人在喝牛奶。
   這兩個人在指著杯裡的牛奶。
   這兩個人中的一個人在指著另一個人。
   這兩個人在騎馬。

08 這兩個人都在喝牛奶。
   這兩個人都在指著杯裡的牛奶。
   這兩個人中祇有一個人在指著甚麼東西。
   這兩個人都在騎馬。

09 這兩個人都不在喝牛奶。
   這兩個人中的一個人在喝牛奶。
   兩個人都在喝牛奶。
   有個人在喝桔汁。

10 這個女人在喝牛奶，但是那個女孩兒沒有。
   這個女孩兒在喝牛奶，但是那個女人沒有。
   這個女人和這個女孩兒都在喝牛奶。
   有個人在喝甚麼東西，但是他喝的不是牛奶。

7-06

quán dōu bù, dōu, liǎng gè

01 zhè gè rén shì nǚ de.
     zhè zhī dòng wù shì gǒu.
     zhè gè rén shì nǚ háir.
     zhè zhī dòng wù shì mǎ.

02 zhè gè rén bú shì hái zi.
     zhè zhī dòng wù bú shì mǎ.
     zhè gè hái zi bú shì nán háir.
     zhè zhī dòng wù bú shì gǒu.

03 zhè xiē rén shì nán de.
     zhè xiē rén shì nǚ de.
     zhè xiē dòng wù shì yú.
     zhè xiē dòng wù shì mǎ.

04 zhè xiē rén quán dōu bú shì nǚ de.
     zhè xiē rén quán dōu bú shì nán de.
     zhè xiē dòng wù quán dōu bú shì mǎ.
     zhè xiē dòng wù quán dōu bú shì yú.

05 zhè xiē hái zi quán dōu shì nán háir.
     zhè xiē hái zi quán dōu bú shì nán háir.
     zhè xiē dòng wù quán dōu shì niú.
     zhè xiē dòng wù quán dōu bú shì niú.

06 zhè xiē hái zi quán dōu bú shì nǚ háir.
     zhè xiē hái zi quán dōu shì nǚ háir.
     zhè xiē dòng wù quán dōu bú shì yú.
     zhè xiē dòng wù quán dōu shì yú.

07 zhè liǎng gè rén zài hē niú nǎi.
     zhè liǎng gè rén zài zhǐ zhe bēi lǐ de niú nǎi.
     zhè liǎng gè rén zhōng de yī gè rén zài zhǐ zhe lìng yī gè rén.
     zhè liǎng gè rén zài qí mǎ.

08 zhè liǎng gè rén dōu zài hē niú nǎi.
     zhè liǎng gè rén dōu zài zhǐ zhe bēi lǐ de niú nǎi.
     liǎng gè rén zhōng zhǐ yǒu yī gè rén zài zhǐ zhe shén me dōng xi.
     zhè liǎng gè rén dōu zài qí mǎ.

09 zhè liǎng gè rén dōu bú zài hē niú nǎi.
     zhè liǎng gè rén zhōng de yī gè rén zài hē niú nǎi.
     liǎng gè rén dōu zài hē niú nǎi.
     yǒu gè rén zài hē jú zhī.

10 zhè gè nǚ rén zài hē niú nǎi, dàn shì nà gè nǚ háir méi yǒu.
     zhè gè nǚ háir zài hē niú nǎi, dàn shì nà gè nǚ rén méi yǒu.
     zhè gè nǚ rén hé zhè gè nǚ háir dōu zài hē niú nǎi.
     yǒu gè rén zài hē shén me dōng xi, dàn shì tā hē de bú shì niú nǎi.

形状、位置；介词；所有、大多数

01　一个绿色的圆
　　一个绿色的长方形
　　一个蓝色的正方形
　　一个蓝色的长方形

02　这个圆在那个长方形的前面。
　　这个正方形在那个三角形的前面。
　　这个圆在那个长方形的后面。
　　这个正方形在那个三角形的后面。

03　这个男孩儿在树的后面。
　　这个男孩儿在树的前面。
　　那杯水在这杯牛奶的后面。
　　这杯水在那杯牛奶的前面。

04　圆是圆形的。
　　球是圆形的。
　　正方形不是圆形的。
　　这座建筑物不是圆形的。

05　这扇窗户是圆形的。
　　这扇窗户是正方形的。
　　这只钟是圆形的。
　　这只钟是正方形的。

06　这个长方形在一个圆的里面。
　　这个长方形在一个正方形的里面。
　　那些蓝花儿周围是黄花儿。
　　那些椅子在那张桌子周围。

07　那些正方形大多数都在那个圆旁边。
　　那个圆在大多数的正方形之上。
　　那些三角形大多数都在那个长方形之上。
　　那些三角形大多数都在那个长方形的里面。

08　那些圆大多数都在那个长方形的周围，但不是所有的
　　　圆都在那个长方形的周围。
　　那些圆全都在那个长方形的周围。
　　那些圆大多数都在那个长方形的前面，但不是所有的
　　　圆都在那个长方形的前面。
　　那些圆全都在那个长方形的前面。

09　那些人全都戴着黄帽子。
　　那些人大多数都戴着黄帽子。
　　那些人全都穿着白衣服。
　　那些人大多数都穿着白衣服。

10　这个圆在那个正方形的前面。
　　这个圆在那个正方形的后面。
　　这个圆在那个正方形之上。
　　这个圆在那个正方形之下。

7-07

形狀、位置；介詞；所有、大多數

01　一個綠色的圓
　　一個綠色的長方形
　　一個藍色的正方形
　　一個藍色的長方形

02　這個圓在那個長方形的前面。
　　這個正方形在那個三角形的前面。
　　這個圓在那個長方形的後面。
　　這個正方形在那個三角形的後面。

03　這個男孩兒在樹的後面。
　　這個男孩兒在樹的前面。
　　那杯水在這杯牛奶的後面。
　　這杯水在那杯牛奶的前面。

04　圓是圓形的。
　　球是圓形的。
　　正方形不是圓形的。
　　這座建築物不是圓形的。

05　這扇窗戶是圓形的。
　　這扇窗戶是正方形的。
　　這隻鐘是圓形的。
　　這隻鐘是正方形的。

06　這個長方形在一個圓的裡面。
　　這個長方形在一個正方形的裡面。
　　那些藍花兒週圍是黃花兒。
　　那些椅子在那張桌子週圍。

07　那些正方形大多數都在那個圓旁邊。
　　那個圓在大多數的正方形之上。
　　那些三角形大多數都在那個長方形之上。
　　那些三角形大多數都在那個長方形的裡面。

08　那些圓大多數都在那個長方形的週圍，但不是所有的
　　　圓都在那個長方形的週圍。
　　那些圓全都在那個長方形的週圍。
　　那些圓大多數都在那個長方形的前面，但不是所有的
　　　圓都在那個長方形的前面。
　　那些圓全都在那個長方形的前面。

09　那些人全都戴著黃帽子。
　　那些人大多數都戴著黃帽子。
　　那些人全都穿著白衣服。
　　那些人大多數都穿著白衣服。

10　這個圓在那個正方形的前面。
　　這個圓在那個正方形的後面。
　　這個圓在那個正方形之上。
　　這個圓在那個正方形之下。

7-07

xíng zhuàng, wèi zhì; jiè cí; suǒ yǒu, dà duō shù

01 yī gè lǜ sè de yuán
   yī gè lǜ sè de cháng fāng xíng
   yī gè lán sè de zhèng fāng xíng
   yī gè lán sè de cháng fāng xíng

02 zhè gè yuán zài nà gè cháng fāng xíng de qián miàn.
   zhè gè zhèng fāng xíng zài nà gè sān jiǎo xíng de qián miàn.
   zhè gè yuán zài nà gè cháng fāng xíng de hòu miàn.
   zhè gè zhèng fāng xíng zài nà gè sān jiǎo xíng de hòu miàn.

03 zhè gè nán háir zài shù de hòu miàn.
   zhè gè nán háir zài shù de qián miàn.
   nà bēi shuǐ zài zhè bēi niú nǎi de hòu miàn.
   zhè bēi shuǐ zài nà bēi niú nǎi de qián miàn.

04 yuán shì yuán xíng de.
   qiú shì yuán xíng de.
   zhèng fāng xíng bú shì yuán xíng de.
   zhè zuò jiàn zhù wù bú shì yuán xíng de.

05 zhè shàn chuāng hu shì yuán xíng de.
   zhè shàn chuāng hu shì zhèng fāng xíng de.
   zhè zhī zhōng shì yuán xíng de.
   zhè zhī zhōng shì zhèng fāng xíng de.

06 zhè gè cháng fāng xíng zài yī gè yuán de lǐ miàn.
   zhè gè cháng fāng xíng zài yī gè zhèng fāng xíng de lǐ miàn.
   nà xiē lán huār zhōu wéi shì huáng huār.
   nà xiē yǐ zi zài nà zhāng zhuō zi zhōu wéi.

07 nà xiē zhèng fāng xíng dà duō shù dōu zài nà gè yuán páng biān.
   nà gè yuán zài dà duō shù de zhèng fāng xíng zhī shàng.
   nà xiē sān jiǎo xíng dà duō shù dōu zài nà gè cháng fāng xíng zhī shàng.
   nà xiē sān jiǎo xíng dà duō shù dōu zài nà gè cháng fāng xíng de lǐ miàn.

08 nà xiē yuán dà duō shù dōu zài nà gè cháng fāng xíng de zhōu wéi, dàn bú shì suǒ yǒu de yuán dōu zài
      nà gè cháng fāng xíng de zhōu wéi.
   nà xiē yuán quán dōu zài nà gè cháng fāng xíng de zhōu wéi.
   nà xiē yuán dà duō shù dōu zài nà gè cháng fāng xíng de qián miàn, dàn bú shì suǒ yǒu de yuán dōu zài
      nà gè cháng fāng xíng de qián miàn.
   nà xiē yuán quán dōu zài nà gè cháng fāng xíng de qián miàn.

09 nà xiē rén quán dōu dài zhe huáng mào zi.
   nà xiē rén dà duō shù dōu dài zhe huáng mào zi.
   nà xiē rén quán dōu chuān zhe bái yī fu.
   nà xiē rén dà duō shù dōu chuān zhe bái yī fu.

10 zhè gè yuán zài nà gè zhèng fāng xíng de qián miàn.
   zhè gè yuán zài nà gè zhèng fāng xíng de hòu miàn.
   zhè gè yuán zài nà gè zhèng fāng xíng zhī shàng.
   zhè gè yuán zài nà gè zhèng fāng xíng zhī xià.

7-08

左、右；满的、空的

01 那个男人在用右手指着什么东西。
那个男人在用左手指着什么东西。
那个男孩儿在用右脚踢球。
那个男孩儿在用左脚踢球。

02 那个男人左手里有糖。
那个男人右手里有糖。
左边的那个杯子里有牛奶。
右边的那个杯子里有牛奶。

03 那个男人左手里有很多糖。
那个男人右手里有很多糖。
左边的那个杯子里装满了牛奶。
右边的那个杯子里装满了牛奶。

04 那个男人左手里有很多糖，但是右手里什么也没有。
那个男人右手里有很多糖，但是左手里什么也没有。
左边的那个杯子里装满了牛奶，但是右边的那个杯子是空的。
右边的那个杯子里装满了牛奶，但是左边的那个杯子是空的。

05 那个杯子是空的。
那个杯子里装满了牛奶。
那个杯子里装满了水。
那个杯子里装满了桔汁。

06 左边的那个杯子里装满了牛奶，而右边的那个杯子里装满了水。
右边的那个杯子里装满了牛奶，左边的那个杯子里也装满了牛奶。
左边的那个杯子里装满了水，但是右边的那个杯子是空的。
右边的那个杯子里装满了水，但是左边的那个杯子是空的。

07 那个男人在门的哪一边？他在左边。
那个男人在门的哪一边？他在右边。
那个男人在数字的哪一边？他在右边。
那个男人在数字的哪一边？他在左边。

08 右边的树上开着许多白花儿。
左边的树上开着许多白花儿。
左边有很多人，但是右边只有几个人。
右边有很多人，但是左边只有几个人。

09 那个女人在用右手写字吗？对，她在用右手写字。
那个女人在用左手写字吗？对，她在用左手写字。
哪个女人在用右手指着什么东西？左边的那个女人。
哪个女人在用左手指着什么东西？右边的那个女人。

7-08

左、右；滿的、空的

01 那個男人在用右手指著甚麼東西。
那個男人在用左手指著甚麼東西。
那個男孩兒在用右腳踢球。
那個男孩兒在用左腳踢球。

02 那個男人左手裡有糖。
那個男人右手裡有糖。
左邊的那個杯子裡有牛奶。
右邊的那個杯子裡有牛奶。

03 那個男人左手裡有很多糖。
那個男人右手裡有很多糖。
左邊的那個杯子裡裝滿了牛奶。
右邊的那個杯子裡裝滿了牛奶。

04 那個男人左手裡有很多糖，但是右手裡甚麼也沒有。
那個男人左手裡有很多糖，但是左手裡甚麼也沒有。
左邊的那個杯子裡裝滿了牛奶，但是右邊的那個杯子是空的。
右邊的那個杯子裡裝滿了牛奶，但是左邊的那個杯子是空的。

05 那個杯子是空的。
那個杯子裡裝滿了牛奶。
那個杯子裡裝滿了水。
那個杯子裡裝滿了桔汁。

06 左邊的那個杯子裡裝滿了牛奶，而右邊的那個杯子裡裝滿了水。
右邊的那個杯子裡裝滿了牛奶，左邊的那個杯子裡也裝滿了牛奶。
左邊的那個杯子裡裝滿了水，但是右邊的那個杯子是空的。
右邊的那個杯子裡裝滿了水，但是左邊的那個杯子是空的。

07 那個男人在門的哪一邊？他在左邊。
那個男人在門的哪一邊？他在右邊。
那個男人在數字的哪一邊？他在右邊。
那個男人在數字的哪一邊？他在左邊。

08 右邊的樹上開著許多白花兒。
左邊的樹上開著許多白花兒。
左邊有很多人，但是右邊只有幾個人。
右邊有很多人，但是左邊只有幾個人。

09 那個女人在用右手寫字嗎？ 對，她在用右手寫字。
那個女人在用左手寫字嗎？ 對，她在用左手寫字。
哪個女人在用右手指著甚麼東西？ 左邊的那個女人。
哪個女人在用左手指著甚麼東西？ 右邊的那個女人。

（继续）

7-08

zuǒ, yòu; mǎn de, kōng de

01 nà gè nán rén zài yòng yòu shǒu zhǐ zhe shén me dōng xi.
   nà gè nán rén zài yòng zuǒ shǒu zhǐ zhe shén me dōng xi.
   nà gè nán háir zài yòng yòu jiǎo tī qiú.
   nà gè nán háir zài yòng zuǒ jiǎo tī qiú.

02 nà gè nán rén zuǒ shǒu lǐ yǒu táng.
   nà gè nán rén yòu shǒu lǐ yǒu táng.
   zuǒ biān de nà gè bēi zi lǐ yǒu niú nǎi.
   yòu biān de nà gè bēi zi lǐ yǒu niú nǎi.

03 nà gè nán rén zuǒ shǒu lǐ yǒu hěn duō táng.
   nà gè nán rén yòu shǒu lǐ yǒu hěn duō táng.
   zuǒ biān de nà gè bēi zi lǐ zhuāng mǎn le niú nǎi.
   yòu biān de nà gè bēi zi lǐ zhuāng mǎn le niú nǎi.

04 nà gè nán rén zuǒ shǒu lǐ yǒu hěn duō táng, dàn shì yòu shǒu lǐ shén me yě méi yǒu.
   nà gè nán rén yòu shǒu lǐ yǒu hěn duō táng, dàn shì zuǒ shǒu lǐ shén me yě méi yǒu.
   zuǒ biān de nà gè bēi zi lǐ zhuāng mǎn le niú nǎi, dàn shì yòu biān de nà gè bēi zi shì kōng de.
   yòu biān de nà gè bēi zi lǐ zhuāng mǎn le niú nǎi, dàn shì zuǒ biān de nà gè bēi zi shì kōng de.

05 nà gè bēi zi shì kōng de.
   nà gè bēi zi lǐ zhuāng mǎn le niú nǎi.
   nà gè bēi zi lǐ zhuāng mǎn le shuǐ.
   nà gè bēi zi lǐ zhuāng mǎn le jú zhī.

06 zuǒ biān de nà gè bēi zi lǐ zhuāng mǎn le niú nǎi, ěr yòu biān de nà gè bēi zi lǐ zhuāng mǎn le shuǐ.
   yòu biān de nà gè bēi zi lǐ zhuāng mǎn le niú nǎi, zuǒ biān de nà gè bēi zi lǐ yě zhuāng mǎn le niú nǎi.
   zuǒ biān de nà gè bēi zi lǐ zhuāng mǎn le shuǐ, dàn shì yòu biān de nà gè bēi zi shì kōng de.
   yòu biān de nà gè bēi zi lǐ zhuāng mǎn le shuǐ, dàn shì zuǒ biān de nà gè bēi zi shì kōng de.

07 nà gè nán rén zài mén de nǎ yī biān? tā zài zuǒ biān.
   nà gè nán rén zài mén de nǎ yī biān? tā zài yòu biān.
   nà gè nán rén zài shù zì de nǎ yī biān? tā zài yòu biān.
   nà gè nán rén zài shù zì de nǎ yī biān? tā zài zuǒ biān.

08 yòu biān de shù shàng kāi zhe xǔ duō bái huār.
   zuǒ biān de shù shàng kāi zhe xǔ duō bái huār.
   zuǒ biān yǒu hěn duō rén, dàn shì yòu biān zhǐ yǒu jǐ gè rén.
   yòu biān yǒu hěn duō rén, dàn shì zuǒ biān zhǐ yǒu jǐ gè rén.

09 nà gè nǚ rén zài yòng yòu shǒu xiě zì ma? duì, tā zài yòng yòu shǒu xiě zì.
   nà gè nǚ rén zài yòng zuǒ shǒu xiě zì ma? duì, tā zài yòng zuǒ shǒu xiě zì.
   nǎ gè nǚ rén zài yòng yòu shǒu zhǐ zhe shén me dōng xi? zuǒ biān de nà gè nǚ rén.
   nǎ gè nǚ rén zài yòng zuǒ shǒu zhǐ zhe shén me dōng xi? yòu biān de nà gè nǚ rén.

(jì xù)

10   有人在门前右边走着。
　　　有人在门前左边走着。
　　　有人在门前左边走着，还有人在门前右边走着。
　　　有人在门前中间走着。

10   有人在門前右邊走著。
　　　有人在門前左邊走著。
　　　有人在門前左邊走著，還有人在門前右邊走著。
　　　有人在門前中間走著。

10 yǒu rén zài mén qián yòu biān zǒu zhe.
    yǒu rén zài mén qián zuǒ biān zǒu zhe.
    yǒu rén zài mén qián zuǒ biān zǒu zhe, hái yǒu rén zài mén qián yòu biān zǒu zhe.
    yǒu rén zài mén qián zhōng jiān zǒu zhe.

7-09

使用更多的介词: 在…上面（上方）、在…下面（下方）等

01 这座桥在马路上面。
这个女人正把球举在头上。
这个男人上方有一座狮子雕塑。
这扇门上方标着门牌号"三百零三"。

02 这条马路在桥下面。
这个女人在球下面。
这个男人在一座狮子雕塑下方。
这扇门在门牌号"三百零三"下方。

03 那个小伙子在伸手够他头上的一顶帽子。
那个小伙子拿着一顶帽子，那顶帽子在他的头下方。
我们能看到下面的火车。
我们能看到上面的火车。

04 这架飞机正在云层上面飞行。
这架飞机正在云层下面飞行。
这架飞机正在雪山前面飞行。
这架飞机正在落日前面飞行。

05 那些人大多数在坐着，但是有一个站着。
那些人大多数在站着，但是有一个坐着。
那些人大多数在上台阶，但是有几个在下台阶。
那些人大多数在下楼，但有几个人在上楼。

06 那些牛大多数躺在地上，但是有几头站着。
那些牛大多数站着，但是有几头躺在地上。
这些人大多数是孩子，但是有几个是成年人。
这些椅子大多数有人坐着，只有几把椅子空着。

07 很多人在下台阶，但是有几个在上台阶。
只有几个人在下楼，但是很多人在上楼。
天空中有很多气球。
天空中只有几个气球。

08 很多人坐在椅子上。
只有两个人坐在椅子上。
只有一个人坐在椅子上。
没有人坐在椅子上。

09 很多人在骑自行车。
只有几个人在骑自行车。
只有一个人在骑自行车。
没有人在骑自行车。

10 这几部电话中只有一部是红色的。
这几部电话中只有一部在使用。
这些枪大多数靠在墙上。
这几支枪全都没靠在墙上。

7-09

使用更多的介詞：在…上面（上方）、在…下面（下方）等

01 這座橋在馬路上面。
這個女人正把球舉在頭上。
這個男人上方有一座獅子雕塑。
這扇門上方標著門牌號"三百零三"。

02 這條馬路在橋下面。
這個女人在球下面。
這個男人在一座獅子雕塑下方。
這扇門在門牌號"三百零三"下方。

03 那個小夥子在伸手夠他頭上的一頂帽子。
那個小夥子拿著一頂帽子，那頂帽子在他的頭下方。
我們能看到下面的火車。
我們能看到上面的火車。

04 這架飛機正在雲層上面飛行。
這架飛機正在雲層下面飛行。
這架飛機正在雪山前面飛行。
這架飛機正在落日前面飛行。

05 那些人大多數在坐著，但是有一個站著。
那些人大多數在站著，但是有一個坐著。
那些人大多數在上臺階，但是有幾個在下臺階。
那些人大多數在下樓，但有幾個人在上樓。

06 那些牛大多數躺在地上，但是有幾頭站著。
那些牛大多數站著，但是有幾頭躺在地上。
這些人大多數是孩子，但是有幾個是成年人。
這些椅子大多數有人坐著，祇有幾把椅子空著。

07 很多人在下臺階，但是有幾個在上臺階。
祇有幾個人在下樓，但是很多人在上樓。
天空中有很多氣球。
天空中祇有幾個氣球。

08 很多人坐在椅子上。
祇有兩個人坐在椅子上。
祇有一個人坐在椅子上。
沒有人坐在椅子上。

09 很多人在騎自行車。
祇有幾個人在騎自行車。
祇有一個人在騎自行車。
沒有人在騎自行車。

10 這幾部電話中祇有一部是紅色的。
這幾部電話中祇有一部在使用。
這些槍大多數靠在牆上。
這幾隻槍全都沒靠在牆上。

7-09

shǐ yòng gèng duō de jiè cí: zài... shàng miàn (shàng fāng), zài... xià miàn (xià fāng) děng

01 zhè zuò qiáo zài mǎ lù shàng miàn.
    zhè gè nǚ rén zhèng bǎ qiú jǔ zài tóu shàng.
    zhè gè nán rén shàng fāng yǒu yī zuò shī zi diāo sù.
    zhè shàn mén shàng fāng biāo zhe mén pái hào "sān bǎi líng sān".

02 zhè tiáo mǎ lù zài qiáo xià miàn.
    zhè gè nǚ rén zài qiú xià miàn.
    zhè gè nán rén zài yī zuò shī zi diāo sù xià fāng.
    zhè shàn mén zài mén pái hào "sān bǎi líng sān" xià fāng.

03 nà gè xiǎo huǒ zi zài shēn shǒu gòu tā tóu shàng de yī dǐng mào zi.
    nà gè xiǎo huǒ zi ná zhe yī dǐng mào zi, nà dǐng mào zi zài tā de tóu xià fāng.
    wǒ men néng kàn dào xià miàn de huǒ chē.
    wǒ men néng kàn dào shàng miàn de huǒ chē.

04 zhè jià fēi jī zhèng zài yún céng shàng miàn fēi xíng.
    zhè jià fēi jī zhèng zài yún céng xià miàn fēi xíng.
    zhè jià fēi jī zhèng zài xuě shān qián miàn fēi xíng.
    zhè jià fēi jī zhèng zài luò rì qián miàn fēi xíng.

05 nà xiē rén dà duō shù zài zuò zhe, dàn shì yǒu yī gè zhàn zhe.
    nà xiē rén dà duō shù zài zhàn zhe, dàn shì yǒu yī gè zuò zhe.
    nà xiē rén dà duō shù zài shàng tái jiē, dàn shì yǒu jǐ gè zài xià tái jiē.
    nà xiē rén dà duō shù zài xià lóu, dàn yǒu jǐ gè rén zài shàng lóu.

06 nà xiē niú dà duō shù tǎng zài dì shàng, dàn shì yǒu jǐ tóu zhàn zhe.
    nà xiē niú dà duō shù zhàn zhe, dàn shì yǒu jǐ tóu tǎng zài dì shàng.
    zhè xiē rén dà duō shù shì hái zi, dàn shì yǒu jǐ gè shì chéng nián rén.
    zhè xiē yǐ zi dà duō shù yǒu rén zuò zhe, zhǐ yǒu jǐ bǎ yǐ zi kōng zhe.

07 hěn duō rén zài xià tái jiē, dàn shì yǒu jǐ gè zài shàng tái jiē.
    zhǐ yǒu jǐ gè rén zài xià lóu, dàn shì hěn duō rén zài shàng lóu.
    tiān kōng zhōng yǒu hěn duō qì qiú.
    tiān kōng zhōng zhǐ yǒu jǐ gè qì qiú.

08 hěn duō rén zuò zài yǐ zi shàng.
    zhǐ yǒu liǎng gè rén zuò zài yǐ zi shàng.
    zhǐ yǒu yī gè rén zuò zài yǐ zi shàng.
    méi yǒu rén zuò zài yǐ zi shàng.

09 hěn duō rén zài qí zì xíng chē.
    zhǐ yǒu jǐ gè rén zài qí zì xíng chē.
    zhǐ yǒu yī gè rén zài qí zì xíng chē.
    méi yǒu rén zài qí zì xíng chē.

10 zhè jǐ bù diàn huà zhōng zhǐ yǒu yī bù shì hóng sè de.
    zhè jǐ bù diàn huà zhōng zhǐ yǒu yī bù zài shǐ yòng.
    zhè xiē qiāng dà duō shù kào zài qiáng shàng.
    zhè jǐ zhī qiāng quán dōu méi kào zài qiáng shàng.

使用更多的动词：跳、爬、看、叼等

01 那个男孩儿要跳了。
那个男孩儿在跳。
那个男孩儿已经跳了。
那个男孩儿在游泳。

02 那个男孩儿要从那些木杆上跳过去。
那个男孩儿在从那些木杆上跳过去。
那个男孩儿已经从那些木杆上跳了过去。
那个男孩儿正在水下游泳。

03 那几个孩子在爬树。
那两个孩子在打滑梯。
那个工人在爬梯子。
那个男孩儿在爬山。

04 他们在往上看。
他们在往下看。
他从窗外朝里看着。
他看着那扇窗户。

05 那个牛仔正尽力在牛身上骑稳。
那个牛仔骑不住那头牛。
那个男孩儿想跳过那个赛马用的跳栏。
那个男孩儿跌倒了。

06 那只狗叼着一只飞盘。
那只狗叼着一顶帽子。
那只狗张着嘴，没有叼什么东西。
那只狗闭着嘴，没有叼什么东西。

07 那只狗正尽力去接那只飞盘。
那只狗已经接住了那只飞盘。
那个牛仔正尽力去抓那头小牛。
那个牛仔已经抓住了那头小牛。

08 那个男人在用绳子。
那个女人在用照相机。
那个男人在用钢笔。
那两个人在划船。

09 他在用绳子爬山。
她在用照相机照相。
他在用钢笔写字。
他们在划船过河。

10 那个牛仔在用绳子去套那头小牛。
那个牛仔在用绳子去绑那头小牛。
那个牛仔在抓那头小牛，但是没有用绳子。
那个牛仔在把那头小牛抬起来。

7-10

使用更多的動詞：跳、爬、看、叼等

01 那個男孩兒要跳了。
那個男孩兒在跳。
那個男孩兒已經跳了。
那個男孩兒在游泳。

02 那個男孩兒要從那些木杆上跳過去。
那個男孩兒在從那些木杆上跳過去。
那個男孩兒已經從那些木杆上跳了過去。
那個男孩兒正在水下游泳。

03 那幾個孩子在爬樹。
那兩個孩子在打滑梯。
那個工人在爬梯子。
那個男孩兒在爬山。

04 他們在往上看。
他們在往下看。
他從窗外朝裡看著。
他看著那扇窗戶。

05 那個牛仔正盡力在牛身上騎穩。
那個牛仔騎不住那頭牛。
那個男孩兒想跳過那個賽馬用的跳欄。
那個男孩兒跌倒了。

06 那隻狗叼著一隻飛盤。
那隻狗叼著一頂帽子。
那隻狗張著嘴，沒有叼甚麼東西。
那隻狗閉著嘴，沒有叼甚麼東西。

07 那隻狗正盡力去接那隻飛盤。
那隻狗已經接住了那隻飛盤。
那個牛仔正盡力去抓那頭小牛。
那個牛仔已經抓住了那頭小牛。

08 那個男人在用繩子。
那個女人在用照相機。
那個男人在用鋼筆。
那兩個人在划船。

09 他在用繩子爬山。
她在用照相機照相。
他在用鋼筆寫字。
他們在划船過河。

10 那個牛仔在用繩子去套那頭小牛。
那個牛仔在用繩子去綁那頭小牛。
那個牛仔在抓那頭小牛，但是沒有用繩子。
那個牛仔在把那頭小牛抬起來。

7-10

shǐ yòng gèng duō de dòng cí: tiào, pá, kàn, diāo děng

01 nà gè nán háir yào tiào le.
nà gè nán háir zài tiào.
nà gè nán háir yǐ jīng tiào le.
nà gè nán háir zài yóu yǒng.

02 nà gè nán háir yào cóng nà xiē mù gān shàng tiào guò qù.
nà gè nán háir zài cóng nà xiē mù gān shàng tiào guò qù.
nà gè nán háir yǐ jīng cóng nà xiē mù gān shàng tiào le guò qù.
nà gè nán háir zhèng zài shuǐ xià yóu yǒng.

03 nà jǐ gè hái zi zài pá shù.
nà liǎng gè hái zi zài dǎ huá tī.
nà gè gōng rén zài pá tī zi.
nà gè nán háir zài pá shān.

04 tā men zài wǎng shàng kàn.
tā men zài wǎng xià kàn.
tā cóng chuāng wài cháo lǐ kàn zhe.
tā kàn zhe nà shàn chuāng hù.

05 nà gè niú zǎi zhèng jìn lì zài niú shēn shàng qí wěn.
nà gè niú zǎi qí bú zhù nà tóu niú.
nà gè nán háir xiǎng tiào guò nà gè sài mǎ yòng de tiào lán.
nà gè nán háir diē dǎo le.

06 nà zhī gǒu diāo zhe yī zhī fēi pán.
nà zhī gǒu diāo zhe yī dǐng mào zi.
nà zhī gǒu zhāng zhe zuǐ, méi yǒu diāo shén me dōng xi.
nà zhī gǒu bì zhe zuǐ, méi yǒu diāo shén me dōng xi.

07 nà zhī gǒu zhèng jìn lì qù jiē nà zhī fēi pán.
nà zhī gǒu yǐ jīng jiē zhù le nà zhī fēi pán.
nà gè niú zǎi zhèng jìn lì qù zhuā nà tóu xiǎo niú.
nà gè niú zǎi yǐ jīng zhuā zhù le nà tóu xiǎo niú.

08 nà gè nán rén zài yòng shéng zi.
nà gè nǚ rén zài yòng zhào xiàng jī.
nà gè nán rén zài yòng gāng bǐ.
nà liǎng gè rén zài huá chuán.

09 tā zài yòng shéng zi pá shān.
tā zài yòng zhào xiàng jī zhào xiàng.
tā zài yòng gāng bǐ xiě zì.
tā men zài huá chuán guò hé.

10 nà gè niú zǎi zài yòng shéng zi qù tào nà tóu xiǎo niú.
nà gè niú zǎi zài yòng shéng zi qù bǎng nà tóu xiǎo niú.
nà gè niú zǎi zài zhuā nà tóu xiǎo niú, dàn shì méi yǒu yòng shéng zi.
nà gè niú zǎi zài bǎ nà tóu xiǎo niú tái qǐ lái.

7-11

運用"正…"、"要…"、"已经…"等表示不同时间发生的事

01 我在跳水。
   我在喝牛奶。
   我正摔下来。
   我在剪纸。

02 我在跳水。
   我已经跳进水里了。
   我在喝牛奶。
   我已经把牛奶喝完了。

03 我正摔下来。
   我已经摔下来了。
   我在剪纸。
   我已经把纸剪完了。

04 我要跳水了。
   我要喝牛奶了。
   我要摔下来了。
   我要剪纸了。

05 我要朝水里跳。
   我在朝水里跳。
   我已经跳进水里了。
   我们在朝水里跳。

06 我们不想跳，他要跳。
   我们不在跳，他在跳。
   我们没有跳，他已经跳下去了。
   我们全都在跳。

07 我要跳，她们不想跳。
   我在跳，她们不在跳。
   我已经跳下去了，她们没有跳。
   我们全都在跳。

08 我要摔下来了。
   我正摔下来。
   我已经摔下来了。
   我要跳水了。

09 我要喝牛奶了。
   我在喝牛奶。
   我已经把牛奶喝完了。
   我要吃面包了。

10 我要吃面包了。
   我在吃面包。
   我已经吃了一点儿面包。
   我戴着帽子。

7-11

運用"正…"、"要…"、"已經…"等表示不同時間發生的事

01 我在跳水。
   我在喝牛奶。
   我正摔下來。
   我在剪紙。

02 我在跳水。
   我已經跳進水裡了。
   我在喝牛奶。
   我已經把牛奶喝完了。

03 我正摔下來。
   我已經摔下來了。
   我在剪紙。
   我已經把紙剪完了。

04 我要跳水了。
   我要喝牛奶了。
   我要摔下來了。
   我要剪紙了。

05 我要朝水裡跳。
   我在朝水裡跳。
   我已經跳進水裡了。
   我們在朝水裡跳。

06 我們不想跳，他要跳。
   我們不在跳，他在跳。
   我們沒有跳，他已經跳下去了。
   我們全都在跳。

07 我要跳，她們不想跳。
   我在跳，她們不在跳。
   我已經跳下去了，她們沒有跳。
   我們全都在跳。

08 我要摔下來了。
   我正摔下來。
   我已經摔下來了。
   我要跳水了。

09 我要喝牛奶了。
   我在喝牛奶。
   我已經把牛奶喝完了。
   我要吃面包了。

10 我要吃面包了。
   我在吃面包。
   我已經吃了一點兒面包。
   我戴著帽子。

7-11

yùn yòng "zhèng...", "yào...", "yǐ jīng..." děng biǎo shì bù tóng shí jiān fā shēng de shì

01 wǒ zài tiào shuǐ.
    wǒ zài hē niú nǎi.
    wǒ zhèng shuāi xià lái.
    wǒ zài jiǎn zhǐ.

02 wǒ zài tiào shuǐ.
    wǒ yǐ jīng tiào jìn shuǐ lǐ le.
    wǒ zài hē niú nǎi.
    wǒ yǐ jīng bǎ niú nǎi hē wán le.

03 wǒ zhèng shuāi xià lái.
    wǒ yǐ jīng shuāi xià lái le.
    wǒ zài jiǎn zhǐ.
    wǒ yǐ jīng bǎ zhǐ jiǎn wán le.

04 wǒ yào tiào shuǐ le.
    wǒ yào hē niú nǎi le.
    wǒ yào shuāi xià lái le.
    wǒ yào jiǎn zhǐ le.

05 wǒ yào cháo shuǐ lǐ tiào.
    wǒ zài cháo shuǐ lǐ tiào.
    wǒ yǐ jīng tiào jìn shuǐ lǐ le.
    wǒ men zài cháo shuǐ lǐ tiào.

06 wǒ men bù xiǎng tiào, tā yào tiào.
    wǒ men bú zài tiào, tā zài tiào.
    wǒ men méi yǒu tiào, tā yǐ jīng tiào xià qù le.
    wǒ men quán dōu zài tiào.

07 wǒ yào tiào, tā men bù xiǎng tiào.
    wǒ zài tiào, tā men bú zài tiào.
    wǒ yǐ jīng tiào xià qù le, tā men méi yǒu tiào.
    wǒ men quán dōu zài tiào.

08 wǒ yào shuāi xià lái le.
    wǒ zhèng shuāi xià lái.
    wǒ yǐ jīng shuāi xià lái le.
    wǒ yào tiào shuǐ le.

09 wǒ yào hē niú nǎi le.
    wǒ zài hē niú nǎi.
    wǒ yǐ jīng bǎ niú nǎi hē wán le.
    wǒ yào chī miàn bāo le.

10 wǒ yào chī miàn bāo le.
    wǒ zài chī miàn bāo.
    wǒ yǐ jīng chī le yī diǎnr miàn bāo.
    wǒ dài zhe mào zi.

复习第七部分

01　那个女孩儿在上船。
　　那个男孩儿正从水里出来。
　　那个男孩儿已经从水里出来了。
　　那个男孩儿要从水里出来了。

02　马平时是驮人的，可这匹马现在没人骑。
　　这匹马驮着人。
　　飞机平时是飞行的，可这架飞机现在没有飞行。
　　飞机平时是飞行的，这架飞机正在飞行。

03　这些骑自行车的人骑得很快。
　　这些骑自行车的人骑得很慢。
　　这架飞机飞得很快。
　　这架飞机在慢慢地移动。

04　现在是冬天，树上有雪。
　　现在是夏天，树是绿色的。
　　现在是夏天，这两个人在游泳池里。
　　现在是秋天，树都黄了，地上全是树叶。

05　这些花儿中有些是黄色的，另外一些是蓝色的。
　　这些花儿全都是黄色的。
　　这两只鸭子中有一只的头是白色的，另一只的头是绿
　　　色的。
　　这些鸭子的头全都是黑色的。

06　这两个人都不在喝牛奶。
　　这两个人中的一个人在喝牛奶。
　　两个人都在喝牛奶。
　　有个人在喝桔汁。

07　这个男孩儿在树的后面。
　　这个男孩儿在树的前面。
　　那杯水在这杯牛奶的后面。
　　这杯水在那杯牛奶的前面。

08　这架飞机正在云层上面飞行。
　　这架飞机正在云层下面飞行。
　　这架飞机正在雪山前面飞行。
　　这架飞机正在落日前面飞行。

09　那个牛仔在用绳子去套那头小牛。
　　那个牛仔在用绳子去绑那头小牛。
　　那个牛仔在抓那头小牛，但是没有用绳子。
　　那个牛仔在把那头小牛抬起来。

10　我们不想跳，他要跳。
　　我们不在跳，他在跳。
　　我们没有跳，他已经跳下去了。
　　我们全都在跳。

7-12

復習第七部分

01　那個女孩兒在上船。
　　那個男孩兒正從水裡出來。
　　那個男孩兒已經從水裡出來了。
　　那個男孩兒要從水裡出來了。

02　馬平時是馱人的，可這匹馬現在沒人騎。
　　這匹馬馱著人。
　　飛機平時是飛行的，可這架飛機現在沒有飛行。
　　飛機平時是飛行的，這架飛機正在飛行。

03　這些騎自行車的人騎得很快。
　　這些騎自行車的人騎得很慢。
　　這架飛機飛得很快。
　　這架飛機在慢慢地移動。

04　現在是冬天，樹上有雪。
　　現在是夏天，樹是綠色的。
　　現在是夏天，這兩個人在游泳池裡。
　　現在是秋天，樹都黃了，地上全是樹葉。

05　這些花兒中有些是黃色的，另外一些是藍色的。
　　這些花兒全都是黃色的。
　　這兩隻鴨子中有一隻的頭是白色的，另一隻的頭是綠
　　　色的。
　　這些鴨子的頭全都是黑色的。

06　這兩個人都不在喝牛奶。
　　這兩個人中的一個人在喝牛奶。
　　兩個人都在喝牛奶。
　　有個人在喝桔汁。

07　這個男孩兒在樹的後面。
　　這個男孩兒在樹的前面。
　　那杯水在這杯牛奶的後面。
　　這杯水在那杯牛奶的前面。

08　這架飛機正在雲層上面飛行。
　　這架飛機正在雲層下面飛行。
　　這架飛機正在雪山前面飛行。
　　這架飛機正在落日前面飛行。

09　那個牛仔在用繩子去套那頭小牛。
　　那個牛仔在用繩子去綁那頭小牛。
　　那個牛仔在抓那頭小牛，但是沒有用繩子。
　　那個牛仔在把那頭小牛抬起來。

10　我們不想跳，他要跳。
　　我們不在跳，他在跳。
　　我們沒有跳，他已經跳下去了。
　　我們全都在跳。

7-12

01　nà gè nǚ háir zài shàng chuán.
　　nà gè nán háir zhèng cóng shuǐ lǐ chū lái.
　　nà gè nán háir yǐ jīng cóng shuǐ lǐ chū lái le.
　　nà gè nán háir yào cóng shuǐ lǐ chū lái le.

02　mǎ píng shí shì tuó rén de, kě zhè pǐ mǎ xiàn zài méi rén qí.
　　zhè pǐ mǎ tuó zhe rén.
　　fēi jī píng shí shì fēi xíng de, kě zhè jià fēi jī xiàn zài méi yǒu fēi xíng.
　　fēi jī píng shí shì fēi xíng de, zhè jià fēi jī zhèng zài fēi xíng.

03　zhè xiē qí zì xíng chē de rén qí de hěn kuài.
　　zhè xiē qí zì xíng chē de rén qí de hěn màn.
　　zhè jià fēi jī fēi de hěn kuài.
　　zhè jià fēi jī zài màn màn de yí dòng.

04　xiàn zài shì dōng tiān, shù shàng yǒu xuě.
　　xiàn zài shì xià tiān, shù shì lǜ sè de.
　　xiàn zài shì xià tiān, zhè liǎng gè rén zài yóu yǒng chí lǐ.
　　xiàn zài shì qiū tiān, shù dōu huáng le, dì shàng quán shì shù yè.

05　zhè xiē huār zhōng yǒu xiē shì huáng sè de, lìng wài yī xiē shì lán sè de.
　　zhè xiē huār quán dōu shì huáng sè de.
　　zhè liǎng zhī yā zi zhōng yǒu yī zhī de tóu shì bái sè de, lìng yī zhī de tóu shì lǜ sè de.
　　zhè xiē yā zi de dōu quán dōu shì hēi sè de.

06　zhè liǎng gè rén dōu bú zài hē niú nǎi.
　　zhè liǎng gè rén zhōng de yī gè rén zài hē niú nǎi.
　　liǎng gè rén dōu zài hē niú nǎi.
　　yǒu gè rén zài hē jú zhī.

07　zhè gè nán háir zài shù de hòu miàn.
　　zhè gè nán háir zài shù de qián miàn.
　　nà bēi shuǐ zài zhè bēi niú nǎi de hòu miàn.
　　zhè bēi shuǐ zài nà bēi niú nǎi de qián miàn.

08　zhè jià fēi jī zhèng zài yún céng shàng miàn fēi xíng.
　　zhè jià fēi jī zhèng zài yún céng xià miàn fēi xíng.
　　zhè jià fēi jī zhèng zài xuě shān qián miàn fēi xíng.
　　zhè jià fēi jī zhèng zài luò rì qián miàn fēi xíng.

09　nà gè niú zǎi zài yòng shéng zi qù tào nà tóu xiǎo niú.
　　nà gè niú zǎi zài yòng shéng zi qù bǎng nà tóu xiǎo niú.
　　nà gè niú zǎi zài zhuā nà tóu xiǎo niú, dàn shì méi yǒu yòng shéng zi.
　　nà gè niú zǎi zài bǎ nà tóu xiǎo niú tái qǐ lái.

10　wǒ men bù xiǎng tiào, tā yào tiào.
　　wǒ men bú zài tiào, tā zài tiào.
　　wǒ men méi yǒu tiào, tā yǐ jīng tiào xià qù le.
　　wǒ men quán dōu zài tiào.

8-01

使用序数词

01 第一个数字是二。
第一个数字是一。
第一个数字是四。
第一个数字是九。

02 第二个数字是九。
第二个数字是八。
第二个数字是五。
第二个数字是六。

03 第三个数字是三。
第四个数字是七。
第四个数字是九。
第三个数字是零。

04 最后一个数字是九。
最后一个数字是三。
最后一个数字是一。
最后一个数字是七。

05 第一个数字是零。
第二个数字是零。
第三个数字是零，第四个数字不是零。
第三个数字是零，第四个数字也是零。

06 最后两个数字都是三。
头两个数字都是二。
最后两个数字都是零。
最后三个数字都是一。

07 第二个数字和第四个数字都是三。
第一个数字和最后一个数字都是三。
第三个数字和最后一个数字都是一。
第一个数字和最后一个数字都是一。

08 头两个数字都是二，最后一个数字是六。
头两个数字都是二，最后一个数字是八。
第一个数字是二，第二个数字是五，第三个数字是
零，最后一个数字是九。
第一个数字是二，第二个数字是五，第三个数字是
零，最后一个数字是七。

09 第二个人和最后一个人都坐着。
第二个人和第三个人都坐着。
第一个人和第四个人都坐着。
第一个人和第二个人都坐着。

10 第一个人和第三个人都站着。
第一个人和最后一个人都站着。
第二个人和第三个人都站着。
第三个人和第四个人都站着。

8-01

使用序數詞

01 第一個數字是二。
第一個數字是一。
第一個數字是四。
第一個數字是九。

02 第二個數字是九。
第二個數字是八。
第二個數字是五。
第二個數字是六。

03 第三個數字是三。
第四個數字是七。
第四個數字是九。
第三個數字是零。

04 最後一個數字是九。
最後一個數字是三。
最後一個數字是一。
最後一個數字是七。

05 第一個數字是零。
第二個數字是零。
第三個數字是零，第四個數字不是零。
第三個數字是零，第四個數字也是零。

06 最後兩個數字都是三。
頭兩個數字都是二。
最後兩個數字都是零。
最後三個數字都是一。

07 第二個數字和第四個數字都是三。
第一個數字和最後一個數字都是三。
第三個數字和最後一個數字都是一。
第一個數字和最後一個數字都是一。

08 頭兩個數字都是二，最後一個數字是六。
頭兩個數字都是二，最後一個數字是八。
第一個數字是二，第二個數字是五，第三個數字是
零，最後一個數字是九。
第一個數字是二，第二個數字是五，第三個數字是
零，最後一個數字是七。

09 第二個人和最後一個人都坐著。
第二個人和第三個人都坐著。
第一個人和第四個人都坐著。
第一個人和第二個人都坐著。

10 第一個人和第三個人都站著。
第一個人和最後一個人都站著。
第二個人和第三個人都站著。
第三個人和第四個人都站著。

8-01

shǐ yòng xù shù cí

01 dì yī gè shù zì shì èr.
    dì yī gè shù zì shì yī.
    dì yī gè shù zì shì sì.
    dì yī gè shù zì shì jiǔ.

02 dì èr gè shù zì shì jiǔ.
    dì èr gè shù zì shì bā.
    dì èr gè shù zì shì wǔ.
    dì èr gè shù zì shì liù.

03 dì sān gè shù zì shì sān.
    dì sì gè shù zì shì qī.
    dì sì gè shù zì shì jiǔ.
    dì sān gè shù zì shì líng.

04 zuì hòu yī gè shù zì shì jiǔ.
    zuì hòu yī gè shù zì shì sān.
    zuì hòu yī gè shù zì shì yī.
    zuì hòu yī gè shù zì shì qī.

05 dì yī gè shù zì shì líng.
    dì èr gè shù zì shì líng.
    dì sān gè shù zì shì líng, dì sì gè shù zì bú shì líng.
    dì sān gè shù zì shì líng, dì sì gè shù zì yě shì líng.

06 zuì hòu liǎng gè shù zì dōu shì sān.
    tóu liǎng gè shù zì dōu shì èr.
    zuì hòu liǎng gè shù zì dōu shì líng.
    zuì hòu sān gè shù zì dōu shì yī.

07 dì èr gè shù zì hé dì sì gè shù zì dōu shì sān.
    dì yī gè shù zì hé zuì hòu yī gè shù zì dōu shì sān.
    dì sān gè shù zì hé zuì hòu yī gè shù zì dōu shì yī.
    dì yī gè shù zì hé zuì hòu yī gè shù zì dōu shì yī.

08 tóu liǎng gè shù zì dōu shì èr, zuì hòu yī gè shù zì shì liù.
    tóu liǎng gè shù zì dōu shì èr, zuì hòu yī gè shù zì shì bā.
    dì yī gè shù zì shì èr, dì èr gè shù zì shì wǔ, dì sān gè shù zì shì líng, zuì hòu yī gè shù zì shì jiǔ.
    dì yī gè shù zì shì èr, dì èr gè shù zì shì wǔ, dì sān gè shù zì shì líng, zuì hòu yī gè shù zì shì qī.

09 dì èr gè rén hé zuì hòu yī gè rén dōu zuò zhe.
    dì èr gè rén hé dì sān gè rén dōu zuò zhe.
    dì yī gè rén hé dì sì gè rén dōu zuò zhe.
    dì yī gè rén hé dì èr gè rén dōu zuò zhe.

10 dì yī gè rén hé dì sān gè rén dōu zhàn zhe.
    dì yī gè rén hé zuì hòu yī gè rén dōu zhàn zhe.
    dì èr gè rén hé dì sān gè rén dōu zhàn zhe.
    dì sān gè rén hé dì sì gè rén dōu zhàn zhe.

第一人称；现在时

01 我在骑马。
我现在不骑马了。
我们在骑自行车。
我们现在不骑自行车了。

02 我们在跑。
我们现在不跑了。
我们在唱歌。
我们现在不唱歌了。

03 我们在唱歌。
我们现在不唱歌了。
我在打扮。
我现在不打扮了。

04 我在吃东西。
我在打电话。
那个既没有打电话也没有吃东西的女人就是我。
那个既没有打电话也没有吃东西的男人就是我。

05 我弹着琴，唱着歌。
我没有唱歌，也没弹琴。
我们笑着，敲着鼓。
我们没敲鼓，也没笑。

06 我们俩都在唱歌。
我们俩都不在唱歌。
我们之中只有一个人在唱歌。
我们六个人都在唱歌。

07 我站在人行道上。
我现在不在人行道上站着了。
我们都打着伞。
我们全都没站着。

08 我们四个人都在走。
我们共有四个人。谁都没有走。
我们三个人都在走。
我们共有三个人。谁都没有走。

09 我们俩都在唱歌。
我们在亲吻。
我们俩没唱歌，也没亲吻。
我站着。我的朋友们全都没站着。

10 我和那个男人都打着伞。
我和那个男人都没打伞。
我和我的儿子都戴着帽子。
我和我的儿子都没戴帽子。

8-02

第一人稱；現在時

01 我在騎馬。
我現在不騎馬了。
我們在騎自行車。
我們現在不騎自行車了。

02 我們在跑。
我們現在不跑了。
我們在唱歌。
我們現在不唱歌了。

03 我們在唱歌。
我們現在不唱歌了。
我在打扮。
我現在不打扮了。

04 我在吃東西。
我在打電話。
那個既沒有打電話也沒有吃東西的女人就是我。
那個既沒有打電話也沒有吃東西的男人就是我。

05 我彈著琴，唱著歌。
我沒有唱歌，也沒彈琴。
我們笑著，敲著鼓。
我們沒敲鼓，也沒笑。

06 我們倆都在唱歌。
我們倆都不在唱歌。
我們之中只有一個人在唱歌。
我們六個人都在唱歌。

07 我站在人行道上。
我現在不在人行道上站著了。
我們都打著傘。
我們全都沒站著。

08 我們四個人都在走。
我們共有四個人，誰都沒有走。
我們三個人都在走。
我們共有三個人，誰都沒有走。

09 我們倆都在唱歌。
我們在親吻。
我們倆沒唱歌，也沒親吻。
我站著，我的朋友們全都沒站著。

10 我和那個男人都打著傘。
我和那個男人都沒打傘。
我和我的兒子都戴著帽子。
我和我的兒子都沒戴帽子。

8-02

dì yī rén chēng; xiàn zài shí

01 wǒ zài qí mǎ.
wǒ xiàn zài bù qí mǎ le.
wǒ men zài qí zì xíng chē.
wǒ men xiàn zài bù qí zì xíng chē le.

02 wǒ men zài pǎo.
wǒ men xiàn zài bù pǎo le.
wǒ men zài chàng gē.
wǒ men xiàn zài bú chàng gē le.

03 wǒ men zài chàng gē.
wǒ men xiàn zài bú chàng gē le.
wǒ zài dǎ bàn.
wǒ xiàn zài bù dǎ bàn le.

04 wǒ zài chī dōng xi.
wǒ zài dǎ diàn huà.
nà gè jì méi yǒu dǎ diàn huà, yě méi yǒu chī dōng xi de nǚ rén jiù shì wǒ.
nà gè jì méi yǒu dǎ diàn huà, yě méi yǒu chī dōng xi de nán rén jiù shì wǒ.

05 wǒ tán zhe qín, chàng zhe gē.
wǒ méi yǒu chàng gē, yě méi tán qín.
wǒ men xiào zhe, qiāo zhe gǔ.
wǒ men méi qiāo gǔ, yě méi xiào.

06 wǒ men liǎ dōu zài chàng gē.
wǒ men liǎ dōu bú zài chàng gē.
wǒ men zhī zhōng zhǐ yǒu yī gè rén zài chàng gē.
wǒ men liù gè rén dōu zài chàng gē.

07 wǒ zhàn zài rén xíng dào shàng.
wǒ xiàn zài bú zài rén xíng dào shàng zhàn zhe le.
wǒ men dōu dǎ zhe sǎn.
wǒ men quán dōu méi zhàn zhe.

08 wǒ men sì gè rén dōu zài zǒu.
wǒ men gòng yǒu sì gè rén, shéi dōu méi yǒu zǒu.
wǒ men sān gè rén dōu zài zǒu.
wǒ men gòng yǒu sān gè rén, shéi dōu méi yǒu zǒu.

09 wǒ men liǎ dōu zài chàng gē.
wǒ men zài qīn wěn.
wǒ men liǎ méi chàng gē, yě méi qīn wěn.
wǒ zhàn zhe, wǒ de péng yǒu men quán dōu méi zhàn zhe.

10 wǒ hé nà gè nán rén dōu dǎ zhe sǎn.
wǒ hé nà gè nán rén dōu méi dǎ sǎn.
wǒ hé wǒ de ér zi dōu dài zhe mào zi.
wǒ hé wǒ de ér zi dōu méi dài mào zi.

8-03

看起来象、几乎所有的、一个、其它、大
多数、全都；指示代词

01　这是一个正方形。
　　这个图形看起来象正方形，但并不是。
　　这是一个三角形。
　　这个图形看起来象三角形，但并不是。

02　这两个人是女人。
　　这两个人看起来象女人，但并不是。它们是人体模
　　　　型。
　　这些人是宇航员。
　　这些人看起来象宇航员，但并不是。

03　这些图形全都是圆的。
　　这些图形全都是三角形。
　　这些图形中有三个是圆的，还有一个是三角形。
　　这些图形中有两个是红色的，还有两个是蓝色的。

04　那个黑色的圆在右上方。
　　那个黑色的圆在左上方。
　　那个黑色的三角形在右下方。
　　那个黑色的三角形在左下方。

05　那些圆中有几个是黑色的。
　　几乎所有的圆都是黄色的，但有一个是黑色的。
　　有几个三角形是黑色的。
　　几乎所有的三角形都是黄色的，但有一个是黑色的。

06　几乎所有的圆都是黄色的。
　　几乎所有的圆都是黑色的。
　　那些三角形全都是黄色的。
　　几乎所有的三角形都是黄色的。

07　几乎所有的圆都是黑色的。
　　几乎所有的圆都是黄色的。
　　有一个圆是蓝色的，其它的都是红色的。
　　有一个圆是红色的。

08　几乎所有的圆都是黄色的，但有两个是蓝色的。
　　有一个圆是黑色的，其它的都是黄色的。
　　那些圆大多数是黑色的，还有一个是绿色的。
　　那些圆大多数是红色的，还有几个是绿色的。

09　那些蓝色的圆大，红色的圆小。
　　那些红色的圆大，蓝色的圆小。
　　那些三角形在那些圆的上面。
　　那些圆在那些三角形的前面。

10　那些黑色的正方形大多数都大，而那些白色的正方形
　　　　全都小。
　　那些黑色正方形全都大，而那些白色的正方形大多数
　　　　都小。
　　那些大三角形中有几个是绿色的，而那些小三角形全
　　　　都是灰色的。
　　那些大三角形全都是绿色的，而那些小三角形中有几
　　　　个是灰色的。

8-03

看起來象、幾乎所有的、一個、其它、大
多數、全都；指示代詞

01　這是一個正方形。
　　這個圖形看起來象正方形，但並不是。
　　這是一個三角形。
　　這個圖形看起來象三角形，但並不是。

02　這兩個人是女人。
　　這兩個人看起來象女人，但並不是。它們是人體模
　　　　型。
　　這些人是宇航員。
　　這些人看起來象宇航員，但並不是。

03　這些圖形全都是圓的。
　　這些圖形全都是三角形。
　　這些圖形中有三個是圓的，還有一個是三角形。
　　這些圖形中有兩個是紅色的，還有兩個是藍色的。

04　那個黑色的圓在右上方。
　　那個黑色的圓在左上方。
　　那個黑色的三角形在右下方。
　　那個黑色的三角形在左下方。

05　那些圓中有幾個是黑色的。
　　幾乎所有的圓都是黃色的，但有一個是黑色的。
　　有幾個三角形是黑色的。
　　幾乎所有的三角形都是黃色的，但有一個是黑色的。

06　幾乎所有的圓都是黃色的。
　　幾乎所有的圓都是黑色的。
　　那些三角形全都是黃色的。
　　幾乎所有的三角形都是黃色的。

07　幾乎所有的圓都是黑色的。
　　幾乎所有的圓都是黃色的。
　　有一個圓是藍色的，其它的都是紅色的。
　　有一個圓是紅色的。

08　幾乎所有的圓都是黃色的，但有兩個是藍色的。
　　有一個圓是黑色的，其它的都是黃色的。
　　那些圓大多數是黑色的，還有一個是綠色的。
　　那些圓大多數是紅色的，還有幾個是綠色的。

09　那些藍色的圓大，紅色的圓小。
　　那些紅色的圓大，藍色的圓小。
　　那些三角形在那些圓的上面。
　　那些圓在那些三角形的前面。

10　那些黑色的正方形大多數都大，而那些白色的正方形
　　　　全都小。
　　那些黑色正方形全都大，而那些白色的正方形大多數
　　　　都小。
　　那些大三角形中有幾個是綠色的，而那些小三角形全
　　　　都是灰色的。
　　那些大三角形全都是綠色的，而那些小三角形中有幾
　　　　個是灰色的。

kàn qǐ lái xiàng, jī hū suǒ yǒu de, yī gè, qí tā, dà duō shù, quán dōu; zhǐ shì dài cí

01 zhè shì yī gè zhèng fāng xíng.
    zhè gè tú xíng kàn qǐ lái xiàng zhèng fāng xíng, dàn bìng bú shì.
    zhè shì yī gè sān jiǎo xíng.
    zhè gè tú xíng kàn qǐ lái xiàng sān jiǎo xíng, dàn bìng bú shì.

02 zhè liǎng gè rén shì nǚ rén.
    zhè liǎng gè rén kàn qǐ lái xiàng nǚ rén, dàn bìng bú shì. tā men shì rén tǐ mó xíng.
    zhè xiē rén shì yǔ háng yuán.
    zhè xiē rén kàn qǐ lái xiàng yǔ háng yuán, dàn bìng bú shì.

03 zhè xiē tú xíng quán dōu shì yuán de.
    zhè xiē tú xíng quán dōu shì sān jiǎo xíng.
    zhè xiē tú xíng zhōng yǒu sān gè shì yuán de, hái yǒu yī gè shì sān jiǎo xíng.
    zhè xiē tú xíng zhōng yǒu liǎng gè shì hóng sè de, hái yǒu liǎng gè shì lán sè de.

04 nà gè hēi sè de yuán zài yòu shàng fāng.
    nà gè hēi sè de yuán zài zuǒ shàng fāng.
    nà gè hēi sè de sān jiǎo xíng zài yòu xià fāng.
    nà gè hēi sè de sān jiǎo xíng zài zuǒ xià fāng.

05 nà xiē yuán zhōng yǒu jǐ gè shì hēi sè de.
    jī hū suǒ yǒu de yuán dōu shì huáng sè de, dàn yǒu yī gè shì hēi sè de.
    yǒu jǐ gè sān jiǎo xíng shì hēi sè de.
    jī hū suǒ yǒu de sān jiǎo xíng dōu shì huáng sè de, dàn yǒu yī gè shì hēi sè de.

06 jī hū suǒ yǒu de yuán dōu shì huáng sè de.
    jī hū suǒ yǒu de yuán dōu shì hēi sè de.
    nà xiē sān jiǎo xíng quán dōu shì huáng sè de.
    jī hū suǒ yǒu de sān jiǎo xíng dōu shì huáng sè de.

07 jī hū suǒ yǒu de yuán dōu shì hēi sè de.
    jī hū suǒ yǒu de yuán dōu shì huáng sè de.
    yǒu yī gè yuán shì lán sè de, qí tā de dōu shì hóng sè de.
    yǒu yī gè yuán shì hóng sè de.

08 jī hū suǒ yǒu de yuán dōu shì huáng sè de, dàn yǒu liǎng gè shì lán sè de.
    yǒu yī gè yuán shì hēi sè de, qí tā de dōu shì huáng sè de.
    nà xiē yuán dà duō shù shì hēi sè de, hái yǒu yī gè shì lǜ sè de.
    nà xiē yuán dà duō shù shì hóng sè de, hái yǒu jǐ gè shì lǜ sè de.

09 nà xiē lán sè de yuán dà, hóng sè de yuán xiǎo.
    nà xiē hóng sè de yuán dà, lán sè de yuán xiǎo.
    nà xiē sān jiǎo xíng zài nà xiē yuán de shàng miàn.
    nà xiē yuán zài nà xiē sān jiǎo xíng de qián miàn.

10 nà xiē hēi sè de zhèng fāng xíng dà duō shù dōu dà, ér nà xiē bái sè de zhèng fāng xíng quán dōu xiǎo.
    nà xiē hēi sè zhèng fāng xíng quán dōu dà, ér nà xiē bái sè de zhèng fāng xíng dà duō shù dōu xiǎo.
    nà xiē dà sān jiǎo xíng zhōng yǒu jǐ gè shì lǜ sè de, ér nà xiē xiǎo sān jiǎo xíng quán dōu shì huī sè de.
    nà xiē dà sān jiǎo xíng quán dōu shì lǜ sè de, ér nà xiē xiǎo sān jiǎo xíng zhōng yǒu jǐ gè shì huī sè de.

8-04

宇宙、地理、国家

01　土星
　　非洲
　　一个女人
　　中国

02　这颗行星叫土星。
　　这个人是女人。
　　这个国家叫中国。
　　这块大陆叫非洲。

03　一颗行星
　　一个人
　　一个国家
　　一块大陆

04　这颗行星是土星。
　　这个人是女孩儿。
　　那个印成红色的国家是英国。
　　这块大陆是北美洲。

05　这块大陆是亚洲。
　　这块大陆是非洲。
　　这块大陆是南美洲。
　　这块大陆是欧洲。

06　这张地图上印成红色的那个国家是巴西。
　　这张地图上印成红色的那个国家是阿根廷。
　　这张地图上印成红色的那个国家是智利。
　　这张地图上印成红色的那个国家是委内瑞拉。

07　美国在这张地图上印成了红色。
　　加拿大在这张地图上印成了红色。
　　墨西哥在这张地图上印成了红色。
　　日本在这张地图上印成了红色。

08　这张地图上印成红色的那个国家是尼日利亚。
　　这张地图上印成红色的那个国家是埃及。
　　这张地图上印成红色的那个国家是阿尔及利亚。
　　这张地图上印成红色的那个国家是坦桑尼亚。

09　德国在欧洲。这张地图上印成红色的那个国家是德
　　国。
　　意大利在欧洲。这张地图上印成红色的那个国家是意
　　大利。
　　印度在亚洲。这张地图上印成红色的那个国家是印
　　度。
　　越南在亚洲。这张地图上印成红色的那个国家是越
　　南。

10　这张地图上印成红色的那个亚洲国家是中国。
　　这张地图上印成红色的那个亚洲国家是朝鲜。
　　这张地图上印成红色的那个欧洲国家是西班牙。
　　俄罗斯在这张地图上印成了红色。俄罗斯横跨欧洲和
　　亚洲。

8-04

宇宙、地理、國家

01　土星
　　非洲
　　一個女人
　　中國

02　這顆行星叫土星。
　　這個人是女人。
　　這個國家叫中國。
　　這塊大陸叫非洲。

03　一顆行星
　　一個人
　　一個國家
　　一塊大陸

04　這顆行星是土星。
　　這個人是女孩兒。
　　那個印成紅色的國家是英國。
　　這塊大陸是北美洲。

05　這塊大陸是亞洲。
　　這塊大陸是非洲。
　　這塊大陸是南美洲。
　　這塊大陸是歐洲。

06　這張地圖上印成紅色的那個國家是巴西。
　　這張地圖上印成紅色的那個國家是阿根廷。
　　這張地圖上印成紅色的那個國家是智利。
　　這張地圖上印成紅色的那個國家是委內瑞拉。

07　美國在這張地圖上印成了紅色。
　　加拿大在這張地圖上印成了紅色。
　　墨西哥在這張地圖上印成了紅色。
　　日本在這張地圖上印成了紅色。

08　這張地圖上印成紅色的那個國家是尼日利亞。
　　這張地圖上印成紅色的那個國家是埃及。
　　這張地圖上印成紅色的那個國家是阿爾及利亞。
　　這張地圖上印成紅色的那個國家是坦桑尼亞。

09　德國在歐洲。這張地圖上印成紅色的那個國家是德
　　國。
　　意大利在歐洲。這張地圖上印成紅色的那個國家是意
　　大利。
　　印度在亞洲。這張地圖上印成紅色的那個國家是印
　　度。
　　越南在亞洲。這張地圖上印成紅色的那個國家是越
　　南。

10　這張地圖上印成紅色的那個亞洲國家是中國。
　　這張地圖上印成紅色的那個亞洲國家是朝鮮。
　　這張地圖上印成紅色的那個歐洲國家是西班牙。
　　俄羅斯在這張地圖上印成了紅色。俄羅斯橫跨歐洲和
　　亞洲。

8-04

yǔ zhòu, dì lǐ, guó jiā

01 tǔ xīng
   fēi zhōu
   yī gè nǚ rén
   zhōng guó

02 zhè kē xíng xīng jiào tǔ xīng.
   zhè gè rén shì nǚ rén.
   zhè gè guó jiā jiào zhōng guó.
   zhè kuài dà lù jiào fēi zhōu.

03 yī kē xíng xīng
   yī gè rén
   yī gè guó jiā
   yī kuài dà lù

04 zhè kē xíng xīng shì tǔ xīng.
   zhè gè rén shì nǚ háir.
   nà gè yìn chéng hóng sè de guó jiā shì yīng guó.
   zhè kuài dà lù shì běi měi zhōu.

05 zhè kuài dà lù shì yà zhōu.
   zhè kuài dà lù shì fēi zhōu.
   zhè kuài dà lù shì nán měi zhōu.
   zhè kuài dà lù shì ōu zhōu.

06 zhè zhāng dì tú shàng yìn chéng hóng sè de nà gè guó jiā shì bā xī.
   zhè zhāng dì tú shàng yìn chéng hóng sè de nà gè guó jiā shì ā gēn tíng.
   zhè zhāng dì tú shàng yìn chéng hóng sè de nà gè guó jiā shì zhì lì.
   zhè zhāng dì tú shàng yìn chéng hóng sè de nà gè guó jiā shì wěi nèi ruì lā.

07 měi guó zài zhè zhāng dì tú shàng yìn chéng le hóng sè.
   jiā ná dà zài zhè zhāng dì tú shàng yìn chéng le hóng sè.
   mò xī gē zài zhè zhāng dì tú shàng yìn chéng le hóng sè.
   rì běn zài zhè zhāng dì tú shàng yìn chéng le hóng sè.

08 zhè zhāng dì tú shàng yìn chéng hóng sè de nà gè guó jiā shì ní rì lì yà.
   zhè zhāng dì tú shàng yìn chéng hóng sè de nà gè guó jiā shì āi jí.
   zhè zhāng dì tú shàng yìn chéng hóng sè de nà gè guó jiā shì ā ěr jí lì yà.
   zhè zhāng dì tú shàng yìn chéng hóng sè de nà gè guó jiā shì tǎn sāng ní yà.

09 dé guó zài ōu zhōu. zhè zhāng dì tú shàng yìn chéng hóng sè de nà gè guó jiā shì dé guó.
   yì dà lì zài ōu zhōu. zhè zhāng dì tú shàng yìn chéng hóng sè de nà gè guó jiā shì yì dà lì.
   yìn dù zài yà zhōu. zhè zhāng dì tú shàng yìn chéng hóng sè de nà gè guó jiā shì yìn dù.
   yuè nán zài yà zhōu. zhè zhāng dì tú shàng yìn chéng hóng sè de nà gè guó jiā shì yuè nán.

10 zhè zhāng dì tú shàng yìn chéng hóng sè de nà gè yà zhōu guó jiā shì zhōng guó.
   zhè zhāng dì tú shàng yìn chéng hóng sè de nà gè yà zhōu guó jiā shì cháo xiǎn.
   zhè zhāng dì tú shàng yìn chéng hóng sè de nà gè ōu zhōu guó jiā shì xī bān yá.
   é luó sī zài zhè zhāng dì tú shàng yìn chéng le hóng sè. é luó sī héng kuà ōu zhōu hé yà zhōu.

街道、人行道

01 那些轿车正在街道上行驶。
那些轿车停在街道上。
人们站在人行道上。
人们走在人行道上。

02 那辆轿车在街道上。
那辆轿车在高速公路上。
那架桥横跨那条高速公路。
那架桥横跨那条河。

03 有两架桥横跨那条公路。
那条路两旁都是树，路上有一辆轿车。
那条路通向那座房子。
那条路通向那座山。

04 那两个人在过铁路。
那两个人站在铁路旁。
那个男人在过街。
那个男人正站在街上。

05 哪几个人正在人行道上骑车？
哪些人正在路上骑车？
有两个人在骑马。他们没在人行道上骑马，也没在路
上骑马。
哪些人正在人行道上，但是什么都没有骑？

06 那些鸟在过人行道。
那条人行道上没有人。
那个男人在骑车过街。
那个男人在坐着轮椅过街。

07 那些鸟在过人行道。
他在跑着过街。
他在骑车过街。
他在坐着轮椅过街。

08 那两排建筑物之间有一条胡同。
那条铁路横跨那条大街。
那辆公共汽车正在人行道上行驶。
那辆公共汽车正在驶过大桥。

09 那个男人正用扫帚打扫街道。
那辆拖拉机正在打扫公路。
那个男人正在街道上的坑里挖土。
那台机器正在街道上挖坑。

10 那条路上到处都是骑车的人。
那条路上到处都是赛跑的人。
那条街上几乎空无一人。
那条人行道上到处都是人。

8-05

街道、人行道

01 那些轎車正在街道上行駛。
那些轎車停在街道上。
人們站在人行道上。
人們走在人行道上。

02 那輛轎車在街道上。
那輛轎車在高速公路上。
那架橋橫跨那條高速公路。
那架橋橫跨那條河。

03 有兩架橋橫跨那條公路。
那條路兩旁都是樹，路上有一輛轎車。
那條路通向那座房子。
那條路通向那座山。

04 那兩個人在過鐵路。
那兩個人站在鐵路旁。
那個男人在過街。
那個男人正站在街上。

05 哪幾個人正在人行道上騎車？
哪些人正在路上騎車？
有兩個人在騎馬。他們沒在人行道上騎馬，也沒在路
上騎馬。
哪些人正在人行道上，但是什麼都沒有騎？

06 那些鳥在過人行道。
那條人行道上沒有人。
那個男人在騎車過街。
那個男人在坐著輪椅過街。

07 那些鳥在過人行道。
他在跑著過街。
他在騎車過街。
他在坐著輪椅過街。

08 那兩排建築物之間有一條胡同。
那條鐵路橫跨那條大街。
那輛公共汽車正在人行道上行駛。
那輛公共汽車正在駛過大橋。

09 那個男人正用掃帚打掃街道。
那輛拖拉機正在打掃公路。
那個男人正在街道上的坑裡挖土。
那臺機器正在街道上挖坑。

10 那條路上到處都是騎車的人。
那條路上到處都是賽跑的人。
那條街上幾乎空無一人。
那條人行道上到處都是人。

8-05

jiē dào, rén xíng dào

01 nà xiē jiào chē zhèng zài jiē dào shàng xíng shǐ.
   nà xiē jiào chē tíng zài jiē dào shàng.
   rén men zhàn zài rén xíng dào shàng.
   rén men zǒu zài rén xíng dào shàng.

02 nà liàng jiào chē zài jiē dào shàng.
   nà liàng jiào chē zài gāo sù gōng lù shàng.
   nà jià qiáo héng kuà nà tiáo gāo sù gōng lù.
   nà jià qiáo héng kuà nà tiáo hé.

03 yǒu liǎng jià qiáo héng kuà nà tiáo gōng lù.
   nà tiáo lù liáng páng dōu shì shù, lù shàng yǒu yī liàng jiào chē.
   nà tiáo lù tōng xiàng nà zuò fáng zi.
   nà tiáo lù tōng xiàng nà zuò shān.

04 nà liǎng gè rén zài guò tiě lù.
   nà liǎng gè rén zhàn zài tiě lù páng.
   nà gè nán rén zài guò jiē.
   nà gè nán rén zhèng zhàn zài jiē shàng.

05 nǎ jǐ gè rén zhèng zài rén xíng dào shàng qí chē?
   nǎ xiē rén zhèng zài lù shàng qí chē?
   yǒu liǎng gè rén zài qí mǎ. tā men méi zài rén xíng dào shàng qí mǎ, yě méi zài lù shàng qí mǎ.
   nǎ xiē rén zhèng zài rén xíng dào shàng, dàn shì shén me dōu méi yǒu qí?

06 nà xiē niǎo zài guò rén xíng dào.
   nà tiáo rén xíng dào shàng méi yǒu rén.
   nà gè nán rén zài qí chē guò jiē.
   nà gè nán rén zài zuò zhe lún yǐ guò jiē.

07 nà xiē niǎo zài guò rén xíng dào.
   tā zài pǎo zhe guò jiē.
   tā zài qí chē guò jiē.
   tā zài zuò zhe lún yǐ guò jiē.

08 nà liǎng pái jiàn zhù wù zhī jiān yǒu yī tiáo hú tòng.
   nà tiáo tiě lù héng kuà nà tiáo dà jiē.
   nà liàng gōng gòng qì chē zhèng zài rén xíng dào shàng xíng shǐ.
   nà liàng gōng gòng qì chē zhèng zài shǐ guò dà qiáo.

09 nà gè nán rén zhèng yòng sào zhou dǎ sǎo jiē dào.
   nà liàng tuō lā jī zhèng zài dǎ sǎo gōng lù.
   nà gè nán rén zhèng zài jiē dào shàng de kēng lǐ wā tǔ.
   nà tái jī qì zhèng zài jiē dào shàng wā kēng.

10 nà tiáo lù shàng dào chù dōu shì qí chē de rén.
   nà tiáo lù shàng dào chù dōu shì sài pǎo de rén.
   nà tiáo jiē shàng jī hū kōng wú yī rén.
   nà tiáo rén xíng dào shàng dào chù dōu shì rén.

8-06

宠物、衣服；名词所有格和代词

01 有个人穿着一件灰毛衣。
有个人穿着一件蓝 T 恤衫。
这些女孩儿穿着黑裙子。
这个男孩儿有一条黑狗。

02 有个人的毛衣是灰色的。
有个人的 T 恤衫是蓝色的。
这些女孩儿的裙子都是黑色的。
这个男孩儿的那只狗是黑色的。

03 这件衬衫是那个男人的。
这件衬衫不是那个男人的。
这两个鼓是那个男人的。
这只狗是那个男孩儿的。

04 这顶帽子是那个女人的。
这顶帽子不是那个女人的。
这件衬衫不是那个男孩儿的。
这件衬衫是一个男孩儿的。

05 这只狗是那个男孩儿的，它是那个男孩儿的宠物。
这只狗是那个女人的，它是那个女人的宠物。
这头熊不属于任何人，它不是宠物。
这头牛是一个农民的，可不是那个农民的宠物。

06 这只宠物很大。
这只宠物很小。
这只动物不是宠物，可是真的。
这只动物不是真的。

07 一顶女式帽子
一顶男式帽子
这件夹克是那个男孩儿的。
这件夹克不是那个男孩儿的。

08 这个女人在抚摩自己的狗。
这个小姑娘在抚摩自己的狗。
这个男人在抚摩那只猫。
这个男人在抚摩自己的狗。

09 这个男人的伞是黑色的。
这两个男人的伞都是黑色的。
这个女人的连衣裙是蓝色的。
这几个女人的连衣裙都是蓝色的。

10 那个男孩儿的狗
那个男孩儿的父亲
那个女孩儿的父亲
那个女孩儿的母亲

8-06

寵物、衣服；名詞所有格和代詞

01 有個人穿著一件灰毛衣。
有個人穿著一件藍 T 恤衫。
這些女孩兒穿著黑裙子。
這個男孩兒有一條黑狗。

02 有個人的毛衣是灰色的。
有個人的 T 恤衫是藍色的。
這些女孩兒的裙子都是黑色的。
這個男孩兒的那隻狗是黑色的。

03 這件襯衫是那個男人的。
這件襯衫不是那個男人的。
這兩個鼓是那個男人的。
這隻狗是那個男孩兒的。

04 這頂帽子是那個女人的。
這頂帽子不是那個女人的。
這件襯衫不是那個男孩兒的。
這件襯衫是一個男孩兒的。

05 這隻狗是那個男孩兒的，它是那個男孩兒的寵物。
這隻狗是那個女人的，它是那個女人的寵物。
這頭熊不屬於任何人，它不是寵物。
這頭牛是一個農民的，可不是那個農民的寵物。

06 這隻寵物很大。
這隻寵物很小。
這隻動物不是寵物，可是真的。
這隻動物不是真的。

07 一頂女式帽子
一頂男式帽子
這件茄克是那個男孩兒的。
這件茄克不是那個男孩兒的。

08 這個女人在撫摩自己的狗。
這個小姑娘在撫摩自己的狗。
這個男人在撫摩那隻貓。
這個男人在撫摩自己的狗。

09 這個男人的傘是黑色的。
這兩個男人的傘都是黑色的。
這個女人的連衣裙是藍色的。
這幾個女人的連衣裙都是藍色的。

10 那個男孩兒的狗
那個男孩兒的父親
那個女孩兒的父親
那個女孩兒的母親

8-06

chǒng wù, yī fú; míng cí suǒ yǒu gé hé dài cí

01 yǒu gè rén chuān zhe yī jiàn huī máo yī.
    yǒu gè rén chuān zhe yī jiàn lán T xù shān.
    zhè xiē nǚ háir chuān zhe hēi qún zi.
    zhè gè nán háir yǒu yī tiáo hēi gǒu.

02 yǒu gè rén de máo yī shì huī sè de.
    yǒu gè rén de T xù shān shì lán sè de.
    zhè xiē nǚ háir de qún zi dōu shì hēi sè de.
    zhè gè nán háir de nà zhī gǒu shì hēi sè de.

03 zhè jiàn chèn shān shì nà gè nán rén de.
    zhè jiàn chèn shān bú shì nà gè nán rén de.
    zhè liǎng gè gǔ shì nà gè nán rén de.
    zhè zhī gǒu shì nà gè nán háir de.

04 zhè dǐng mào zi shì nà gè nǚ rén de.
    zhè dǐng mào zi bú shì nà gè nǚ rén de.
    zhè jiàn chèn shān bú shì nà gè nán háir de.
    zhè jiàn chèn shān shì yī gè nán háir de.

05 zhè zhī gǒu shì nà gè nán háir de, tā shì nà gè nán háir de chǒng wù.
    zhè zhī gǒu shì nà gè nǚ rén de, tā shì nà gè nǚ rén de chǒng wù.
    zhè tóu xióng bù shǔ yú rèn hé rén, tā bú shì chǒng wù.
    zhè tóu niú shì yī gè nóng mín de, kě bú shì nà gè nóng mín de chǒng wù.

06 zhè zhī chǒng wù hěn dà.
    zhè zhī chǒng wù hěn xiǎo.
    zhè zhī dòng wù bú shì chǒng wù, kě shì zhēn de.
    zhè zhī dòng wù bú shì zhēn de.

07 yī dǐng nǚ shì mào zi
    yī dǐng nán shì mào zi
    zhè jiàn jiá kè shì nà gè nán háir de.
    zhè jiàn jiá kè bú shì nà gè nán háir de.

08 zhè gè nǚ rén zài fǔ mó zì jǐ de gǒu.
    zhè gè xiǎo gū niang zài fǔ mó zì jǐ de gǒu.
    zhè gè nán rén zài fǔ mó nà zhī māo.
    zhè gè nán rén zài fǔ mó zì jǐ de gǒu.

09 zhè gè nán rén de sǎn shì hēi sè de.
    zhè liǎng gè nán rén de sǎn dōu shì hēi sè de.
    zhè gè nǚ rén de lián yī qún shì lán sè de.
    zhè jǐ gè nǚ rén de lián yī qún dōu shì lán sè de.

10 nà gè nán háir de gǒu
    nà gè nán háir de fù qīn
    nà gè nǚ háir de fù qīn
    nà gè nǚ háir de mǔ qīn

8-07

形容词的比较级和最高级

01 这个女人比这个男人年纪大。
这个男人比这个女人年纪大。
这个男孩儿比这个女孩儿高。
这个女孩儿比这个男孩儿高。

02 一个年轻女人
这个女人年纪较大，但不是年纪最大的。
年纪最大的女人
一个小男孩儿

03 年纪最大的男孩儿
这个男孩儿年纪较小，但不是最小的。
年纪最小的男孩儿
他比这些男孩儿年纪大，他是一个男人。

04 这架飞机飞得最高。
这架飞机飞得很低，离地面很近。
这架飞机飞得很低，但不是最低的。
这架飞机没有飞，它在地面上。

05 哪只狗的颜色最深？
哪只狗的鼻子最短？
哪只狗的颜色最浅？
哪只狗跑得最快？

06 哪个孩子看起来最高兴？
哪个孩子看起来最不高兴？
哪个孩子跑得最快？
哪个孩子头发最长？

07 这只狗身上的花点比另一只狗的少。
这只狗身上的花点比另一只狗的多。
这只豹子身上的花点比两只狗哪一条的都多。
这只虎身上有条纹，但没有花点。

08 这只动物身上的花点最少。
这只动物身上的花点较多，但不是最多的。
这只动物是这些动物中身上花点最多的。
这只动物身上有条纹，但没有花点。

09 从马身上跳到牛身上是很危险的。
士兵打仗是很危险的。
骑马不是很危险的。
坐在家里一点都不危险。

10 谁飞得最高？
谁跑得最快？
谁身上最湿？
谁感到最冷？

8-07

形容詞的比較級和最高級

01 這個女人比這個男人年紀大。
這個男人比這個女人年紀大。
這個男孩兒比這個女孩兒高。
這個女孩兒比這個男孩兒高。

02 一個年輕女人
這個女人年紀較大，但不是年紀最大的。
年紀最大的女人
一個小男孩兒

03 年紀最大的男孩兒
這個男孩兒年紀較小，但不是最小的。
年紀最小的男孩兒
他比這些男孩兒年紀大，他是一個男人。

04 這架飛機飛得最高。
這架飛機飛得很低，離地面很近。
這架飛機飛得很低，但不是最低的。
這架飛機沒有飛，它在地面上。

05 哪隻狗的顏色最深？
哪隻狗的鼻子最短？
哪隻狗的顏色最淺？
哪隻狗跑得最快？

06 哪個孩子看起來最高興？
哪個孩子看起來最不高興？
哪個孩子跑得最快？
哪個孩子頭髮最長？

07 這隻狗身上的花點比另一隻狗的少。
這隻狗身上的花點比另一隻狗的多。
這隻豹子身上的花點比兩隻狗哪一條的都多。
這隻虎身上有條紋，但沒有花點。

08 這隻動物身上的花點最少。
這隻動物身上的花點較多，但不是最多的。
這隻動物是這些動物中身上花點最多的。
這隻動物身上有條紋，但沒有花點。

09 從馬身上跳到牛身上是很危險的。
士兵打仗是很危險的。
騎馬不是很危險的。
坐在家裡一點都不危險。

10 誰飛得最高？
誰跑得最快？
誰身上最濕？
誰感到最冷？

8-07

xíng róng cí de bǐ jiào jí hé zuì gāo jí

01   zhè gè nǚ rén bǐ zhè gè nán rén nián jì dà.
      zhè gè nán rén bǐ zhè gè nǚ rén nián jì dà.
      zhè gè nán háir bǐ zhè gè nǚ háir gāo.
      zhè gè nǚ háir bǐ zhè gè nán háir gāo.

02   yī gè niáng qīng nǚ rén
      zhè gè nǚ rén nián jì jiào dà, dàn bú shì nián jì zuì dà de.
      nián jì zuì dà de nǚ rén
      yī gè xiǎo nán háir

03   nián jì zuì dà de nán háir
      zhè gè nán háir nián jì jiào xiǎo, dàn bú shì zuì xiǎo de.
      nián jì zuì xiǎo de nán háir
      tā bǐ zhè xiē nán háir nián jì dà, tā shì yī gè nán rén.

04   zhè jià fēi jī fēi de zuì gāo.
      zhè jià fēi jī fēi de hěn dī, lí dì miàn hěn jìn.
      zhè jià fēi jī fēi de hěn dī, dàn bú shì zuì dī de.
      zhè jià fēi jī méi yǒu fēi, tā zài dì miàn shàng.

05   nǎ zhī gǒu de yán sè zuì shēn?
      nǎ zhī gǒu de bí zi zuì duǎn?
      nǎ zhī gǒu de yán sè zuì qiǎn?
      nǎ zhī gǒu pǎo de zuì kuài?

06   nǎ gè hái zi kàn qǐ lái zuì gāo xìng?
      nǎ gè hái zi kàn qǐ lái zuì bù gāo xìng?
      nǎ gè hái zi pǎo de zuì kuài?
      nǎ gè hái zi tóu fà zuì cháng?

07   zhè zhī gǒu shēn shàng de huā diǎn bǐ lìng yī zhī gǒu de shǎo.
      zhè zhī gǒu shēn shàng de huā diǎn bǐ lìng yī zhī gǒu de duō.
      zhè zhī bào zi shēn shàng de huā diǎn bǐ liǎng zhī gǒu nǎ yī tiáo de dōu duō.
      zhè zhī hǔ shēn shàng yǒu tiáo wén, dàn méi yǒu huā diǎn.

08   zhè zhī dòng wù shēn shàng de huā diǎn zuì shǎo.
      zhè zhī dòng wù shēn shàng de huā diǎn jiào duō, dàn bú shì zuì duō de.
      zhè zhī dòng wù shì zhè xiē dòng wù zhōng shēn shàng huā diǎn zuì duō de.
      zhè zhī dòng wù shēn shàng yǒu tiáo wén, dàn méi yǒu huā diǎn.

09   cóng mǎ shēn shàng tiào dào niú shēn shàng shì hěn wēi xiǎn de.
      shì bīng dǎ zhàng shì hěn wēi xiǎn de.
      qí mǎ bú shì hěn wēi xiǎn de.
      zuò zài jiā lǐ yī diǎn dōu bù wēi xiǎn.

10   shéi fēi de zuì gāo?
      shéi pǎo de zuì kuài?
      shéi shēn shàng zuì shī?
      shéi gǎn dào zuì lěng?

8-08

近 、远；形容词的比较级形式

01 这架飞机在地面上。
这架飞机离地面很近。
这架飞机离地面很高。
这艘船在水上。

02 这些赛跑的人彼此站得很近。
这些赛跑的人彼此站得很远。
这些飞机飞行时，彼此距离很近。
这两架飞机飞行时，彼此距离很远。

03 这些羊呆在一起。
这只羊没有和其它羊在一起。
这些牛呆在一起。
这两头牛离得很远。

04 这两个人走路时，彼此距离很近。
这两个人走路时，彼此距离很远。
这两个人坐得很近。
这两个人坐得很远。

05 这个穿白衣服的男孩儿离穿蓝衣服的男孩儿很近。
这个穿白衣服的男孩儿离穿蓝衣服的男孩儿不近。
那只风筝离这个男人很近。
那只风筝离这个男人很远。

06 火离得很近。
火离得很远。
这匹马离得很近。
那匹马离得很远。

07 这座城堡离那些房子很近。
那个堡垒离所有的房子都很远。
这个男人离水很近。
这个男人离水很远。

08 这张照片里的两个牛仔离得很近。
这张照片里的两个牛仔离得很远。
有一张脸离得很近。
有一张脸离得很远。

09 那辆车比那个男人离这儿近一些。
那个男人比那辆车离这儿近一些。
那辆红车比黄车离这儿近一些。
那辆红车比黄车离这儿远一些。

10 那个男人比那辆车离这儿远一些。
那辆轿车比那个男人离这儿远一些。
那辆黄车比红车离这儿远一些。
那辆黄车比红车离这儿近一些。

8-08

近、遠；形容詞的比較級形式

01 這架飛機在地面上。
這架飛機離地面很近。
這架飛機離地面很高。
這艘船在水上。

02 這些賽跑的人彼此站得很近。
這些賽跑的人彼此站得很遠。
這些飛機飛行時，彼此距離很近。
這兩架飛機飛行時，彼此距離很遠。

03 這些羊呆在一起。
這隻羊沒有和其它羊在一起。
這些牛呆在一起。
這兩頭牛離得很遠。

04 這兩個人走路時，彼此距離很近。
這兩個人走路時，彼此距離很遠。
這兩個人坐得很近。
這兩個人坐得很遠。

05 這個穿白衣服的男孩兒離穿藍衣服的男孩兒很近。
這個穿白衣服的男孩兒離穿藍衣服的男孩兒不近。
那隻風箏離這個男人很近。
那隻風箏離這個男人很遠。

06 火離得很近。
火離得很遠。
這匹馬離得很近。
那匹馬離得很遠。

07 這座城堡離那些房子很近。
那個堡壘離所有的房子都很遠。
這個男人離水很近。
這個男人離水很遠。

08 這張照片裡的兩個牛仔離得很近。
這張照片裡的兩個牛仔離得很遠。
有一張臉離得很近。
有一張臉離得很遠。

09 那輛車比那個男人離這兒近一些。
那個男人比那輛車離這兒近一些。
那輛紅車比黃車離這兒近一些。
那輛紅車比黃車離這兒遠一些。

10 那個男人比那輛車離這兒遠一些。
那輛轎車比那個男人離這兒遠一些。
那輛黃車比紅車離這兒遠一些。
那輛黃車比紅車離這兒近一些。

8-08

jìn, yuǎn; xíng róng cí de bǐ jiào jí xíng shì

01 zhè jià fēi jī zài dì miàn shàng.
   zhè jià fēi jī lí dì miàn hěn jìn.
   zhè jià fēi jī lí dì miàn hěn gāo.
   zhè sōu chuán zài shuǐ shàng.

02 zhè xiē sài pǎo de rén bǐ cǐ zhàn de hěn jìn.
   zhè xiē sài pǎo de rén bǐ cǐ zhàn de hěn yuǎn.
   zhè xiē fēi jī fēi xíng shí, bǐ cǐ jù lí hěn jìn.
   zhè liǎng jià fēi jī fēi xíng shí, bǐ cǐ jù lí hěn yuǎn.

03 zhè xiē yáng dāi zài yī qǐ.
   zhè zhī yáng méi yǒu hé qí tā yáng zài yī qǐ.
   zhè xiē niú dāi zài yī qǐ.
   zhè liǎng tóu niú lí de hěn yuǎn.

04 zhè liǎng gè rén zǒu lù shí, bǐ cǐ jù lí hěn jìn.
   zhè liǎng gè rén zǒu lù shí, bǐ cǐ jù lí hěn yuǎn.
   zhè liǎng gè rén zuò de hěn jìn.
   zhè liǎng gè rén zuò de hěn yuǎn.

05 zhè gè chuān bái yī fu de nán háir lí chuān lán yī fu de nán háir hěn jìn.
   zhè gè chuān bái yī fu de nán háir lí chuān lán yī fu de nán háir bú jìn.
   nà zhī fēng zhēng lí zhè gè nán rén hěn jìn.
   nà zhī fēng zhēng lí zhè gè nán rén hěn yuǎn.

06 huǒ lí de hěn jìn.
   huǒ lí de hěn yuǎn.
   zhè pǐ mǎ lí de hěn jìn.
   nà pǐ mǎ lí de hěn yuǎn.

07 zhè zuò chéng bǎo lí nà xiē fáng zi hěn jìn.
   nà gè bǎo lěi lí suǒ yǒu de fáng zi dōu hěn yuǎn.
   zhè gè nán rén lí shuǐ hěn jìn.
   zhè gè nán rén lí shuǐ hěn yuǎn.

08 zhè zhāng zhào piàn lǐ de liǎng gè niú zǎi lí de hěn jìn.
   zhè zhāng zhào piàn lǐ de liǎng gè niú zǎi lí de hěn yuǎn.
   yǒu yī zhāng liǎn lí de hěn jìn.
   yǒu yī zhāng liǎn lí de hěn yuǎn.

09 nà liàng chē bǐ nà gè nán rén lí zhèr jìn yī xiē.
   nà gè nán rén bǐ nà liàng chē lí zhèr jìn yī xiē.
   nà liàng hóng chē bǐ huáng chē lí zhèr jìn yī xiē.
   nà liàng hóng chē bǐ huáng chē lí zhèr yuǎn yī xiē.

10 nà gè nán rén bǐ nà liàng chē lí zhèr yuǎn yī xiē.
   nà liàng jiào chē bǐ nà gè nán rén lí zhèr yuǎn yī xiē.
   nà liàng huáng chē bǐ hóng chē lí zhèr yuǎn yī xiē.
   nà liàng huáng chē bǐ hóng chē lí zhèr jìn yī xiē.

位置；介词

01　一家银行
　　一家饭店
　　一座机场
　　一个游戏场

02　这座图书馆在那家银行旁边。
　　这座教堂在那家银行旁边。
　　这家医院在那个游戏场旁边。
　　这座加油站在那个游戏场旁边。

03　这座犹太教堂在那家饭店对过儿。
　　这家鞋店在那家饭店对过儿。
　　这家药店在那座加油站对过儿。
　　这家超级市场在那座加油站对过儿。

04　这座宾馆在那所医院旁边。
　　这座宾馆在那所医院对过儿。
　　这个游戏场在那所医院旁边。
　　这个游戏场在那所医院对过儿。

05　从这家银行往前走，拐个弯儿就是这家面包店。
　　从这家银行往前走，拐弯儿就是这座电影院。
　　从这家银行往前走，过一条街就是这家面包店。
　　从这家银行往前走，过一条街就是这座电影院。

06　这个地铁站在那家银行对过。
　　这个地铁站在那家银行旁边。
　　从这家银行往前走，拐弯儿就是这个地铁站。
　　从这家银行往前走，过一条街就是这个地铁站。

07　从这个游戏场往前走，拐弯儿就是这座教堂。
　　这座犹太教堂在那个游戏场旁边。
　　这座清真寺在那个游戏场对过。
　　这座印度寺庙和那个游戏场在同一条街上。

08　这家面包店在那家银行旁边。
　　这座监狱在那家银行旁边。
　　从这家银行往前走，拐弯儿就是这所警察局。
　　这所警察局在那家银行旁边。

09　这家工厂在那个火车站旁边。
　　这所大学在那个游戏场旁边。
　　这家饭店在那个火车站旁边。
　　这所医院在那个游戏场旁边。

10　这座机场在那家工厂旁边。
　　这家面包店在那座宾馆对过。
　　这家面包店在那座电影院对过。
　　这所大学在那座宾馆对过。

8-09

位置；介詞

01　一家銀行
　　一家飯店
　　一座機場
　　一個游戲場

02　這座圖書館在那家銀行旁邊。
　　這座教堂在那家銀行旁邊。
　　這家醫院在那個游戲場旁邊。
　　這座加油站在那個游戲場旁邊。

03　這座猶太教堂在那家飯店對過　兒。
　　這家鞋店在那家飯店對過兒。
　　這家藥店在那座加油站對過兒。
　　這家超級市場在那座加油站對過兒。

04　這座賓館在那所醫院旁邊。
　　這座賓館在那所醫院對過兒。
　　這個游戲場在那所醫院旁邊。
　　這個游戲場在那所醫院對過兒。

05　從這家銀行往前走，拐個彎兒就是這家面包店。
　　從這家銀行往前走，拐彎兒就是這座電影院。
　　從這家銀行往前走，過一條街就是這家面包店。
　　從這家銀行往前走，過一條街就是這座電影院。

06　這個地鐵站在那家銀行對過。
　　這個地鐵站在那家銀行旁邊。
　　從這家銀行往前走，拐彎兒就是這個地鐵站。
　　從這家銀行往前走，過一條街就是這個地鐵站。

07　從這個游戲場往前走，拐彎兒就是這座教堂。
　　這座猶太教堂在那個游戲場旁邊。
　　這座清真寺在那個游戲場對過。
　　這座印度寺廟和那個游戲場在同一條街上。

08　這家面包店在那家銀行旁邊。
　　這座監獄在那家銀行旁邊。
　　從這家銀行往前走，拐彎兒就是這所警察局。
　　這所警察局在那家銀行旁邊。

09　這家工廠在那個火車站旁邊。
　　這所大學在那個游戲場旁邊。
　　這家飯店在那個火車站旁邊。
　　這所醫院在那個游戲場旁邊。

10　這座機場在那家工廠旁邊。
　　這家面包店在那座賓館對過。
　　這家面包店在那座電影院對過。
　　這所大學在那座賓館對過。

8-09

wèi zhì; jiè cí

01   yī jiā yín háng
     yī jiā fàn diàn
     yī zuò jī chǎng
     yī gè yóu xì chǎng

02   zhè zuò tú shū guǎn zài nà jiā yín háng páng biān.
     zhè zuò jiào táng zài nà jiā yín háng páng biān.
     zhè jiā yī yuàn zài nà gè yóu xì chǎng páng biān.
     zhè zuò jiā yóu zhàn zài nà gè yóu xì chǎng páng biān.

03   zhè zuò yóu tài jiào táng zài nà jiā fàn diàn duì guòr.
     zhè jiā xié diàn zài nà jiā fàn diàn duì guòr.
     zhè jiā yào diàn zài nà zuò jiā yóu zhàn duì guòr.
     zhè jiā chāo jí shì chǎng zài nà zuò jiā yóu zhàn duì guòr.

04   zhè zuò bīn guǎn zài nà suǒ yī yuàn páng biān.
     zhè zuò bīn guǎn zài nà suǒ yī yuàn duì guòr.
     zhè gè yóu xì chǎng zài nà suǒ yī yuàn páng biān.
     zhè gè yóu xì chǎng zài nà suǒ yī yuàn duì guòr.

05   cóng zhè jiā yín háng wǎng qián zǒu, guǎi gè wānr jiù shì zhè jiā miàn bāo diàn.
     cóng zhè jiā yín háng wǎng qián zǒu, guǎi wānr jiù shì zhè zuò diàn yǐng yuàn.
     cóng zhè jiā yín háng wǎng qián zǒu, guò yī tiáo jiē jiù shì zhè jiā miàn bāo diàn.
     cóng zhè jiā yín háng wǎng qián zǒu, guò yī tiáo jiē jiù shì zhè zuò diàn yǐng yuàn.

06   zhè gè dì tiě zhàn zài nà jiā yín háng duì guò.
     zhè gè dì tiě zhàn zài nà jiā yín háng páng biān.
     cóng zhè jiā yín háng wǎng qián zǒu, guǎi wānr jiù shì zhè gè dì tiě zhàn.
     cóng zhè jiā yín háng wǎng qián zǒu, guò yī tiáo jiē jiù shì zhè gè dì tiě zhàn.

07   cóng zhè gè yóu xì chǎng wǎng qián zǒu, guǎi wānr jiù shì zhè zuò jiào táng.
     zhè zuò yóu tài jiào táng zài nà gè yóu xì chǎng páng biān.
     zhè zuò qīng zhēn sì zài nà gè yóu xì chǎng duì guò.
     zhè zuò yìn dù sì miào hé nà gè yóu xì chǎng zài tóng yī tiáo jiē shàng.

08   zhè jiā miàn bāo diàn zài nà jiā yín háng páng biān.
     zhè zuò jiān yù zài nà jiā yín háng páng biān.
     cóng zhè jiā yín háng wǎng qián zǒu, guǎi wānr jiù shì zhè suǒ jǐng chá jú.
     zhè suǒ jǐng chá jú zài nà jiā yín háng páng biān.

09   zhè jiā gōng chǎng zài nà gè huǒ chē zhàn páng biān.
     zhè suǒ dà xué zài nà gè yóu xì chǎng páng biān.
     zhè jiā fàn diàn zài nà gè huǒ chē zhàn páng biān.
     zhè suǒ yī yuàn zài nà gè yóu xì chǎng páng biān.

10   zhè zuò jī chǎng zài nà jiā gōng chǎng páng biān.
     zhè jiā miàn bāo diàn zài nà zuò bīn guǎn duì guòr.
     zhè jiā miàn bāo diàn zài nà zuò diàn yǐng yuàn duì guòr.
     zhè suǒ dà xué zài nà zuò bīn guǎn duì guòr.

8-10

方向: 去…怎么走？

01　去这个火车站怎么走？
　　走到这家银行后，向右转，再往前走，过一条街就到了。

　　去这个火车站怎么走？
　　走到这家银行后，向左转，再往前走，过一条街就到了。

　　去这个火车站怎么走？
　　走到这座图书馆后，向左转，再往前走，就在第二个街口那儿。

　　去这个火车站怎么走？
　　走到这座图书馆后，向右转，再往前走，过一条街就到了。

02　去这所警察局怎么走？
　　走到这座教堂后，向右转，往前走，警察局就在第四个街口那儿。

　　去这所警察局怎么走？
　　走到这座教堂后，向左转，往前走，警察局就在第四个街口那儿。

　　去这所警察局怎么走？
　　走到这座教堂后，向右转，往前走，警察局就在第二个街口那儿。

　　去这所警察局怎么走？
　　走到这座教堂后，向左转，往前走，警察局就在第二个街口那儿。

03　去这家医院怎么走？
　　往前走，到第二个街口那家饭店后，向右转，再往前走，医院就在第三个街口那儿。

　　去这家医院怎么走？
　　往前走，到第四个街口那家饭店后，向右转，过一条街就到医院了。

　　去这家医院怎么走？
　　往前走，到第三个街口那家饭店后，向左转，再往前走，医院就在第三个街口那儿。

　　去这家医院怎么走？
　　往前走，到第四个街口那家饭店后，向左转，过一条街就到医院了。

8-10

方向：去…怎麼走？

01　去這個火車站怎麼走？
　　走到這家銀行後，向右轉，再往前走，過一條街就到了。

　　去這個火車站怎麼走？
　　走到這家銀行後，向左轉，再往前走過一條街就到了。

　　去這個火車站怎麼走？
　　走到這座圖書館後，向左轉，再往前走，就在第二個街口那兒。

　　去這個火車站怎麼走？
　　走到這座圖書館後，向右轉，再往前走，過一條街就到了。

02　去這所警察局怎麼走？
　　走到這座教堂後，向右轉，往前走，警察局就在第四個街口那兒。

　　去這所警察局怎麼走？
　　走到這座教堂後，向左轉，往前走，警察局就在第四個街口那兒。

　　去這所警察局怎麼走？
　　走到這座教堂後，向右轉，往前走，警察局就在第二個街口那兒。

　　去這所警察局怎麼走？
　　走到這座教堂後，向左轉，往前走，警察局就在第二個街口那兒。

03　去這家醫院怎麼走？
　　往前走，到第二個街口那家飯館後，向右轉，再往前走，醫院就在第三個街口那兒。

　　去這家醫院怎麼走？
　　往前走，到第四個街口那家飯店後，向右轉，過一條街就到醫院了。

　　去這家醫院怎麼走？
　　往前走，到第三個街口那家飯店後，向左轉，再往前走，醫院就在第三個街口那兒。

　　去這家醫院怎麼走？
　　往前走，到第四個街口那家飯店後，向左轉，過一條街就到醫院了。

（继续）

8-10

fāng xiàng: qù...zěn me zǒu?

01 qù zhè gè huǒ chē zhàn zěn me zǒu?
    zǒu dào zhè jiā yín háng hòu, xiàng yòu zhuǎn, zài wǎng qián zǒu, guò yī tiáo jiē jiù dào le.

    qù zhè gè huǒ chē zhàn zěn me zǒu?
    zǒu dào zhè jiā yín háng hòu, xiàng zuǒ zhuǎn, zài wǎng qián zǒu, guò yī tiáo jiē jiù dào le.

    qù zhè gè huǒ chē zhàn zěn me zǒu?
    zǒu dào zhè zuò tú shū guǎn hòu, xiàng zuǒ zhuǎn, zài wǎng qián zǒu, jiù zài dì èr gè jiē kǒu nàr.

    qù zhè gè huǒ chē zhàn zěn me zǒu?
    zǒu dào zhè zuò tú shū guǎn hòu, xiàng yòu zhuǎn, zài wǎng qián zǒu, guò yī tiáo jiē jiù dào le.

02 qù zhè suǒ jǐng chá jú zěn me zǒu?
    zǒu dào zhè zuò jiào táng hòu, xiàng yòu zhuǎn, wǎng qián zǒu, jǐng chá jú jiù zài dì sì gè jiē kǒu nàr.

    qù zhè suǒ jǐng chá jú zěn me zǒu?
    zǒu dào zhè zuò jiào táng hòu, xiàng zuǒ zhuǎn, wǎng qián zǒu, jǐng chá jú jiù zài dì sì gè jiē kōu nàr.

    qù zhè suǒ jǐng chá jú zěn me zǒu?
    zǒu dào zhè zuò jiào táng hòu, xiàng yòu zhuǎn, wǎng qián zǒu, jǐng chá jú jiù zài dì èr gè jiē kǒu nàr.

    qù zhè suǒ jǐng chá jú zěn me zǒu?
    zǒu dào zhè zuò jiào táng hòu, xiàng zuǒ zhuǎn, wǎng qián zǒu, jǐng chá jú jiù zài dì èr gè jiē kōu nàr.

03 qù zhè jiā yī yuàn zěn me zǒu?
    wǎng qián zǒu, dào dì èr gè jiē kǒu nà jiā fàn diàn hòu, xiàng yòu zhuǎn, zài wǎng qián zǒu, yī yuàn jiù
        zài dì sān gè jiē kǒu nàr.

    qù zhè jiā yī yuàn zěn me zǒu?
    wǎng qián zǒu, dào dì sì gè jiē kǒu nà jiā fàn diàn hòu, xiàng yòu zhuǎn, guò yī tiáo jiē jiù dào yī yuàn
        le.

    qù zhè jiā yī yuàn zěn me zǒu?
    wǎng qián zǒu, dào dì sān gè jiē kǒu nà jiā fàn diàn hòu, xiàng zuǒ zhuǎn, zài wǎng qián zǒu, yī yuàn
        jiù zài dì sān gè jiē kǒu nàr.

    qù zhè jiā yī yuàn zěn me zǒu?
    wǎng qián zǒu, dào dì sì gè jiē kǒu nà jiā fàn diàn hòu, xiàng zuǒ zhuǎn, guò yī tiáo jiē jiù dào yī yuàn
        le.

(jì xù)

04　去这个地铁站怎么走？
　　走到第二个街口那家面包店后，向左转，再往前走，
　　地铁站就在第二个街口左边。

　　去这个地铁站怎么走？
　　走到第二个街口那家面包店后，向左转，再往前走，
　　地铁站就在第二个街口右边。

　　去这个地铁站怎么走？
　　走到第三个街口那家宾馆后，向右转，再往前走，地
　　铁站就在第二个街口右边。

　　去这个地铁站怎么走？
　　走到第三个街口那家宾馆后，向右转，再往前走，地
　　铁站就在第二个街口左边。

05　去这个游戏场怎么走？
　　走到第二个街口那座清真寺后，向左转，再往前走，
　　游戏场就在第三个街口右边。

　　去这个游戏场怎么走？
　　走到第三个街口那座清真寺后，向左转，再往前走，
　　游戏场就在第二个街口右边。

　　去这个游戏场怎么走？
　　往前走，过三条街，游戏场就在第四个街口左边。

　　去这个游戏场怎么走？
　　往前直走，过三条街，游戏场就在第四个街口右边。

06　去这个火车站怎么走？
　　顺着这条街往前走，路过这所学校，到了警察局后，
　　向右转，再往前走，火车站就在第二个街口那儿。

　　去这个火车站怎么走？
　　顺着这条街往前走，路过这所学校，到了警察局后，
　　向左转，再往前走，火车站就在第二个街口那儿。

　　去这个火车站怎么走？
　　顺着这条街往前走，路过这家医院，到了警察局后，
　　向右转，再往前走，火车站就在第二个街口那儿。

　　去这个火车站怎么走？
　　顺着这条街往前走，路过这家医院，到了警察局后，
　　向左转，再往前走，火车站就在第二个街口那儿。

04　去這個地鐵站怎麼走？
　　走到第二個街口那家面包店後，向左轉，再往前走，
　　地鐵站就在第二個街口左邊。

　　去這個地鐵站怎麼走？
　　走到第二個街口那家面包店後，向左轉，再往前走，
　　地鐵站就在第二個街口右邊。

　　去這個遊戲場怎麼走？
　　往前走，過三條街，遊戲場就在第四個街口左邊。

　　去這個地鐵站怎麼走？
　　走到第三個街口那家賓館後，向右轉，再往前走，地
　　鐵站就在第二個街口左邊。

05　去這個遊戲場怎麼走？
　　走到第二個街口那座清真寺後，向左轉，再往前走，
　　遊戲場就在第三個街口右邊。

　　去這個遊戲場怎麼走？
　　走到第三個街口那座清真寺後，向左轉，再往前走，
　　遊戲場就在第二個街口右邊。

　　去這個遊戲場怎麼走？
　　往前直走，過三條街，遊戲場就在第四個街口左邊。

　　去這個遊戲場怎麼走？
　　往前直走，過三條街，游戲場就在第四個街口右邊。

06　去這個火車站怎麼走？
　　順著這條街往前走，路過這所學校，到了警察局後，
　　向右轉，再往前走，火車站就在第二個街口那兒。

　　去這個火車站怎麼走？
　　順著這條街往前走，路過這所學校，到了警察局後，
　　向左轉，再往前走，火車站就在第二個街口那兒。

　　去這個火車站怎麼走？
　　順著這條街往前走，路過這家醫院，到了警察局後，
　　向右轉，再往前走，火車站就在第二個街口那兒。

　　去這個火車站怎麼走？
　　順著這條街往前走，路過這家醫院，到了警察局後，
　　向左轉，再往前走，火車站就在第二個街口那兒。

（继续）

04 qù zhè gè dì tiě zhàn zěn me zǒu?
zǒu dào dì èr gè jiē kǒu nà jiā miàn bāo diàn hòu, xiàng zuǒ zhuǎn, zài wǎng qián zǒu, dì tiě zhàn jiù
zài dì èr gè jiē kǒu zuǒ biān.

qù zhè gè dì tiě zhàn zěn me zǒu?
zǒu dào dì èr gè jiē kǒu nà jiā miàn bāo diàn hòu, xiàng zuǒ zhuǎn, zài wǎng qián zǒu, dì tiě zhàn jiù
zài dì èr gè jiē kǒu yòu biān.

qù zhè gè dì tiě zhàn zěn me zǒu?
zǒu dào dì sān gè jiē kǒu nà jiā bīn guǎn hòu, xiàng yòu zhuǎn, zài wǎng qián zǒu, dì tiě zhàn jiù zài dì
èr gè jiē kǒu yòu biān.

qù zhè gè dì tiě zhàn zěn me zǒu?
zǒu dào dì sān gè jiē kǒu nà jiā bīn guǎn hòu, xiàng yòu zhuǎn, zài wǎng qián zǒu, dì tiě zhàn jiù zài dì
èr gè jiē kǒu zuǒ biān.

05 qù zhè gè yóu xì chǎng zěn me zǒu?
zǒu dào dì èr gè jiē kǒu nà zuò qīng zhēn sì hòu, xiàng zuǒ zhuǎn, zài wǎng qián zǒu, yóu xì chǎng jiù
zài dì sān gè jiē kǒu yòu biān.

qù zhè gè yóu xì chǎng zěn me zǒu?
zǒu dào dì sān gè jiē kǒu nà zuò qīng zhēn sì hòu, xiàng zuǒ zhuǎn, zài wǎng qián zǒu, yóu xì chǎng jiù
zài dì èr gè jiē kǒu yòu biān.

qù zhè gè yóu xì chǎng zěn me zǒu?
wǎng qián zǒu, guò sān tiáo jiē, yóu xì chǎng jiù zài dì sì gè jiē kǒu zuǒ biān.

qù zhè gè yóu xì chǎng zěn me zǒu?
wǎng qián zhí zǒu, guò sān tiáo jiē, yóu xì chǎng jiù zài dì sì gè jiē kǒu yòu biān.

06 qù zhè gè huǒ chē zhàn zěn me zǒu?
shùn zhe zhè tiáo jiē wǎng qián zǒu, lù guò zhè suǒ xué xiào, dào le jǐng chá jú hòu, xiàng yòu zhuǎn,
zài wǎng qián zǒu, huǒ chē zhàn jiù zai dì èr gè jiē kǒu nàr.

qù zhè gè huǒ chē zhàn zěn me zǒu?
shùn zhe zhè tiáo jiē wǎng qián zǒu, lù guò zhè suǒ xué xiào, dào le jǐng chá jú hòu, xiàng zuǒ zhuǎn,
zài wǎng qián zǒu, huǒ chē zhàn jiù zài dì èr gè jiē kǒu nàr.

qù zhè gè huǒ chē zhàn zěn me zǒu?
shùn zhe zhè tiáo jiē wǎng qián zǒu, lù guò zhè jiā yī yuàn, dào le jǐng chá jú hòu, xiàng yòu zhuǎn, zài
wǎng qián zǒu, huǒ chē zhàn jiù zài dì èr gè jiē kǒu nàr.

qù zhè gè huǒ chē zhàn zěn me zǒu?
shùn zhe zhè tiáo jiē wǎng qián zǒu, lù guò zhè jiā yī yuàn, dào le jǐng chá jú hòu, xiàng zǒu zhuǎn, zài
wǎng qián zǒu, huǒ chē zhàn jiù zài dì èr gè jiē kǒu nàr.

(jì xù)

07 去这所大学怎么走？
顺着这条街往前走，路过左边的教堂，到了加油站后，向左转，再往前走，大学就在第二个街口右边。

去这所大学怎么走？
顺着这条街往前走，路过右边的教堂，到了加油站后，向左转，再往前走，大学就在第二个街口右边。

去这所大学怎么走？
顺着这条街往前走，路过左边的医院，到了加油站后，向左转，再往前走，大学就在第二个街口右边。

去这所大学怎么走？
顺着这条街往前走，路过右边的医院，到了加油站后，向左转，再往前走，大学就在第二个街口右边。

08 去这所教堂怎么走？
顺着这条街往前走，路过这座图书馆，到了学校后，向右转，再往前走，教堂就在第二个街口左边。

去这所教堂怎么走？
顺着这条街往前走，路过这个游戏场，到了鞋店后，向右转，再往前走，教堂就在第二个街口右边。

去这所教堂怎么走？
顺着这条街往前走，路过这所学校，到了这座图书馆后，向右转，再往前走，教堂就在第二个街口右边。

去这所教堂怎么走？
顺着这条街往前走，路过这家鞋店，到了游戏场后，向右转，再往前走，教堂就在第二个街口右边。

07 去這所大學怎麼走？
順著這條街往前走，路過左邊的教堂，到了加油站後，向左轉，再往前走，大學就在第二個街口右邊。

去這所大學怎麼走？
順著這條街往前走，路過右邊的教堂，到了加油站後，向左轉，再往前走，大學就在第二個街口右邊。

去這所大學怎麼走？
順著這條街往前走，路過左邊的醫院，到了加油站後，向左轉，再往前走，大學就在第二個街口右邊。

去這所大學怎麼走？
順著這條街往前走，路過右邊的醫院，到了加油站後，向左轉，再往前走，大學就在第二個街口右邊。

08 去這所教堂怎麼走？
順著這條街往前走，路過這座圖書館，到了學校後，向右轉，再往前走，教堂就在第二個街口左邊。

去這所教堂怎麼走？
順著這條街往前走，路過這個遊戲場，到了鞋店後，向右轉，再往前走，教堂就在第二個街口右邊。

去這所教堂怎麼走？
順著這條街往前走，路過這所學校，到了這座圖書館後，向右轉，再往前走，教堂就在第二個街口右邊。

去這所教堂怎麼走？
順著這條街往前走，路過這家鞋店，到了遊戲場後，向右轉，再往前走，教堂就在第二個街口右邊。

（继续）

07 qù zhè suǒ dà xué zěn me zǒu?
    shùn zhe zhè tiáo jiē wǎng qián zǒu, lù guò zuǒ biān de jiào táng, dào le jiā yóu zhàn hòu, xiàng zuǒ
    zhuǎn, zài wǎng qián zǒu, dà xué jiù zài dì èr gè jiē kǒu yòu biān.

    qù zhè suǒ dà xué zěn me zǒu?
    shùn zhe zhè tiáo jiē wǎng qián zǒu, lù guò yòu biān de jiào táng, dào le jiā yóu zhàn hòu, xiàng zuǒ
    zhuǎn, zài wǎng qián zǒu, dà xué jiù zài dì èr gè jiē kǒu yòu biān.

    qù zhè suǒ dà xué zén me zǒu?
    shùn zhe zhè tiáo jiē wǎng qián zǒu, lù guò zuǒ biān de yī yuàn, dào le jiā yóu zhàn hòu, xiàng zuǒ
    zhuǎn, zài wǎng qián zǒu, dà xué jiù zài dì èr gè jiē kǒu yòu biān.

    qù zhè suǒ dà xué zěn me zǒu?
    shùn zhe zhè tiáo jiē wǎng qián zǒu, lù guò yòu biān de yī yuàn, dào le jiā yóu zhàn hòu, xiàng zuǒ
    zhuǎn, zài wǎng qián zǒu, dà xué jiù zài dì èr gè jiē kǒu yòu biān.

08 qù zhè suǒ jiào táng zěn me zǒu?
    shùn zhe zhè tiáo jiē wǎng qián zǒu, lù guò zhè zuò tú shū guǎn, dào le xué xiào hòu, xiàng yòu zhuǎn,
    zài wǎng qián zǒu, jiào táng jiù zai dì èr gè jiē kǒu zuǒ biān.

    qù zhè suǒ jiào táng zěn me zǒu?
    shùn zhe zhè tiáo jiē wǎng qián zǒu, lù guò zhè gè yóu xì chǎng, dào le xié diàn hòu, xiàng yòu zhuǎn,
    zài wǎng qián zǒu, jiào táng jiù zài dì èr gè jiē kǒu yòu biān.

    qù zhè suǒ jiào táng zěn me zǒu?
    shùn zhe zhè tiáo jiē wǎng qián zǒu, lù guò zhè suǒ xué xiào, dào le zhè zuò tú shū guǎn hòu, xiàng yòu
    zhuǎn, zài wǎng qián zǒu, jiào táng jiù zài dì èr gè jiē kǒu yòu biān.

    qù zhè suǒ jiào táng zěn me zǒu?
    shùn zhe zhè tiáo jiē wǎng qián zǒu, lù guò zhè jiā xié diàn, dào le yóu xì chǎng hòu, xiàng yòu zhuǎn,
    zài wǎng qián zǒu, jiào táng jiù zài dì èr gè jiē kǒu yòu biān.

(jì xù)

09　去这个加油站怎么走？
　　去这个加油站的路现在不通。转弯，往回走，然后右转。往前走，在下一个街口右转。再往前走三条横街，在第四个街口右转。再往前走，在下一个街口右转，就到加油站了。

　　去这个加油站怎么走？
　　去这个加油站的路现在不通。转弯，往回走，然后左转。往前走，在下一个街口左转。再往前走三条横街，在第四个街口左转。再往前走，在下一个街口左转，就到加油站了。

　　去这个加油站怎么走？
　　去这个加油站的路现在不通。转弯，往回走，然后右转。往前走，在下一个街口右转。再往前走三条横街，在第四个街口右转。再往前走，在下一个街口左转，就到加油站了。

　　去这个加油站怎么走？
　　去这个加油站的路现在不通。转弯，往回走，然后左转。往前走，在下一个街口左转。再往前走三条横街，在第四个街口左转。再往前走，在下一个街口左转，加油站就在你左边。

10　去这家医院怎么走？
　　顺着这条街往前走到分叉口那儿，然后右转。

　　去这家医院怎么走？
　　顺着这条街往前走到分叉口那儿，然后左转。

　　去这家医院怎么走？
　　顺着这条街走到头，然后左转。再往前走，医院就在第四街口左边。

　　去这家医院怎么走？
　　顺着这条街走到头，然后右转。再往前走，医院就在第四街口右边。

09　去這個加油站怎麼走？
　　去這個加油站的路現在不通。轉彎，往迴走，然後右轉。往前走，在下一個街口右轉。再往前走三條橫街，在第四個街口右轉。再往前走，在下一個街口右轉，就到加油站了。

　　去這個加油站怎麼走？
　　去這個加油站的路現在不通。轉彎，往迴走，然後左轉。往前走，在下一個街口左轉。再往前走三條橫街，在第四個街口左轉，再往前走，在下一個街口左轉，就到加油站了。

　　去這個加油站怎麼走？
　　去這個加油站的路現在不通。轉彎，往迴走，然後右轉。往前走，在下一個街口右轉。再往前走三條橫街，在第四個街口右轉。再往前走，在下一個街口左轉，就到加油站了。

　　去這個加油站怎麼走？
　　去這個加油站的路現在不通。轉彎，往迴走，然後左轉。往前走，在下一 個街口左轉。再往前走三條橫街，在第四個街口左轉。再往前走，在下一個街口左轉，加油站就在你左邊。

10　去這家醫院怎麼走？
　　順著這條街往前走到分岔口那兒，然後右轉。

　　去這家醫院怎麼走？
　　順著這條街往前走到分岔口那兒，然後左轉。

　　去這家醫院怎麼走？
　　順著這條街走到頭，然後左轉。再往前走，醫院就在第四街口左邊。

　　去這家醫院怎麼走？
　　順著這條街走到頭，然後右轉。再往前走，醫院就在第四街口右邊。

09 qù zhè gè jiā yóu zhàn zěn me zǒu?
    qù zhè gè jiā yóu zhàn de lù xiàn zài bù tōng. zhuǎn wān, wǎng huí zǒu, rán hòu yòu zhuǎn. wǎng qián
    zǒu, zài xià yī gè jiē kǒu yòu zhuǎn. zài wǎng qián zǒu sān tiáo héng jiē, zài dì sì gè jiē kǒu yòu
    zhuǎn. zài wǎng qián zǒu, zài xià yī gè jiē kǒu yòu zhuǎn, jiù dào jiā yóu zhàn le.

    qù zhè gè jiā yóu zhàn zěn me zǒu?
    qù zhè gè jiā yóu zhàn de lù xiàn zài bù tōng. zhuǎn wān, wǎng huí zǒu, rán hòu zuǒ zhuǎn. wǎng qián
    zǒu, zài xià yī gè jiē kǒu zuǒ zhuǎn. zài wǎng qián zǒu sān tiáo héng jiē, zài dì sì gè jiē kǒu zuǒ
    zhuǎn. zài wǎng qián zǒu, zài xià yī gè jiē kǒu zuǒ zhuǎn, jiù dào jiā yóu zhàn le.

    qù zhè gè jiā yóu zhàn zěn me zǒu?
    qù zhè gè jiā yóu zhàn de lù xiàn zài bù tōng. zhuǎn wān, wǎng huí zǒu, rán hòu yòu zhuǎn. wǎng qián
    zǒu, zài xià yī gè jiē kǒu yòu zhuǎn. zài wǎng qián zǒu sān tiáo héng jiē, zài dì sì gè jiē kǒu yòu
    zhuǎn. zài wǎng qián zǒu, zài xià yī gè jiē kǒu zuǒ zhuǎn, jiù dào jiā yóu zhàn le.

    qù zhè gè jiā yóu zhàn zěn me zǒu?
    qù zhè gè jiā yóu zhàn de lù xiàn zài bù tōng. zhuǎn wān, wǎng huí zǒu, rán hòu zuǒ zhuǎn. wǎng qián
    zǒu, zài xià yī gè jiē kǒu zuǒ zhuǎng. zài wǎng qián zǒu sān tiáo héng jiē, zài dì sì gè jiē kǒu zuǒ
    zhuǎng, zài wǎng qián zǒu, zài xià yī gè jiē kǒu zuǒ zhuǎng, jiā yóu zhàn jiù zài nǐ zuǒ biān.

10 qù zhe jiā yī yuàn zěn me zǒu?
    shùn zhe zhè tiáo jiē wǎng qián zǒu dào fēn chà kǒu nàr, rán hòu yòu zhuǎn.

    qù zhè jiā yī yuàn zěn me zǒu?
    shùn zhe zhè tiáo jiē wǎng qián zǒu dào fēn chà kǒu nàr, rán hòu zuǒ zhuǎn.

    qù zhè jiā yī yuàn zěn me zǒu?
    shùn zhe zhè tiáo jiē zǒu dào tóu, rán hòu zuǒ zhuǎn. zài wǎng qián zǒu, yī yuàn jiù zài dì sì jiē kǒu zuǒ
    biān.

    qù zhè jiā yī yuàn zěn me zǒu?
    shùn zhe zhè tiáo jiē zǒu dào tóu, rán hòu yòu zhuǎn. zài wǎng qián zǒu, yī yuàn jiù zài dì sì jiē kǒu yòu
    biān.

使用更多的动词：参加、戴、看等

01 我们在参加自行车比赛。
我们刚才参加了自行车比赛。
我戴着帽子。
我刚才戴着帽子。

02 我在看书。
我刚才在看书。
我在钓鱼。
我刚才在钓鱼。

03 我在跳绳。这两个男孩儿在摇绳。
我们刚才在跳绳。
我在喝水。
我刚才在喝水。

04 我和两个儿子在挖地。
我和两个儿子刚才在挖地。
我在爬梯子。
我已经爬着梯子上去了。

05 我穿着一件衬衫，可是衬衫太小了。
我刚才穿了一件衬衫，可是衬衫太小了。
我穿着自己的衬衫。
我穿着我爸爸刚才穿着的那件衬衫。

06 我在弹吉他。
我刚才在弹吉他。
我拿着吉他。
我刚才拿着吉他，现在这个男孩儿拿着它。

07 我要把猫抱起来。
我正把猫抱起来。
我已经把猫抱了起来，正把它抱在怀里。
我在看报纸。

08 我要穿连衣裙。
我在穿连衣裙。
我已经穿上了连衣裙。
我在穿 T 恤衫。

09 我要往头上浇水。
我在往头上浇水。
我要看书。
我在看书。

10 我们要赛跑了。
我们在赛跑。
我们已经赛跑完了。
我在赛跑。

8-11

使用更多的動詞：參加、戴、看等

01 我們在參加自行車比賽。
我們剛才參加了自行車比賽。
我戴著帽子。
我剛才戴著帽子。

02 我在看書。
我剛才在看書。
我在釣魚。
我剛才在釣魚。

03 我在跳繩，這兩個男孩兒在搖繩。
我們剛才在跳繩。
我在喝水。
我剛才在喝水。

04 我和兩個兒子在挖地。
我和兩個兒子剛才在挖地。
我在爬梯子。
我已經爬著梯子上去了。

05 我穿著一件襯衫，可是襯衫太小了。
我剛才穿了一件襯衫，可是襯衫太小了。
我穿著自己的襯衫。
我穿著我爸爸剛才穿著的那件襯衫。

06 我在彈吉他。
我剛才在彈吉他。
我拿著吉他。
我剛才拿著吉他，現在這個男孩兒拿著它。

07 我要把貓抱起來。
我正把貓抱起來。
我已經把貓抱了起來，正把它抱在懷裡。
我在看報紙。

08 我要穿連衣裙。
我在穿連衣裙。
我已經穿上了連衣裙。
我在穿 T 恤衫。

09 我要往頭上澆水。
我在往頭上澆水。
我要看書。
我在看書。

10 我們要賽跑了。
我們在賽跑。
我們已經賽跑完了。
我在賽跑。

8-11

shǐ yòng gèng duō de dòng cí: cān jiā, dài, kàn děng

01 wǒ men zài cān jiā zì xíng chē bǐ sài.
wǒ men gāng cái cān jiā le zì xíng chē bǐ sài.
wǒ dài zhe mào zi.
wǒ gāng cái dài zhe mào zi.

02 wǒ zài kàn shū.
wǒ gāng cái zài kàn shū.
wǒ zài diào yú.
wǒ gāng cái zài diào yú.

03 wǒ zài tiào shéng, zhè liǎng gè nán háir zài yáo shéng.
wǒ men gāng cái zài tiào shéng.
wǒ zài hē shuǐ.
wǒ gāng cái zài hē shuǐ.

04 wǒ hé liǎng gè ér zi zài wā dì.
wǒ hé liǎng gè ér zi gāng cái zài wā dì.
wǒ zài pá tī zi.
wǒ yǐ jīng pá zhe tī zi shàng qù le.

05 wǒ chuān zhe yī jiàn chèn shān, kě shì chèn shān tài xiǎo le.
wǒ gāng cái chuān le yī jiàn chèn shān, kě shì chèn shān tài xiǎo le.
wǒ chuān zhe zì jǐ de chèn shān.
wǒ chuān zhe wǒ bà bà gāng cái chuān zhe de nà jiàn chèn shān.

06 wǒ zài tán jí tā.
wǒ gāng cái zài tán jí tā.
wǒ ná zhe jí tā.
wǒ gāng cái ná zhe jí tā, xiàn zài zhè gè nán háir ná zhe tā.

07 wǒ yào bǎ māo bào qǐ lái.
wǒ zhèng bǎ māo bào qǐ lái.
wǒ yǐ jīng bǎ māo bào le qǐ lái, zhèng bǎ tā bào zài huái lǐ.
wǒ zài kàn bào zhǐ.

08 wǒ yào chuān lián yī qún.
wǒ zài chuān lián yī qún.
wǒ yǐ jīng chuān shàng le lián yī qún.
wǒ zài chuān T xù shān.

09 wǒ yào wǎng tóu shàng jiāo shuǐ.
wǒ zài wǎng tóu shàng jiāo shuǐ.
wǒ yào kàn shū.
wǒ zài kàn shū.

10 wǒ men yào sài pǎo le.
wǒ men zài sài pǎo.
wǒ men yǐ jīng sài pǎo wán le.
wǒ zài sài pǎo.

复习第八部分

01 第二个数字和第四个数字都是三。
第一个数字和最后一个数字都是三。
第三个数字和最后一个数字都是一。
第一个数字和最后一个数字都是一。

02 我弹着琴，唱着歌。
我没有唱歌，也没弹琴。
我们笑着，敲着鼓。
我们没敲鼓，也没笑。

03 那些黑色的正方形大多数都大，而那些白色的正方形
全都小。
那些黑色正方形全都大，而那些白色的正方形大多数
都小。
那些大三角形中有几个是绿色的，而那些小三角形全
都是灰色的。
那些大三角形全都是绿色的，而那些小三角形中有几
个是灰色的。

04 这张地图上印成红色的那个亚洲国家是中国。
这张地图上印成红色的那个亚洲国家是朝鲜。
这张地图上印成红色的那个欧洲国家是西班牙。
俄罗斯在这张地图上印成了红色。俄罗斯横跨欧洲和
亚洲。

05 有两架桥横跨那条公路。
那条路两旁都是树，路上有一辆轿车。
那条路通向那座房子。
那条路通向那座山。

06 这只狗是那个男孩儿的，它是那个男孩儿的宠物。
这只狗是那个女人的，它是那个女人的宠物。
这头熊不属于任何人，它不是宠物。
这头牛是一个农民的，可不是那个农民的宠物。

07 这架飞机飞得最高。
这架飞机飞得很低，离地面很近。
这架飞机飞得很低，但不是最低的。
这架飞机没有飞，它在地面上。

08 这两个人走路时，彼此距离很近。
这两个人走路时，彼此距离很远。
这两个人坐得很近。
这两个人坐得很远。

8-12

復習第八部分

01 第二個數字和第四個數字都是三。
第一個數字和最後一個數字都是三。
第三個數字和最後一個數字都是一。
第一個數字和最後一個數字都是一。

02 我彈著琴，唱著歌。
我沒有唱歌，也沒彈琴。
我們笑著，敲著鼓。
我們沒敲鼓，也沒笑。

03 那些黑色的正方形大多數都大，而那些白色的正方形
全都小。
那些黑色正方形全都大，而那些白色的正方形大多數
都小。
那些大三角形中有幾個是綠色的，而那些小三角形全
都是灰色的。
那些大三角形全都是綠色的，而那些小三角形中有幾
個是灰色的。

04 這張地圖上印成紅色的那個亞洲國家是中國。
這張地圖上印成紅色的那個亞洲國家是朝鮮。
這張地圖上印成紅色的那個歐洲國家是西班牙。
俄羅斯在這張地圖上印成了紅色。俄羅斯橫跨歐洲和
亞洲。

05 有兩架橋橫跨那條公路。
那條路兩旁都是樹，路上有一輛轎車。
那條路通向那座房子。
那條路通向那座山。

06 這隻狗是那個男孩兒的，它是那個男孩兒的寵物。
這隻狗是那個女人的，它是那個女人的寵物。
這頭熊不屬於任何人，它不是寵物。
這頭牛是一個農民的，可不是那個農民的寵物。

07 這架飛機飛得最高。
這架飛機飛得很低，離地面很近。
這架飛機飛得很低，但不是最低的。
這架飛機沒有飛，它在地面上。

08 這兩個人走路時，彼此距離很近。
這兩個人走路時，彼此距離很遠。
這兩個人坐得很近。
這兩個人坐得很遠。

（继续）

8-12

fù xí dì bā bù fen

01 dì èr gè shù zì hé dì sì gè shù zì dōu shì sān.
    dì yī gè shù zì hé zuì hòu yī gè shù zì dōu shì sān.
    dì sān gè shù zì hé zuì hòu yī gè shù zì dōu shì yī.
    dì yī gè shù zì hé zuì hòu yī gè shù zì dōu shì yī.

02 wǒ tán zhe qín, chàng zhe gē.
    wǒ méi yǒu chàng gē, yě méi tán qín.
    wǒ men xiào zhe, qiāo zhe gǔ.
    wǒ men méi qiāo gǔ, yě méi xiào.

03 nà xiē hēi sè de zhèng fāng xíng dà duō shù dōu dà, ér nà xiē bái sè de zhèng fāng xíng quán dōu xiǎo.
    nà xiē hēi sè zhèng fāng xíng quán dōu dà, ér nà xiē bái sè de zhèng fāng xíng dà duō shù dōu xiǎo.
    nà xiē dà sān jiǎo xíng zhōng yǒu jǐ gè shì lǜ sè de, ér nà xiē xiǎo sān jiǎo xíng quán dōu shì huī sè de.
    nà xiē dà sān jiǎo xíng quán dōu shì lǜ sè de, ér nà xiē xiǎo sān jiǎo xíng zhōng yǒu jǐ gè shì huī sè de.

04 zhè zhāng dì tú shàng yìn chéng hóng sè de nà gè yà zhōu guó jiā shì zhōng guó.
    zhè zhāng dì tú shàng yìn chéng hóng sè de nà gè yà zhōu guó jiā shì cháo xiǎn.
    zhè zhāng dì tú shàng yìn chéng hóng sè de nà gè ōu zhōu guó jiā shì xī bān yá.
    é luó sī zài zhè zhāng dì tú shàng yìn chéng le hóng sè. é luó sī héng kuà ōu zhōu hé yà zhōu.

05 yǒu liǎng jià qiáo héng kuà nà tiáo gōng lù.
    nà tiáo lù liǎng páng dōu shì shù, lù shàng yǒu yī liàng jiào chē.
    nà tiáo lù tōng xiàng nà zuò fáng zi.
    nà tiáo lù tōng xiàng nà zuò shān.

06 zhè zhī gǒu shì nà gè nán háir de, tā shì nà gè nán háir de chǒng wù.
    zhè zhī gǒu shì nà gè nǚ rén de, tā shì nà gè nǚ rén de chǒng wù.
    zhè tōu xióng bù shǔ yú rèn hé rén, tā bú shì chǒng wù.
    zhè tóu niú shì yī gè nóng mín de, kě bú shì nà gè nóng mín de chǒng wù.

07 zhè jià fēi jī fēi de zuì gāo.
    zhè jià fēi jī fēi de hěn dī, lí dì miàn hěn jìn.
    zhè jià fēi jī fēi de hěn dī, dàn bú shì zuì dī de.
    zhè jià fēi jī méi yǒu fēi, tā zài dì miàn shàng.

08 zhè liǎng gè rén zǒu lù shí, bǐ cǐ jù lí hěn jìn.
    zhè liǎng gè rén zǒu lù shí, bǐ cǐ jù lí hěn yuǎn.
    zhè liǎng gè rén zuò de hěn jìn.
    zhè liǎng gè rén zuò de hěn yuǎn.

(jì xù)

09 去这所大学怎么走？
　　顺着这条街往前走，路过左边的教堂，到了加油站后，向左转，再往前走，大学就在第二个街口右边。

　　去这所大学怎么走？
　　顺着这条街往前走，路过右边的教堂，到了加油站后，向左转，再往前走，大学就在第二个街口右边。

　　去这所大学怎么走？
　　顺着这条街往前走，路过左边的医院，到了加油站后，向左转，再往前走，大学就在第二个街口右边。

　　去这所大学怎么走？
　　顺着这条街往前走，路过右边的医院，到了加油站后，向左转，再往前走，大学就在第二个街口右边。

10 我穿着一件衬衫，可是衬衫太小了。
　　我刚才穿了一件衬衫，可是衬衫太小了。
　　我穿着自己的衬衫。
　　我穿着我爸爸刚才穿着的那件衬衫。

09 去這所大學怎麼走？
　　順著這條街往前走，路過左邊的教堂，到了加油站後，向左轉，再往前走，大學就在第二個街口右邊。

　　去這所大學怎麼走？
　　順著這條街往前走，路過右邊的教堂，到了加油站後，向左轉，再往前走，大學就在第二個街口右邊。

　　去這所大學怎麼走？
　　順著這條街往前走，路過左邊的醫院，到了加油站後，向左轉，再往前走，大學就在第二個街口右邊。

　　去這所大學怎麼走？
　　順著這條街往前走，路過右邊的醫院，到了加油站後，向左轉，再往前走，大學就在第二個街口右邊。

10 我穿著一件襯衫，可是襯衫太小了。
　　我剛才穿了一件襯衫，可是襯衫太小了。
　　我穿著自己的襯衫。
　　我穿著我爸爸剛才穿著的那件襯衫。

（继续）

09 qù zhè suǒ dà xué zěn me zǒu?
    shùn zhe zhè tiáo jiē wǎng qián zǒu, lù guò zuǒ biān de jiào táng, dào le jiā yóu zhàn hòu, xiàng zuǒ zhuǎn, zài wǎng qián zǒu, dà xué jiù zài dì èr gè jiē kǒu yòu biān.

    qù zhè suǒ dà xué zěn me zǒu?
    shùn zhe zhè tiáo jiē wǎng qián zǒu, lù guò yòu biān de jiào táng, dào le jiā yóu zhàn hòu, xiàng zuǒ zhuǎn, zài wǎng qián zǒu, dà xué jiù zài dì èr gè jiē kǒu yòu biān.

    qù zhè suǒ dà xué zén me zǒu?
    shùn zhe zhè tiáo jiē wǎng qián zǒu, lù guò zuǒ biān de yī yuàn, dào le jiā yóu zhàn hòu, xiàng zuǒ zhuǎn, zài wǎng qián zǒu, dà xué jiù zài dì èr gè jiē kǒu yòu biān.

    qù zhè suǒ dà xué zěn me zǒu?
    shùn zhe zhè tiáo jiē wǎng qián zǒu, lù guò yòu biān de yī yuàn, dào le jiā yóu zhàn hòu, xiàng zuǒ zhuǎn, zài wǎng qián zǒu, dà xué jiù zài dì èr gè jiē kǒu yòu biān.

10 wǒ chuān zhe yī jiàn chèn shān, kě shì chèn shān tài xiǎo le.
    wǒ gāng cái chuān le yī jiàn chèn shān, kě shì chèn shān tài xiǎo le.
    wǒ chuān zhe zì jǐ de chèn shān.
    wǒ chuān zhe wǒ bà bà gāng cái chuān zhe de nà jiàn chèn shān.